BY DEGREES

Richard Moses

National Library of Canada Cataloguing in Publication Data

Moses, Richard, 1933-
    By degrees : around the world by tramp freighter / written by Richard Moses.
ISBN 1-4120-0507-8
    1. Moses, Richard, 1933- --Journeys. 2. Voyages around the world. I. Title.
G440.M66A3 2003   910.4'1   C2003-903233-7

TRAFFORD

This book was published *on-demand* in cooperation with Trafford Publishing.
On-demand publishing is a unique process and service of making a book available for retail sale to the public taking advantage of on-demand manufacturing and Internet marketing.
On-demand publishing includes promotions, retail sales, manufacturing, order fulfilment, accounting and collecting royalties on behalf of the author.

Suite 6E, 2333 Government St., Victoria, B.C. V8T 4P4, CANADA

Phone	250-383-6864	Toll-free	1-888-232-4444 (Canada & US)
Fax	250-383-6804	E-mail	sales@trafford.com
Web site	www.trafford.com	TRAFFORD PUBLISHING IS A DIVISION OF TRAFFORD HOLDINGS LTD.
Trafford Catalogue #03-0876		www.trafford.com/robots/03-0876.html

10   9   8   7   6   5   4   3   2

For Renand

PRELUDE

Here is the story of the realization of a long-held dream: actually "belonging" to a freighter, a great ship that would travel from point A back to point A by moving ever eastward around the globe, that would carry me with it—my own floating hotel—so that wherever I went, whatever exotic port I visited, my "home" would be but a taxi ride away—or even closer. Even greater: it would take me to "down to the sea".

When I broached the subject to my prairie-born wife ten years or so ago, her response to the idea of three or four months on the ocean, let alone on a freighter, was a hearty, "Bon Voyage!"

There was a false start in 2001; a last minute health concern that cancelled the trip virtually at the foot of the gangway (no doctors on freighters). There were always the daunting Canadian currency exchange rates; but over it all was the absolute and very persuasive fact that "I ain't gettin' any younger!" And this was one of those things I *had* to do!

Brought up in a Methodist parsonage I was well-acquainted with my long-standing finicky food preferences, but figured that Polish meals prepared by a Filipino cook would just be part of the adventure. (Gulp!) Nevertheless, from the first inkling of a plan, a hot air popcorn popper went at the top of my list of stuff to take: one of my favorite foods would be available, just in case.

As the days at sea went by, I made a point of copying into the handwritten journal (the "urtext" for what follows) the actual latitude and longitude—the position—of the ship as I found it on our GPS/radar screen at noon each day, or when we entered a port. Once in while, I had to consult a map or chart for the numbers.

I want to say thanks to some folks. First to Roberta Shapiro, splendid, patient friend, who read through the raw first draft, making comments, suggestions and occasionally leaving in her wake, phrases like, "Surely, you jest!" Then to son Dan Moses, for his wizardry at the computer keyboard and his mysterious knowledge of things cyberspatial, including of course the fantastic (!) web site; to Charles Buchwald (PeregrineNewMedia) whose imaginative expertise and professional touch created the cover; and finally to the indomitable Florence Reid who gave the thing a final proofing, and tried her best to convince me that it was worth the paper it's printed on.

So, if you're ready, we're off across the seas and oceans—for days and nights, weeks on end, months even; by ever-shifting time zones, and of course, by degrees.

RBM – 9/15/03

33°30'N x 112°W (Phoenix)

April 9, 2002 Airborne! At last! But, it won't make any difference now. This plane is already an hour late leaving Phoenix en route from Vancouver to Houston where it is now 8:54 p.m., or, by the 24 hour clock, 2054 hrs. (CDT). Flying time to Houston is 2 hours, 20 minutes. I knew this was going to be a tight squeeze—runway to ship—but a makeable one. Now "This is your captain speaking . . . " has shot my safety margin all to hell. Which means that, almost certainly—figuring time to round up the baggage (if it's there!), phone the ship's agent, and nail a cab for the half hour (or so) ride from the George Bush airport to the Port of Houston—*I am going to miss the boat!*

This is not just a figure of speech: this "boat" is the ship which, I had hoped, was going to take me clean around the world, a voyage of "19 to 20 weeks", stopping at "20 ports or more", and which, to the best of my knowledge, is scheduled—as much as a tramp freighter can be scheduled—to sail from the Port of Houston's Pier 16 at midnight, i.e., 2400 hrs. *tonight—three hours and six minutes from right now!*

It's 2212; I've finished my book and read everything in the New Yorker including curtain times for every Broadway show. Nothing to do but sit here going 524 miles an hour and fret over what to do first if we ever actually do get to Houston: (1) the phone, (2) the cab, (3) the bags. I decide I will blow an extra twenty bucks for the cabby if he or she can get me to the ship on time.

2302, we're about to land. 58 minutes to get to the dock.

29°30'N x 95°W (Houston)

2310: We're down. But rolling, rolling, rolling, turning, more rolling, then stop, and all the other "geese" stand up in the aisle and don't move for five minutes, then shuffle *slowly* out the door.

When I am able, I race down the ramp, down the corridor, into the baggage hall (will my unique and absolutely crucial baggage be there?). Not yet, it isn't. I head for the taxi rank: *there is no taxi rank!* More coming, says the lady. Try the telephone; can't get through to the agent. Back to the carousel. Ah, one bag! AHA! The other one! Drag and drop at the now-existing taxi rank.

At 2325 I say to the first cabby in line: "I've got to get to the Port of Houston, Pier 16, Turning Basin Terminal. Know where that is?"

"Well, lemme see. Uh—geez, I'm not too sure—umm..."

"It's somewhere near Clinton – "

"Oh, yeah, I know the place."

"There's an extra twenty in it if you can get me there by midnight."

And we're off! 80 mph, nearly empty freeways, not a cop in sight. I have no idea which direction we're going, but the driver seems to know; keeps encouraging me to think positive. I'm thinking of how I can get to Beaumont, Texas, the ship's next port, in the middle of the night. I look at my watch, count out dollars, ready for a quick exit just in case we do make it. More freeway, more exits, finally: "<u>PORT OF HOUSTON</u>".

At exactly 2356 we pull up to the main gate, tell the guard who we are, where we are going. He *slowly* checks his clip board. "Hmmmm, lemme see here—you said BIBI? Pier 16?. 'Scuse me—", and he turns *slowly* away to check out an exiting truck on the other side. Then back to us and more page riffling, "What's the name a' that ship again? BIBI? Hmmmm. Nope, I got no ship up there at all."

"Let's go anyway," I say to the cabby. It is now—

2358, and I can see it all in my head: even if the ship *is* there, lines have been singled up; the pilot is aboard; tugs are nudging; the ship is moving slowly away from Pier 16. But there is still just a chance: maybe a slight delay of some sort, and I have flown a good 2,000 miles today to get here, so both of us lean forward from the edges of our seats, and barrel along the empty port road: Pier 28.Pier 25 (these are actually enormous warehouses or "sheds"). Pier 22. Pier 19. I say, "Blast your horn, let 'em know we're coming"

"Horn's busted," says my concentrating cabby, "sounds like a sick cow."

Approaching the Pier 19 shed now, straining for a view of—what?—an empty quay, a bereft wharf?

But, as we clear the last corner: LO AND BEHOLD! THERE SHE IS!   Lit up like Times Square, huge dark green hull and, emblazoned on her bows: BIBI. "MY SHIP," I holler, "YOU MADE IT!", clapping the cabby on his shoulder. "She's still here!" We beetle across the vast and deserted quay.

It is exactly 2400 hrs.—12 midnight!

But the gangway is pulled up three or four feet off the quay; several men are gathered; a pickup truck stands empty. "She's getting ready to leave!" I mutter to myself through clenched teeth, as we haul the bags out of the trunk. I reward the cabby generously, dash to the foot of the gangway. A Filipino crewman is standing by, no doubt wondering who is this frantic, bearded oddball. "I'm a

2

passenger; sorry I'm late, but I have to get on this ship!" I gasp. He grabs a bag, signals up to the deck and the gangway is lowered slightly. Another seaman clambers down and grabs the other bag. I teeter up the sloping stairway after them, and am at last, actually, really, standing on the deck of my very own ship! I made it! I'm here! I had told the folks back home that I would believe this trip only when I was planted firmly on the deck,   and, almost unbelievably, here I am!

The seamen move me and the bags in through the doorway and onto a tiny elevator. The gate is slammed and we rise five stories to E Deck where I am hustled down the corridor to wait while one of the crewmen enters a door marked CAPTAIN and points uncertainly at this midnight apparition. The Master himself emerges, we both talk at the same time, saying the obvious things; he beckons and I enter. I take a seat; the room is full of men—some uniforms, some suits—and a lot of papers. I notice very little; am still feeling unreal that I am actually aboard this ship—and just in the absolute nick of time!

Soon the men leave, the Polish Captain beckons again, and we head off down the corridor to the elevator with the crewmen and the big bags. We ride down to C deck and approach my cabin, "#5". Still somewhat breathless, I say to the Captain, "The ship is just about to leave, right?"

"No," he says, "we just got in."

Just got in! *Just got in?* "Uh—just arrived?", I manage.

"There was fog," he says, "couldn't come up Ship Canal until tonight; we sail tomorrow—probably midnight."

The ship just arrived! It won't sail for 24 hours! I have busted several nerve endings, endangered my aorta, and blown a precious twenty, and the ship *just arrived!*

I recover sufficiently to ask, just as casually, "Are the other passengers aboard?" "No," he answers, "you are only passenger until Hamburg." Zowee! Any other surprises to exercise the flexibility I am urged by all the Line's literature to maintain?

Yes! But this one is very pleasant indeed: my cabin. Designed originally for a Chief Steward who is no longer included in the ship's company, it is in fact a suite. I enter a small office with a window looking to starboard, a broad counter beneath the window, two filing cabinets, a separate desk with telephone, and a comfy-looking armchair. Hooks on the wall hold a big puffy life jacket and a hardhat, and, opposite, a large colour print of a mighty lighthouse being pummeled by a rogue wave. A door leads into the combination day- and bedroom: large bed (plenty wide and longer than a queen-sized), fine couch, small fridge and a built-in desk-hutch-wardrobe with bolted-down VCR and TV, telephone, and, best of all, two large windows looking forward over the ship's hatches, cranes and

3

derricks. Off the bedroom a bath with shower stall and other advisable mod cons. All in all more than 300 square feet of living space in which to spend the next four or five months.

Still breathing heavily, I teeter back down the gangway and go in search of a telephone, call the wifely Ellen, who of course can't wait to tell me that the ship just got in and won't leave for 24 hours, and I don't have to hurry or worry. When the fog closed in, it seems, the Rickmers Linie agent called Freighter World Cruises (my bookers), who then called Vicky Blevins at Uniglobe Travel on Salt Spring Island, who left a message for Ellen, but, alas, too late: we were on our way, and then I was aloft, and it never occurred to me to phone back from Phoenix. (Lesson: Keep checking until you walk up that gangway!)

About eleven hours ago, at 1330 hrs., we bid farewell at the Vancouver airport after catching the 0630 ferry from Long Harbour, Salt Spring to Tsawwassen, Vancouver's ferry port. Everything went well until the snag in Phoenix. Well, there was that striking moment at the Vancouver check-in counter when I innocently asked, "These bags are going through to Houston, right?" And the agent, looking a bit startled, took a quick look at the tags he was attaching to those very bags. "Oops", he said, "I got 'em going to Albuquerque—and I got the wrong name, too. Sorry. Glad you mentioned it." *Albuquerque?* The mind boggles at what that foul-up might have meant! But now, with all bags accounted for and the important phone call behind me, I can really start to relax, and again I climb the swaying gangway, heading for my new home where I fall all the way down into the first of who knows how many night's sleep aboard the wandering BIBI.

2.

4/10 The view from one of my fine forward-looking windows: an ant farm! All five ship's cranes and the big derrick plus a gigantic shore crane are hard at work; at least a hundred men bustle about; fork lifts of all sizes, huge flatbed trucks, even rail cars, move—from my vantage point—like Tonka toys on this enormous quay. We are discharging huge steel structures, like parts of a bridge. They were piled on the hatch covers; they filled several hold spaces: they are, I discover, the skeleton of a new parking garage for Houston, and they came from some place in Asia. I am compelled to watch this circus of swinging metal; I *must* watch—if only to make sure they get it right.

I am up at 0700 for breakfast, served from 0730 to 0830 so as to catch crew members before they go on their four hour watch at 0800, as well as those just coming off watch. I am told by the Steward that I can have anything I want—eggs, bacon, ham, sausage, cereal, toast, a variety of juices—or everything! As I sit marveling at my eggs ("over and smashed") a ship glides past the

4

mess room window. It is the MV LEON, the very ship I was booked on before being switched (and upgraded!) to the good ship BIBI. LEON, built in 1979, the same year as her sisters BIBI and MERIDA, has been ordered back to Asia with cargo from the U.S. This is a rare occurrence, to have two of the sisters, which should have been following each other around the globe at decent intervals, together in the same port.

As soon as possible I don my garden variety "work" gloves against the "oily, rusty, greasy, dirty, sooty" (it says in my pre-boarding instruction sheet) surfaces of many parts of the ship, especially the hand rails on the gangway, leave the stevedores to their own devices, and pick my way over the ant hill to inspect MV LEON which has tied up just ahead of us at Pier 17. Of course, her superstructure, cranes, derricks, house, and funnel housing are identical to ours, but the poor thing needs a coat of paint so badly that even four months and about a thousand ships later, back in Houston, I have to conclude I have never seen a worse-looking ship. But never mind: I find it bad form to be too critical of the appearance of a ship as hard-working as she. And there, high up on LEON's E deck aft staircase stands a woman apparently sketching the scene below. I lurk about our sister ship's stern and finally catch the sketcher and a male companion leaving the ship for a taxi that has pulled up. Grabbing a quick word, I announce that I am about to start the voyage they have apparently just completed.

"Yes," she purrs: "137 days! And it was marvelous! Your biggest expense will be taxi fares from ports into cities along the way." So saying, they climb aboard their taxi and make for the city. (A month or so later, my son Dan, who has devised a web site to follow my progress, is combing cyberspace for anything having to do with this ship or this trip and he comes across a site set up by "Bandit" who regales his readers, in quite colourful language, with tales of his and his mother's recent trip on a tramp freighter—and he has photos! Dan immediately gets his permission to borrow some for his site and discovers they were taken on the LEON. And "Bandit" and his sketching Mum were apparently the very persons I saw into the waiting cab!)

Meanwhile, our stevedores seem to be doing fine, but I can see why "flexibility" is the key word when it comes to general cargo freighters. A truck turns out to be too short for the great steel frames being unloaded. Nothing happens for 15 minutes until a bigger truck is found; now they can't discharge from the forward hold: a rail car must be pushed out of the way: 20 minutes. Etc. It is all fascinating to watch. Speed is naturally of the essence, but care in placing and lashing is even more important. Everything I see is monstrous in scale and as the trip unfolds I continue to be impressed at the ingenuity of humans in designing and building unbelievably huge,

5

enormous, gigantic machines to assist their own comparatively puny efforts. I get quite used to watching gargantuan cranes and derricks handle 150-ton "modules" and v - e - r - y s - l - o - w - l - y lift and gently place them on waiting vehicles. I will never tire of watching this process.

The ship carries five 20-ton cranes (that is, each of them can lift 20 tons at a time), but four of them are mounted in pairs on revolving pedestals and can be linked, both then operable from one cab, their great hooks detached and their cables shackled to a single even larger hook, Voila! A 40-ton crane! 'Midships is the 250-ton Stuelcken derrick used for very heavy lifts. (A crane is defined as "a swinging arm attached to a vertical axis", while a derrick is "a long, moving beam pivoted at the base of a vertical stationary beam and guided by ropes running on pulleys".) The BIBI actually has five derricks: the "jumbo" Stuelcken, and four other beams attached to its support towers that are too lightweight to be used, get in the way, have to be painted and maintained, and are going to be got rid of, or so I am told. The cranes can revolve fully so as to work out of hatches fore and aft of their mountings. The Stuelcken jumbo, though mounted between hatches three and four, can be cleverly "flipped" to service either.

I quickly revise my opinion that general cargo ships like the BIBI are fast becoming anachronisms—eclipsed by the giant container ships now plying the seas. Watching what came out of this ship, and later what goes into it, it becomes obvious that there are thousands and thousands of tons of cargo that could never be carried in containers. (In fact, the Rickmers Line was just completing the first of nine new Super General Cargo ships 100 feet longer than the BIBI and able to handle virtually any kind of cargo: general, like us, liquid [e.g. cooking oil], bulk [e.g. fertilizer], refrigerated, roll-on [e.g., cars and trucks], containers—in short, just about anything that requires long distance totage.)

At lunch, served again to straddle the watches, from 1130 to 1230, I learn that after Beaumont, our next port will be Tampa, then straight to Hamburg—no East Coast U.S. stops at all—a bit of a disappointment, but I remember about that "flexibility" thing.

Took a long walk along the quay this afternoon, through vast and echoing pierside sheds filled to the rafters with bales of cotton. Returned to discover an ice cream truck with cheery bells ringing pulled up among the stacks of steel. Perfect!

Not very hungry at supper tonight, but before I can suggest a "not very much" plate, the alert Steward has placed before me a healthy helping of braised beef, spaghetti made of little larva-like pasta, and really excellent French fries! I may do all right after all with my fussy, Protestant "meat and potatoes" preferences. Still, I'm glad I packed the popcorn popper—just in case. I clean the plate, swallow all the bottled water I can manage, swig some OJ and keep my orange for later. As a rule, no desserts are served on these ships, but fresh fruit is a nice alternative.

Two strange men are at the table tonight. They are not Polish, as are the other officers—as they made haste to point out; they are Greek and represent Technomar, the company that actually operates this ship. Technomar, based in Athens, is under contract to Double C Shipping of Limassol, Cyprus, BIBI's port of registration—her "hailport". Double C owns 55% of BIBI, but Technomar provides officers and crew and in all other ways manages the voyages: full provisioning—everything from fuel oil and cable grease to oranges for everyone, orange coveralls for the crew, and books and videos for the library. Double C purchased the ship from Rickmers, which company, upon discovering that general cargo hauling might after all be lucrative, bought back 45%. It seems now, with a tightening market (since, we were told, the 9/11 catastrophe) there may be more reconsidering. In any case, another five years of service may put paid to the circumnavigational life of "my" ship, which would then be sold to a smaller "coasting" line. And five years or so after that, she may just end up at the ship breaker's yard. Apparently 30 to 35 years is about the life span of a ship. Maintenance, replacement of parts, etc. just become too expensive.

In any case, here was Technomar in the flesh, just playing Inspector General and seeing how things were going. The Greeks would disembark in Tampa, and I sensed that any tears shed by our bunch would probably be crocodile.

Still—into the evening now—that steel for future parkers is being lifted away. When the decks are cleared of the huge grids, hatches are opened to reveal yet more steel! Soon a dozen ponderous, swinging crane loads empty what I just assume is the "hold", but, before my very eyes, the floor of the "hold" suddenly begins to fold itself flat against the bulkhead to reveal more space beneath and, you guessed it, *more steel!* The bottom space, where the ribs of the ship can be seen is, in fact, the hold itself; the upper area is the 'tween decks.

Also emerging from these immense spaces today: three huge steam generators weighing 507,482 lbs. each. I am already forming the habit of checking weights, contents, destinations, etc. whenever I can get near the cargo on shore; I was never invited into the hold spaces: tricky getting in and out—through small hatches in the deck and straight down steel ladders—probably a safely and insurance thing), and two 4 ton ship anchors. The generators are laid gently atop super-strong articulated railroad flat cars and—never mind "lashing", chaining, or tying down—actually welded right to the floor of the car—a common practice, it seems.

Also had my tour of the ship this afternoon, the Captain my guide: former radio room (now satellite telephone, personal computers, etc.—the radios are now on the bridge and there is no longer a Radio Officer), conference room, various lounges, laundry facilities, etc., and lastly, the bridge, located above E deck. I will be welcome there anytime. He leaves all the "engineering stuff" for the Chief Engineer to present. I look forward to that.

I can't seem to relax yet, seem to want to be on the go all the time, except when I sit down for a minute to read my book and start to nod off. The promised CD player is not in evidence in the cabin. With the great stack of disks I brought, I foresee possible panic without music to my ears. I mention this to the Captain and he promises to have one ready when we provision in Antwerp. In the meantime, I must contrive some way to make do for the month or more until we get there.

This has been a fine day! The ship is even more intriguing than I had imagined, its workings fascinating, the accommodations excellent, the food more than adequate. I am thoroughly enjoying this adventure. Then it occurs to me: the ship is still tied to the pier; it hasn't moved an inch; the voyage hasn't even started!

It is nearly midnight; the last pieces of steel are extracted and simply piled on the quay—no trucks about at this hour. Cranes are lowered into their "nests", and hooks wrestled with and finally lashed down by Filipino crewmen only inches taller than the hooks; the big derrick, first hauled into its straight-up position—almost 176 feet high—then lowered to 45° so it won't bump the bridges and cable crossings on the Houston Ship Canal; hatches are hydraulically closed and latched, and the ship is made ready to sail. A tugboat hoots into place, the pilot comes aboard, deck lights are doused; our crew stands by on poop deck and bow to take in the twelve giant hawsers tying us to Houston—six fore and six aft—and, on shore, a small squad of rather rotund longshoremen stands by to hoist the lines from the bollards and drop them with a splash into the harbour so our winches can reel them in. To me it is almost unbearably exciting; to the rest, just routine work.

4/11   At 0045 I am peering over the rail when, almost imperceptibly, the gap between ship and shore begins to widen: *we are moving!* Five hundred and eighty-four feet of ship, 17,000 tons heavy, is actually moving! The voyage has begun! We are starting to circle the world!   One day, four or five months from now, we will be tugged and nudged back into this very spot, and will prepare to discharge one small piece of cargo—me!

8

Our speed increases slightly as tug at stern and bow thruster forward combine to take us out into the stream, and soon I can feel the deep throb and pulse as our 15,000 hp engine begins to turn the 19 foot propeller and move us into the start of this nearly 25,000 mile voyage, ever easting through 24 time zones until we arrive right back where we began.

We have moved down the Canal for 2 1/2 hours now, with another two or three hours to go, then we'll cross Galveston Bay and enter the Gulf of Mexico. The passage is slow and quiet and fascinating, a variety of ships and industries, many oil refineries with their gas flares brightening the night, but my own brightness is dimming rapidly. I know I should be "on watch" so as not to miss anything, but it's the eyes and especially the eyelids that are betraying me. I'm sorry, but the Captain, the Second Officer, the helmsman and the pilot will just have to manage the ship on their own for a while. I crumple onto the big bed and let the slow pulse of the engine and the graceful movement of my ship lull me into a second sound sleep aboard the BIBI.

3.

I wake with a new motion to the ship—for some reason it feels like we are backing up: vibration, a sort of juddering—like a ferry in a sharp turn. At the window the sun is bright, the sea green, the bow wave lovely to look at, and there is no land in sight. This is the Gulf of Mexico! And this is the ship moving at speed, probably 18 knots or so. We are not backing up, not turning, but running straight and true. But what is this racket? I have dreamed of being lullabied to sleep by the deep rumble of the engine; instead I am rattled awake by a cacophony that will surely plague to distraction my sleeping hours. Is *this* what a ship sounds like underway? I am inside a spinning clothes drier! With a pair of size 12 runners banging and bumping around with me! Is this it for 140 days? I return to bed, roll over—*and sleep again!*

I wake. All seems quiet. I discover that the multifarious noises happen only now and then when one or more of the air compressors kicks in. The main engine sounds are right where they should be: way down there grumbling away. And I discover that noises on a ship are gotten used to; in fact, they quickly become a lullaby—even (or perhaps especially) during the day! There is but a gentle motion to the ship; the sea is calm with only a modest swell. Hey, this may not be so bad after all! I have skipped breakfast, but will make do with last night's orange and drink the water purloined from the ship's fridge last evening. When we tie up in Beaumont today I will taxi someplace and pick up a few things, though the shopping list now contains 16 items, including popcorn of course—I brought none with me on the plane: too heavy—and the least expensive CD player I can find—just in case the Antwerp connection doesn't come through, and in any case, to tide me over.

Suddenly, out the front window, I am appalled to see a seaman scaling one of the 100 foot derrick support towers. The rungs of his ladder are simply welded to the outside of the tower, but up he goes to lash fast one of those pesky lightweight derrick beams.

I also discover that my shower, which should spray, simply dribbles; the cold water tap on my sink spins wantonly when I need it; there are no hangers in the wardrobe, and no plug for the sink—a major drawback with spring-loaded taps and only two hands—a demonstration that one hand does indeed wash the other.

Oil rigs all around us. As I get to know this ship and her crew, I have a little *satori*: we landlubbers are quite accustomed, especially us ferry riders, to thinking of a ship as merely a means to an end. It gets us places (or doesn't!), brings us things; it is a method of transportation. But it suddenly seems to me that a ship is only incidentally that: not just a means, it is a sort of miraculous end in itself. A community, sufficient, with a life of its own: it breathes and circulates, moves, ingests, processes, excretes (very carefully and very "greenly"). It is a living being and just happens to carry cargo and people. It is easy to understand why ships are "shes", why we begin to think of these largest of all moving entities as nourishing and caring, and somehow even alive.

We have stopped. Must wait first for an anchorage spot, then for a tug and the pilot to make the long, long passage to the inland port of Beaumont. Will I ever get to attack my provisions list? It is bound to be a short stop here, just some cargo to offload, nothing to pick up. I am already beginning to detect a rather strange world trading pattern in this voyage, strange inasmuch as the United States is generally considered "the greatest" industrial nation on earth. We discharged cargo in Houston; we will discharge cargo in Beaumont; more cargo will be left in Tampa, and when we cross the Atlantic the ship will be "in ballast"—empty! A freighter leaving the United States for Europe and carrying nothing? Yup. We start to load up again in Europe, deliver the goods to the Middle East and perhaps to Singapore, Thailand, Viet Nam, and some to China, at which point we are nearly empty again! Load up in China, Korea, Japan and deliver a nearly full shipload to the United States! Then "deadhead" across the Atlantic to start the run all over again. Sort of

10

makes you stop and think. With all the steel mills and the plethora of industry in the States and the costs of packing and shipping, it is obviously still less expensive to purchase and ship an entire parking garage from Asia to America, generators and boilers and huge "modules" from Japan and China for Beaumont and Tampa. Something is amiss here.

BIBI's bridge

Made my first excursion to the bridge this morning. The "bridge" is of course a room—the control centre of ship, usually located above all the decks on top of the "house". Apparently the name derives from the necessity, on the earliest steam-powered ships, of constructing a literal bridge across the ship from which to steer. It is not a real bridge any more, nor is it the "wings" that stretch out from the bridge proper to provide views while docking, loading, etc.

I am welcomed on this bridge, and devour the sights and sounds: great control panels for lights (a special one labeled SUEZ CANAL LIGHTS), horns, autopilot; the ship's wheel in the centre—not the large, spoked wheel we have come to expect on ships, but an affair about the size of a car steering wheel with the top third removed. Steering, except when "maneuvering" in and out of anchorages, ports and berths, is done electronically using the GPS (Global Positioning System), gyro compass, computers, etc. and consists of setting a course—say, 53°, switching on the autopilot, then watching either of the two radar screens and peering out the windows to make sure we don't run into anything. This applies, by the way, 24 hours a day, around the clock. There is always an officer on the bridge on watch.

The "after" section of the bridge (not shown) is the chart "room". I have long been fascinated by marine charts (much different from plain old maps) and could read them by the hour. The ship's lockers contain hundreds and hundreds of charts, charts for every ocean, sea, channel, canal and almost every port in the world, in various scales. With their insets, notes, and updates—an infinity of information, you can lose yourelf in these charts! The crew quickly gets used to this old bearded guy "navigating" his way across a chart with dividers and parallel rulers to calculate directions and distances. (A rumor began that I was either a retired captain or the new owner of the ship!) At night, the chart room is curtained off from the control bridge, as the latter needs to be darkened, very much as a car's interior must remain unlit at night. Later, I would observe the interplay on the bridge as pilot, Captain, mate and helmsman work together to get the ship to its berth.

Have decided that, in the manner of old, I will take a daily "noon fix" from the GPS and plot it on my big world map. Sometimes I will "fix" our position when we actually arrive in a port—or "port", as in Phoenix. Here's the first one from the GPS.

30°10'N x 94°W (at sea)

After a delicious lunch of chicken, etc., I begin what will become a compulsive and continuous exploration of the ship. This expedition turns up a plastic chair on the deck just aft of the bridge. I find no real deck chairs yet on the ship—those chaise longue types.

But we are still at anchor, waiting for our entry into Beaumont. My shopping expedition may be fading fast, and there are certain things which no amount of scrounging will turn up on the ship—like popcorn! I sit outside in my newfound plastic chair on a bright, sunny afternoon and get to thinking about all this. Somebody asked me if I had guide books to all the countries and places on the trip. I don't. Why not? Perhaps one reason was my focus on the ship itself—and the sea. I have long known I wanted to make this trip and how, but the exact reason for it I've never actually explained—even to myself. Very complicated. Has to do, naturally, with the womb-like nature of a ship (or a train, for that matter), comforting sounds, gentle motion, the security of a cozy space, plenty to eat, lots of time with nothing else happening. But it's also the idea of "keeping going", of constant motion, new places every day—every hour! I can easily understand the father of a friend who, on family trips, was so reluctant to stop the car for anything that they have albums full of blurry pictures taken from moving car windows.

And it also has to do with ships.

Ships have a history as long as man himself. A ship is a miracle of design, construction, engineering, grace, and beauty. This ship, after carrying thousands of tons of steel and generators, and a great deal more, accomplished the miracle of crossing the Pacific and made possible the building of a new parking facility, the production of hundreds of megawatts of electric power, and, let's not forget, the safe anchoring of a new ship—or ships—with those two huge anchors. Then, looking at first incredibly huge, monumentally heavy, seemingly welded in place and totally incapable of travelling anyplace at anytime, it actually started to move, to glide, gracefully to leave its rock-ribbed "permanent" berth and embark on a voyage which would circle the globe. It became, itself, a miracle!

And sitting here like a decoy duck not moving an inch makes another point. In the world out there when there is a delay, as there was in Phoenix for me on the plane, dozens of schedules are disrupted, most of all the plane's. Here, on this tramp freighter, we sit for several hours. Schedule? What schedule? This ship has no schedule (although it does try). It goes where and when it can. When it gets there, it's there. Late? No such thing. "On time?" Always!

4.

30°30'N x 94°W (Beaumont)

At 2200 we finally reach Beaumont—it must be near Chicago! It took us more than five hours to traverse the Sabine and Neches Rivers, lakes and canals. Nice slow trip. Spent most of my time on the bridge with the pilot, a personable fellow with a belt line rivaling his state's border. Have seen a good deal of abdominal acreage in the past few days.

This routine is wearing me down! I am never relieved by a new "watch", am "on duty" all the time. Must see everything, do everything. But we do eat! Breakfast as big as you want plus two full meals a day. Juice, bottled water, soup, salad, meat, potatoes, vegetable and invariably fruit of some kind. No desserts except now and then a dish of ice cream or, as the journey continues, a slice of apple pie once, and now and then a piece of rather strange cake—but cake all the same. One mess hall, actually more like a communal dining room, serves western food for the Polish officers and crew, passengers, and other "westerners" who may come aboard from time to time, and on the other side of the ship, a second mess offers Filipino foods for the rest of the crew. We eat restaurant style,

13

but with only one thing on the menu, the officers generally eating very fast, passengers and visitors lingering a bit longer. But meals are not "sittings"—diners come and go anytime during the allotted serving hour, following the established routine of wishing others "Good appetite" when arriving and "Thank you" or "Excuse" when departing. The white-coated Steward, who is the "waiter", graciously serving plates to each "customer", gently assigns each new arrival a place at the long table and that place is "reserved" for the rest of the voyage. Helpings are more than generous and later we get into the habit of asking for "only 50%, please".

Have yet to try the VCR or the TV and haven't had a rousing game of solitaire or tackled a crossword puzzle; will wait 'til I get really bored.

4/12 Well, from a newly discovered, if slightly scary, observation post on "G Deck" atop the bridge, I have supervised all the really heavy unloading—2 great coolers from us and a huge "splitter" from a barge next door (we have the biggest lifter in the area) for a refinery. One huge module required a special lifting frame that came right with it, probably weighing several tons itself, and in all likelihood will now become scrap metal. I realize, watching the lifting and loading and unloading activity, that right from the design stage, methods of lifting and carrying must be built right into these enormous components, and the whole package cannot be larger than the hatch through which it must fit. As we touch port after port, it becomes obvious that when it comes to shipping, e.g., an entire paper mill, not only must the hundreds of components large and small be manufactured, they must then be carefully packed in wooden boxes. Surely, a totally separate company—a boxing outfit—does this job, then labels each crate as to destination, contents, exact size and weight. The amount of sturdy wood used for these boxes will surely keep many a family warm for most of a winter.

But now I await a cab to whisk me to Parkdale Mall in Beaumont (learned about it from the pilot) where I will pick up an increasingly long list of small stuff.

For a $10 flat fee (for seamen—that's me!), the driver guides me through beautiful downtown Beaumont (which now "has only lawyers in it"), out to where "the real stores are", and delivers me into the largest "mall" I've ever seen. It spreads over a thousand acres of former cotton field, the stores being largely separate. Enclosed malls? No need—this is hot weather Texas! On a hunch I suggest the local Wal-Mart, and sure enough, every single thing I need, including a $24 stereo/CD player, and to my immense relief, even though it isn't my brand, *six pounds of popcorn*, is found in Sam Walton's famous emporium. Waiting for the cab to take me

14

back, this being my first time away from the ship, I experience the first of many such panics: *it won't be there when I return!* Though I know we won't sail until at least midnight—and probably tomorrow.

Back "home" again, I unpack my treasures, warm up the CD player and fill the cabin with glorious music: so *that's* what's been missing! I realize, not for the first time, that life without music is no life at all, and, to celebrate, set about whipping up a mess of popcorn. I stopper up the sink, distribute my new hangers, and generally relish the dozen or more tiny things that will balance out my contentment level. It's not that I forgot stuff; I deliberately didn't bring certain things—like several pounds of popcorn, butter, salt, etc., and then discovered those other missing things in the cabin. By the way, I rarely use real butter on my popcorn, but to my dismay, I found that Becel—the only passable substitute—seems to be available only in Canada. Pity! I picked up at Wal-Mart what looked like a substitute, but it turned out to be about 90% water, so I chucked it out and asked the Steward for the "loan" of some butter. "A pound?" he asked. "Oh, no, but half a pound would be nice". And he produced it. I am just about to plug in the popper when there is a knock at the door. It is the Steward himself, Renand Mercado, again, looking about 19 (he is really 31 with a wife and child back home), with a great tub full of goodies to make my little fridge "more attractive". He fills it with big bottles of water, boxes of juice, 12 cans of Coke, 2 lemons, cartons of yogurt and a jar of raspberry preserves. Renand will become my absolute favorite crewman—and not because of the goodies: as the months pass, he will prove to be fiercely intelligent, highly perceptive, possessed of an incomparable sense of humour, adept at card tricks and other magicks. He will also be "the man" on the ship who will bring linens and towels, and a number of other items down the line. I press upon him a bag of fresh popcorn. In return, I suggest he call me "Moses" instead of "Sir". The end product of this negotiation, for the rest of the voyage, is: "Sir Moses" or "Sir Richard". I like the sound of either.

I had been told that the ship would have a library and a collection of videos, and it surely does, in the officers lounge just off the dining room. Several new books and tapes had been donated by Freighter World Cruises, the agency I dealt with in booking this passage. But in my own cabin I also found a collection of about 20 books—all in German, including a Desmond Bagley, a James Clavell, a selection of Japanese folk tales, and "*Abenteuer Alaska*" by Pierre Berton. Since I had brought along 17 paperbacks from the Salt Spring Library book sale, I decided not to try one of the *Deutscher Bücher* just yet, and schlepped them all down to the central library. Passengers sort of understand that the books and other library items they bring aboard will probably be left there for future travelers. I left a great wad of sampler CDs that I hope will be enjoyed by newcomers.

With all my new goodies, plus the glorious music and a $7 folding stool I thought might come in handy, I'm beginning to feel right at home in my suite. Still, I can't help but look at all of this through Ellen's eyes—and perhaps those of other women as well. It is hard to imagine Ellen clambering onto and then up the swaying, staircase known as the gangway, let alone down, especially when the thing is raised a couple or three feet off the ground, not swung away from the ship, you find yourself looking straight down the steps into open water, there is no one to make adjustments, and a nimble leap onto the raised edge of the quay is required to alight. My Ellen is also addicted to quietness. Quietness on this ship? Not so's you'd notice! Then there is walking—one of her favorite things—but here, on decks inevitably dirty, oily, sooty, fraught with trippable hooks, eyes and other weldings just where you're about to put a foot, mere strolling becomes something of an adventure. Care and concentration are required wherever one goes. There is also the fact that for my nurse wife, cleanliness *is* godliness, and while "shipshape" and "Bristol fashion" can certainly be applied to the decks and rigging, "clean" probably can't be. Over everything external is an inevitable greasy mix of salt, oil, and soot, and to touch virtually anything outside is to find one's hands greasy and sort of clammy-feeling—a coating that will not come off without a thorough washing with hot water and soap. One simply gets used to donning gloves (garden or work variety) when venturing forth. (You do learn after a bit just what to touch and what to avoid in walking the decks.) Naturally, everyone working on deck wears not only gloves, but coveralls, heavy boots that *must* be removed before entering living spaces (the grunge is also very difficult to remove from the carpeted floors.) Mind you, the insides of the ship—corridors, stairways, etc., are immaculate and kept that way. The internal staircases are very effectively railed on both sides, but are steep, with risers slightly higher than normal and steps a bit narrower than usual—or maybe it just seems like that.

There were other events and anomalies as the voyage proceeded that brought to mind Ellen's very wise, I think, response some years ago when I issued my invitation and she replied with her usual keen intuition. Then there were those times, particularly rolling 30° or more and watching "secure" items flying around the cabin, when I wondered if *I'd* made the right choice. Or should "*Bon voyage*" have been my reaction, too?

Speaking of "shipshape", the BIBI is in her 23rd year, has had a full life and a hard one, but no matter how many coats of paint are applied, it is always time to start all over again.

Mechanisms, hatch covers, valves and vents all now look completely painted shut and immovable. Not so. Everything works. It must! Every cable, hatch, latch, lever, button, airway, winch, chain and cable has to work or the ship will fail to function, to carry out its miraculous cargo haulage. There is rust, of course; there would be rust if the ship had been painted yesterday! Rust is an ever-vigilant, never-resting attacker of any ship. But you cannot tell a ship by its rust streaks. BIBI's sister, the MV LEON, appears to be a classic "rust bucket", her paint chipped and worn, her original colour hard to guess at, but never mind; inside, she too is ship-shape and Bristol fashion—and she works!

There are many wonders apparent on and around the ship. The immensity of its size, the unbelievable strength of its cranes and winches and derrick, the relative puniness of the tiny men in their hard hats and the amazing knowledge they demonstrate in getting things done using their brains and the ship's brawn. Only once in a while is human brute strength called upon. Rigging the lifting frame this morning meant lifting 4 1/2 inch thick, 30 foot long cable bights and hooking them to enormous shackles that probably weighed 70 lbs. each. I watched three men wrestle one such linkage into position. The image was reminiscent of the flag-raising on Iwo Jima. This is not to mention the danger if even one of those giant shackles fell on a foot! I keep well back and out of the way.

The cranes and great Stuelcken derrick move with gargantuan ponderousness and grace, giving even more emphasis to their strength. Unloading the big coolers today, when the derrick reached out to place the load on a flatcar, the entire ship took on a definite starboard list and my pen rolled off the desk. Don't tell me this isn't a whole heap more interesting than watching containers being loaded or unloaded. In fact, later in the voyage one of the Supercargoes (the name used for the Supervisor of Cargo), said to us passengers one day, "You think we do all this for your entertainment?" "Absolutely!" we chorused, "And we thank you!"

4/13 We are again reaching the Gulf, passing some giant, beached oil rigs waiting to be towed out or retired. I held out 'til about 2200 last evening and finally—after three days "on watch" collapsed. Woke up a couple of times when internals altered—mine or the ship's. At 0205 they were still unloading; at 0400 we were moving, all deck lights doused, all cranes secured.

We will soon hit the Gulf and rev up to FULL AHEAD. Am anxious to feel again the effects of full speed. The ship, by the way, has really only eight speeds: four ahead and four astern. FULL, HALF, SLOW, and DEAD SLOW. I can still hear the Captain's voice bellowing from one of the wings to the Officer (he who actually controls the "throttle"), standing next to the helmsman: "HALF

AHEAD!", and the Officer's return shout, "HALF AHEAD, SIR!".
While the traditional "engine telegraph" is in place, a simple switch
on the bridge console makes it possible—and more convenient—to
control the engine's speed instantly from "upstairs" without the need
for an engineer waiting below decks to receive and repeat the signal.
This was the usual arrangement. Of course, the "ninth
directive"—STOP ENGINES—was always a welcome cry; it meant we
had arrived.

No idea when we will reach Tampa. Waiting now for the Fitter
to fix my plumbing—the ship's that is. Never thought I'd be this
eager for a shower. Here comes one of those beautiful, speedy, husky
little boats to take our pilot away. I'll go watch.

Heading 177°, speed 17 knots. We have yet to leave the
Safety Fairway leading into and out of Beaumont and turn to port. I
figure the course at about 90° to Tampa.

Was wondering about the nesting of the cranes and derricks
when at sea. The big derrick is hoisted straight up (unless we need
to pass under bridges or cables), but each crane has a "nest" on its
own special platform where boom and hook are secured.

Captain says, "Tonight we make bar-r-r-becue!" Steaks,
chops?

Am still tired; may have to (gasp) have a nap today! I realize
this is part of the dream coming true—a dream born of falling asleep
on ferries, only to be rudely awakened by a deckhand banging on
your window, obviously over-anxious to keep traffic moving! Some
nerve! Ahh, to be on a moving ship and just drop off. As it were.

1 1/2 days to Tampa we are told. We just turned east to head
for the Florida city. So far the ship moves like one of those B.C.
ferries: no seas running, very little swell. Weather altogether
beautiful. Nearing noon now; must head down for lunch, but I really
just want to sleep!

5.

29°30'N x 93°45'W (at sea)

Course 80°, speed 17.8 knots, seas Force 2. Gorgeous,
gorgeous day! Ship on autopilot; only the Chief Officer (1st Mate),
one of the Greeks and me on the bridge. English is the official
language of the sea lanes—radio contacts, pilots, all personnel
generally communicate in English, but interpersonal chat is another
matter. Occasionally on the bridge I have heard simultaneous
conversations in Polish, Tagalog, Greek, English—and after
Hamburg, there'll be German!

Back in the cabin I have noticed the infrequent aroma of oil, probably filtering through the air conditioning; now the scent of burning charcoal—the BBQ has begun! Is this the life, or what?

Mind you, I'm not counting any chickens—barbecued or not—we have yet to cross two oceans, the Bay of Biscay, the Arabian Sea, the Mediterranean and sundry other bodies of those waters that make up two-thirds of the earth's surface. I am ever conscious of my stash of seasickness remedies including two acupressure elastic bracelets reputed to be the last word in seagoing tummy health.

Outstanding BBQ! Pork chops, chicken, that very good sausage, rice, salad, coke, etc. All out on the breezy poop deck (from the French *"poupe"*, Italian *"poppa"*. Latin *"puppis"* —"the stern of a ship; on sailing ships, a raised deck at the stern", on this ship a large flat area, the location of vents and winches for handling shore lines, and, for tonight's purposes, a metal canopy covering a rustic picnic table; a home-made "gym" consisting of a set of rusty, but workable barbells, and a pulley rigged for lifting weights; a split 50 gallon drum for the fire. The poop deck is also the open air workshop for welding, cutting and anything else the Fitter has to fix. Wonderful sitting at the stern as the sun sets. Several ships pass, freighters, tankers, even a big white liner heading for New Orleans. Do those passengers have any inkling that here on this old freighter there is another passenger who is having as much or more fun than they are? And, by the way, on that big orange tanker: do *they* have BBQs on *their* fantail? BOOM!

Have been fiddling with the new "World Band", i.e. short-wave, radio I brought along, trying the antenna in different places. Really too early to "DX" properly, should wait 'til after sundown, but—Voila!—all of sudden there is "Quirks and Quarks" from RCI/CBC! Nice treat.

Ah, the darkened bridge. Ghostly figures—three of us, I think—moving about in and out of the dim glow of the radar scopes. Oil rigs on every hand; ships passing in the night. Sun disappearing. Still smells like the BBQ up here.

4/14 Another bright, sunny, calm day. We are heading east so the sun pours into my two front windows. Seem to have caught up on my sleep. Sleeping here not unlike on a train. Gentle motion (so far!) and always the dull rumble of movement along the tracks or, here, the engine down below, plus the air moving through the ducts. Our bows are shouldering aside the waves, plowing on. The waves don't seem to mind at all; they leap and tumble almost gaily: a little diversion in their otherwise rather humdrum day.

19

Already this morning the #4 hatch covers have been cleared of spacer or bracing planks, and I can hear sounds of work—on a steel ship, a the sound of a hammer goes a long way. Makes me feel oddly inadequate, very privileged and a bit sheepish: I'm the only one among the 24 crew members with no job! Work never stops on a ship like this—chipping, painting, repairing, oiling, greasing

Well! That's a mistake I won't make again! Forgot to set my watch ahead an hour last night, so when I got down to breakfast I was all alone. But Renand fixed me Sunday morning bacon and eggs anyway, without saying a word. I must learn to notice the little sign hanging over the clock in the dining room: "ADVANCE CLOCKS ONE HOUR TONIGHT!" It will be there at least 23 more times before I'm back. I now have three separate times going: GMT on the SW radio, PDT on an old watch hanging from the rail around the book shelf for back home, and the current hour on my wrist.

Just had a call from the Captain: could I come to his cabin for a talk. Uh oh! I'm in trouble! Having too much fun!

Nope, he just wanted to give me the ship's dope sheet (see Postlude) with all the info I'd been wondering about—just a little late, is all. Now I'll know where not to go and when. He—Grzegorz Wasielewski—is as shy with me as I am with him. But a very nice fellow. Showed me the boxes and boxes of files and paperwork he has to keep; this as a prelude to asking me to sign a copy of the regs so he could file it away!

29°N x 90°W (at sea)

Lunch is finished. One feels almost a responsibility to eat, even though not particularly hungry. Today, beef chunks in gravy on mashed potatoes, and for "dessert"—a hunk of watermelon, thus beginning The Great Watermelon Saga!. There are, on the long mess table, islands of condiments, sauces, etc. and today I counted eighteen different items, including the salt and pepper, plus nifty toothpick dispensers.
Now I'll take a stroll around the deck.

Or not. Got up to the bridge (to report my intentions) just in time for the rain to begin and the radar to show "big rain" just ahead. So I stayed put as we forged on, right through a couple of squalls that in my sailboating days would have had us battening down everything and dousing canvas. Here? Nice! Ship all clean now.

20

Funny about our "company" men from Technomar. One is the Marine Superintendent, the other the Engineering Supervisor. They are getting off in Tampa and I sense again a certain relief at that event. They are OK, but still "foreigners" to the ship's company (even more foreign than me!) and they are "management", and they speak a language that nobody understands, and they sort of lurk here and appear there, and I have overheard a heated word or two from time to time. As to my poor shower's need for repair, the Captain smiles when I suggest in lowered tones: "When the Greeks are gone." And around him faces light up and heads nod as if I have discovered some deep secret they would never have let out.

Well, it looks like Tampa by 0300 tomorrow morning, then discharge and leave by midnight on Monday the 15th. I am discovering that night and day, dark and light hold no significance for freighters: in fact, we are more likely to enter and leave ports in the middle of the night than in daylight. That's ok, but it plays havoc with the sleep of a guy who has to be on watch all the time!

After Tampa it's an eleven day run to Hamburg which puts us in there on April 26 or so. But of course we will remain Flexible!

There, by jing! This is a day to remember, a day that will live *in familia*. (Ellen will love this!) Finally got so desperate to have a shower (a week since) that I dove into the stall and *fixed* the damn thing myself! Well, not really. At least it didn't scald me (there is a sign in the stall reading PLEASE CHECK COLD WATER BEFORE ENTERING SHOWER—apparently at times there *is* no cold water) even if it did only dribble and drool almost like it didn't have a shower head. But, I'm clean!

What brought it all about was my half hour (six turns) around the deck soaking up sun and salt and sweat (the rains have gone, the sun is out, the sea and sky once again blue and the bow wave creamy white). After the shower, had a wee kip, just dozing over a book on my great sofa. Hey, it's all part of the dream; besides it's the ship's fault: it keeps putting me to sleep.

Am picking up a word or two of Tagalog (accent on the middle syllable), the Philippine language: "Selamat" is "Thank you". That's it so far.

Oh dear! Something for supper that looked decidedly unappetizing. Saw the Chief Officer eating a huge plate of mashed potatoes and beef (from lunch) so decided to ask for that instead—and got it! Then looked over: he had polished off the beef and was now on his "unappetizing" supper plate! I discovered later that the Chief never comes down to lunch, but has the Steward save his plate, so that at supper he has a choice—or a combination! I agree with him: sometimes there tends to be just too much to eat. Of

21

course, in this case, he ate them both! This Chief Officer, a husky, prize-fighter type with a brush cut, who at first makes me want to just stand back, is Waldemar Watracz, already showing signs of being an unusual fellow.

Coming back to the cabin, I still have the feeling there may be a message on the phone or an e-mail (emm) from cyberspace, or perhaps even someone to talk to, but, alas, there is only this journal.

Movie time!

Brought back a video movie; I'll just see if all this hardware really works.

It does! After a bit of fussing, AUTUMN IN NEW YORK is ready to roll.

Latest nugget of info: the two Polish Fitters on board are father and son. They will depart in Hamburg to be replaced by a single Fitter, reducing the crew to 23.

"Well, they spit in our eye again!" says one of the Greeks. Yep, we have to drop anchor just outside the channel into Tampa Bay—that's in maybe half an hour—and wait 'til 0100 when the pilot will come out and get us. Then maybe four or five hours to the wharf—about dawn, I would say. Shoot! I was going to stay up and watch the entry, but now I don't think so. See, I'm pooping out already!

Renand brought me a real deck chair tonight—a reclining, longue type with wheels and cushion and everything! He is a special guy—the chair almost as heavy as he!

One of our 7 1/2 ton anchors has rumbled and rattled into these Florida waters and we are at rest, lit up like a bright island.

6.

4/15   Woke at 0205 (no rest for the wary) to find us moving in the Fairway with Tampa still far away. Awake again at 0715; we are tied up at a berth that looks like the end of the world; sounds of heavy equipment BEEP BEEP BEEPing, and cranes already at work. Will not go down to breakfast; juice and pills here, maybe some popcorn, then search for a phone.

17°45'N x 82°30'W (Tampa)

Well, that takes the cake! Here we are tied up at what looks like "elegant" Tampa's scrap metal yard. Just on the starboard quarter a huge power plant with immense piles of coal waiting to make steam and electricity. Except for the twenty feet or so along the edge, our wharf is dirt. And as if that weren't enough, the berth isn't long enough for us—no place to secure bow lines except for a couple of long springs, so a tug is camped on the port bow holding us against the mole; it will remain there, engine running, prop turning—an aerobic exercise in pushing this 17,000 ton ship nowhere—'til we leave! Wonder what that's costing somebody.

There should be a phone fairly close, but probably no chance of getting into town. No real need. Pelicans gliding and swooping, crashing themselves into the sea pursuing a tasty morsel, then rising straight up into flight.

Called home: Ell and son Dan at about 1300 (EDT). Sudden rain around us now; unloading not yet finished. The trailers

23

handling the giant modules we are disgorging are extraordinary. One has 96 wheels arranged in sets and each set can be independently steered—like a hook and ladder fire truck.

Huge liner JUBILEE just leaving the port. Do I wish I were on it? Not a bit of it!

Long walk along the road past the TECO (Tampa Electrical Company) power plant—huge and scarifying with great gouts of steam blasting out, and the usual (I'm getting used to this on the trip) gargantuan everything—giant stacks, immense coolers and generators and great big noise. This is where those huge modules are going—and why we are camped out on our close-by mini-pier. The enormous things must also have come from Asia someplace,

Was stopped and quizzed by two security guards about what I'm doing, especially with the camera. I have no pass, nothing to prove I'm with the ship, so will start carrying my ticket which says it all. I am in a United States still jittery after 9/11. Incidentally, when I entered the Captain's cabin, back there in Houston, he was in the process of receiving news that because of a new regulation enacted "yesterday", no one on the ship without a U.S. Visa would be allowed ashore—a real blow to most of the crew who had been almost a month at sea—and who would now get no shore leave between Japan and Europe. And, here in Tampa, one of the young fellows who had been on hand to take our lines at 0300 this morning, was assigned to "guard" our gangway so that no "unauthorized personnel" could *leave* the ship. (Mostly he lolled out of the hot sun under an air compressor nearby.) I even had a bit of a problem myself. After all, I didn't have a visa either.

Big Mama derrick is sick—nobody at supper but the Captain and me, everybody trying to fix it—seven more modules to come out. Captain says we will try to get away about noon tomorrow then it's straight to Hamburg, and maybe Antwerp, then perhaps a port or two in Italy. So it looks like Hamburg on or about the 27th of April.

4/16 Big Mama back in action. Another module just moving away. Takes about an hour to unload one of them. Skipped breakfast. (I know, I know—"A better breakfast makes you feel better A - L - L - L day long. "Cream of Wheat, it's so good to eat . . . da dee dum dee dee dee dum" I *know* all that!). So nice to sleep in.

More watermelon for lunch! That's three times. But who's counting? NEWS: We'll pick up *three* passengers in Hamburg—a couple and one single fellow, *and* we'll probably stop in "Newport, England" on the way there! Called Ell as a surprise and got my friend Tony's phone number in Broadstairs, Kent, just in case there's time.

Well, they are offloading the last of the modules now; a couple of small ten ton boilers to go and we will be off. The conundrum of seafaring, I'm beginning to realize, is how much I look forward to entering a port and tying up, and then how much I look forward to untying and leaving for the open sea!

It seems to take forever for Big Mama to reach down into the hold and bring forth the last unit of cargo for TECO, a huge boiler. The giant truck carrying it away gives a last blast of farewell as it eases down the road.

And then, as if by magic, all the shore crews leave at what seems like triple speed! Fork lifts roar around picking up gear, and suddenly a great wind comes up! Dust fills the air, nearly blotting out the setting sun dead ahead. It seems to add a sense of drama and excitement to the scene: all the scurrying and the blowing and the running about: something momentous is about to happen.

There are always last minute people who have to come aboard and leave again. The Greeks leave and we gaily wave them on. The pilot arrives with his little bag and his purposeful air. He disappears inside. By tradition, he will bring the Captain a copy of today's newspaper and the Captain will tender him a small gift, a carton of Marlboros, for example, or a bottle of something. The linesmen pile out of their van (reminding me of circus clowns with their tiny car) and stand by the lines.

Now I ask you: is there anything more downright exciting than the departure of a ship? (A train maybe, but, no . . .) Even if you're not on it. But if you are . . . ! The leave-taking is infinitely slow in starting; almost imperceptibly , the great wall of the ship begins to move away from the quay. The last line, a stern spring, is loosed and winched aboard and the movement increases. The patient pushing tug alongside ceases its nudging and backs away, and the almost insufferable noises of that power plant, a cement loading dock, and the emptying of a barge astern, just fade away, and soon I can hear the rush of the bow wave as the ship picks up speed. Of course we are "late" getting away, but what is "late" when there is no schedule?

But we are away—and a-weigh!—not to stop for nine days to England, or eleven to Hamburg.

Found a makeshift doormat today—every cabin seems to have one—and mounted one of the elegant calling cards Dan made for me on the outside of the door. Class!

We have probably a good day's sailing down the west coast of Florida and around the Keys, then into "The Big O", as we used to call it in our little sailboats off Rhode Island. What then? Even in fine weather the ship will encounter a swell, usually gentle and long and, in a small boat, almost unnoticed until the boat ahead seems to disappear. On our NNE course it will probably lift the ship just slightly and lower it gracefully again. Then there is the chance of unfine weather. I am prepared, I think.

We have dropped the pilot. There's a job! It's one thing to know the territory by heart in the dark, and guide a huge freighter out of the harbour, but then just to step over the rail of a ship moving at 13 knots, onto a "Jacob's" ladder (just rope and wood or composition rungs) and climb down 20 feet of flat steel ship side, step gingerly onto the bouncing pilot boat also moving at speed: uh huh! And these pilots are not all Spring chickens, either!

4/17   Awake at 0738 (I have a talking clock and have but to reach out to where I know it is without even opening an eye and the little man inside it tells me the time—the alarm plays that familiar theme from the Boccherini String Quintet!). A *bad* nightmare last night! Somehow I had gotten myself, in the dream, into someplace on the ship, some obscure place where a sort of hatch clanged shut and no one would ever find me, and I couldn't get out, and it was pitch dark. I awoke totally disoriented. Knew I was on the ship, but was trapped! Felt around in the dark, found a light fixture, turned it on. Lo, I was in my own berth, in my own cabin. Still very scary! Will leave a light on in the "office" from now on. Ellen made me pack a nightlight, at which I, of course, scoffed merrily, but it wouldn't work when I tried it. Something about the ship's power system, I think. Noticed, too, that it takes longer to pop the corn in my hot air popper. Undernourished electricity.
Now heading 183°, almost due south and in a couple of hours will turn to 127° (as laid out by the Second Officer, the official navigator, on the big chart upstairs) and start around the Keys. Speed 18.3 knots Another beautiful, calm morning.

Flying fish!

25°30'N x 82°30'W (at sea)

Lunch: chicken pieces, pasta "maggoti" (well, it looks like little insect eggs!), an apple, and—WHOA! Jet plane just flew over—*low*!

Can't stay awake. Siesta time.

Chief Officer Waldek is on the bridge when I go up about 1700. He's very talkative, very funny. Stories of stowaways, his family—wife, 3 year old daughter, Rose "who talks too much". They will come aboard at Hamburg along with other wives and

26

visitors—"may have to eat in shifts". BIBI now making over 20 knots on a heading of 75° up Florida's east coast. No land in sight. Ship stays well offshore—50 miles or more.

Lovely sunset. A way to go before clearing the Grand Bahama Bank and turning east for Europe. I find myself thinking: "It just doesn't get any better than this!". Then at other times: "What the heck am I doing?" Can I really hang on here for four more *months*? I do realize that after this long Atlantic passage, the next ones will be much shorter, one or two days, until we leave Asia for the trans-Pacific run.

I do miss the sort of wide open verbal communication I'm used to. All aboard try mightily and sometimes delightfully, but it's still a Polish/English or Tagalog/English struggle for all of us. And here come the Germans!

7.

4/18 Grayish morning—ah, there's the sun, just peeking over the horizon. Oops—gone! Just behind a cloud: great Beethoven sky above. We have definitely turned east, but seas no more than (Beaufort Scale) Force 1 or 2 and the Atlantic swell is causing a delightful rising and falling of the ship—more motion than heretofore.

My little Salt Spring compass points in a general direction but is at least 15° off—far too much metal around it. Ship's compasses must be "boxed" regularly and adjusted for this phenomenon.

I'll skip breakfast again (Don't start!), take my pills and head up to the bridge to see where we are.

I may eat these words soon enough, but right now, I feel I could go on like this forever. One of the wondrous things about it is that during the night while I am fast asleep, the ship just goes on and on, making almost 20 nautical miles an hour, never slowing, never stopping, just plowing on: I really don't have to watch every mile go by!

Well, they have rolled out "Mr. Big"—the chart of the North Atlantic Ocean. Much smaller scale, so we seem—with the hourly position marks—to be just inching across this vast space. It appears to be about 3,800 miles from Key West to Bishop's Rock at the tip of England, which means that at, say, 18 NM/hr. we should be there in 211 hours which is about 9 days. Just what they said. Beautiful day, small fishing boats, a motor yacht, blips on radar, but too far away to see their cause. Easy to figure distance on the chart: one

27

degree of longitude at the Equator equals 60 nautical miles, so what's with all this metric business?

27°30'N x 79°30'W (at sea)

Ahh! Did my laps around the deck—6 or 7—half hour's worth. For lunch: "Chicken Loolipops (sic)", according to Steward Renand. This is a very clever reworking of chicken wings made by taking the large wing bone, pushing all the meat up to one end (where it seems mysteriously to remain), then dropping the whole thing into deep fat. Excellent! Always a special treat, from Erlito Ratio, the cook. Stout fellow! Literally!

We are taking a slightly longer, more southern, route across the pond; better weather—not for me, but for the ship, which is "in ballast" or empty and thus more gingerly afoot. Normal efficient speed in ballast would be about 18.5 knots which we are doing, but with following seas and wind the ship has actually whizzed along at 23 knots! Good! They "want us in Hamburg"! Captain wryly remarks that our "schedule" may put us in Hamburg on a holiday or "no-work" weekend, which would put us in Antwerp in time for a Belgian "no-work!" weekend. which in turn would bring us into Genoa just in time for an Italian "no-work" weekend! Ah, these European holidays! Like catching the first red traffic light. He doesn't mind the schedule per se—he just hates to sit around. Me, too.

Am becoming real friends with Chief Officer Watracz who has the 0400-0800 and 1600 to 2000 watches ("That way I can see sun come up and sun go down.") He speaks wonderfully accented and nearly always accurate (sometimes intentionally hilarious) English, is something of a philosopher, a story teller, and a real comedian. He breezes into supper, when he is briefly relieved for it at 1800, with a hearty *"Guten Mor-r-r-gen!"* which is, he says, the only German he knows, Of course, there are no German speakers aboard yet, so he is safe. He is very well-read, a cinema buff and a music lover. I find myself gravitating to the bridge when he is on watch (except for four o'clock in the morning!) and we are having some remarkable conversations. He smokes like a chimney, but I just stay upwind.

The ocean tonight is like Fulford Harbour on Salt Spring, just a barely perceptible rise and fall of the ship. No wind at all, though we are supposed to get some tomorrow. Last trip, the ship, I am told, went directly from Japan to Panama—18 days! Well, as long as I have plenty of popcorn when we start out.

The sea is as flat as the Canadian prairies, that is, not really—but gently undulating with a gradual rise and fall, as the sun

28

sets behind us. It could be St. Mary Lake on my Island except that it goes on forever. Not a ship in sight; just water, water everywhere.

Renand is cleaning the cabin, which he will do once a week if I let him—I won't. Bathroom is all tiled and with the high sill in the doorway can be doused with a hose and thoroughly swabbed out. He just takes off his shoes and socks and wades in. He tells me that before going to sea he worked in a 5 star hotel owned by Emelda Marcos. I say, "The shoe lady?" And he laughs.

Last visit to the bridge for Day 10. Totally dark forward of the night curtain except for radar and instrument glow. Sliding door to starboard wing is open; night air is warm. An eerie feeling being on this huge ship, plunging through the pitch black night with only the reaching radar to guide us. Must stop walking the deck; gives me too much energy.

4/19 Awake early. Quite a restless night, tossing and turning, waking. No reason—perhaps the two doze-offs during the day, maybe the exercise around the deck. Very little motion to the ship and the sound is much like that of a freight train crossing as you wait in your car—a sort of dull roar, plus of course the constant vibration that pervades everything and which you get used to in short order. The ship is simply alive and letting you know it.

Did not really come around until 0951, according to my tiny talking timepiece, but lay abed reflecting: a strange dream. A whole clutch of us, Joan from next door at home, and others, were being deported! We were catching busses, etc. to the airport. I had only a small backpack. Before we got on the plane, it suddenly occurred to me—hey, wait a minute—I'm a Canadian citizen; you can't deport me! End of dream. Hmmm.

Thoughts while waiting for the corn to pop:
Another little insight: how slowly we lose our "scheduling" instinct. Of course, it takes several days to wind down when starting any vacation—especially after a hair-raising departure like mine, but there is something more about this voyage. First was the obvious truism that this ship was on no schedule—and they meant that! Fog, a broken crane, a no-work weekend. Doesn't matter. *There is no schedule!* But witness the fellow in Tampa whose job it must have been to oversee the unloading of all those modules and boilers. Knickers all in a knot when it went slower than he felt "necessary". They had probably been waiting several weeks, if not months, for the cargo, so what difference would a another few hours make? But he was in a tizzy. He had not yet reached Stage One: It will all get done, but only when it gets done. (The Tao takes it one step further: Nothing is done; yet nothing is left undone.)

29

Then yesterday, Stage Two became apparent. Learning that the ocean crossing would take eleven days, I gasped mentally. Eleven days out of sight of land, out of touch with the world. I immediately began to figure when it would end, how far we had gone, how far yet to go. Then on the bridge I asked Waldemar (Waldek for short; *not* Valdy!) about the 18 day trip from Japan to Panama. 18 days! He made me to understand that he preferred to be at sea rather than in port. Of course! "At sea" is what this ship is all about; it means the quiet routine of sailing, regular watches, regular, if tough, work. "In port" is an interruption of the journey; it means confusion, more and irregular work and hours, pressure, loading, lashing, discharging, etc. etc. and I suddenly realized that Stage Two was upon me. True, it is the ports and the cargo that make this life possible, but these are seamen, mariners; it is the voyage, the time at sea, that makes the life they chose. In a hurry to get there? Not at all! Eighteen days? Wonderful! The sea time is not, again, just a means to an end: it is an end in itself. Stage Two: Getting there is *all* the fun!

So perhaps another dollop of my impatience has begun to fade. This is, after all, *the* big life adventure that we men seem to crave. For many it was the war(s). For my dad it was. So why am I, even unconsciously, trying to hurry it along? One reason perhaps is that these "great adventures" are always "abnormal" or dangerous or at least decidedly different. Don't tell me the fellow high on Everest, freezing and struggling, doesn't wish he were back in good old normal Moose Jaw. But even if offered the chance he would not go: he's *got* to be right where he is! There are moments even now when I find myself thinking about getting back home, yet at the same time, feeling: don't rush me.

It's just that we have these built in (or developed) alarm clocks that make us hurry. I have no doubt that on returning to "civilization" I will probably revert to type and pick up my impatience where it left off, but for now—be cool! Do not rush to the end of a minute or an hour or a day. Let yourself be carried at its pace. It is not a race; only in music can you beat time.

Ahh, a batch of popcorn, ice cold Coke, a good book and the roll of the sea. How could I ask for anything more—except maybe some good company.

Continuing strange: only a little while can elapse without having to give in to the urge to look out the window, so I put down the book, rise from this terrific sofa and turn to gaze forward over BIBI's bow. Voila! *Ocean!* More ocean; water to the end of the earth. I watch for many minutes, then go about my business only to have the whole process begin again in usually not more than 20 minutes.

8.

29°03'N x 75°06'W (at sea)

NEWS! We now have *two* ports in Great Britain: "Newport, England", on the Bristol Channel, and Immingham on England's east coast. Big event coming up soon: we sail off one chart and onto another (is this *still* my impatience showing?). The new one shows no land at all on it, only water.

Just thinking of the passengers who will board at Hamburg—whenever we happen to get there!—going through the same "flexibility" as I did: daily dispatches and updates, and now a new port added making the ship even later getting there. Tenterhooks is the name of this game—at least until you are on board.

I am taken back to my own tenterhooks in the days and weeks, even years, before Ellen and I boarded Salt Spring Island's Long Harbour ferry at 0630 on April 9 to start this nutty journey. I had discovered the existence of freighter travel sometime back in the mists of time and with an inborn attraction to ships and boats, had wondered if that might be a good way to see something of the world. Again, somehow I found out about TravLtips, (see Internet) a New York outfit whose main function is booking freighter trips and publishing a bi-monthly eponymous magazine with ship listings and articles by folks who have been there and done that.

Through TT, I actually booked a three month container ship circumnavigation leaving on January 18, 2001. This trip, would circle the world the other way—clockwise—leaving New York and heading for Panama, etc. I had been having some internal problems (that's not a euphemism: it's about the best diagnosis that four different doctors could come up with) and some wonky test results, but otherwise feeling about 99% ok. Still, I was advised to see just one more specialist on our Island. The only appointment available was on January 17, the very day we were to leave for Vancouver where I would catch the plane for New York the next day. All packed and genuinely ready for the trip—volunteer responsibilities covered, friends farewelled, arrangements made at home for Ellen to woman the fort—and on the way to the Long Harbour ferry, we stopped at the doctor's office. After a good deal of poking and prodding, questions and more-or-less answers, he called us together. "We have a decision to make," says he. "If this were a trip to Toronto, that's one thing; but you plan to be at sea for three months with no doctor. I'm not sure I'd recommend it. But it's up to you." We conferred and we concurred. And drove back home. And ordered a pizza, and I cancelled everything while Ellen sat in the car and wept, and I tried to "come back home". It took me more than a month. I simply hid out and gradually, like a ghostly wraith, began to appear again. A "Moses sighting" became an island phenomenon to be whispered about through the blackberry bushes.

Some thought, "Well, that's the end of *his* big world trip!" But, 'way down deep, I knew better: it was something I simply *had* to do. The money—from the propitious sale of a house in Oakville, Ontario 13 years before—was still there (the entire called-off trip fare recovered through cancellation insurance—don't leave home without it!) burning a hole in the bank account. My health had stabilized, but how long would the bod hold up? We never discovered what that little "pain" was. The doctors all said, "When you find out, would you let us know?"

And a new circumnavigational opportunity was being advertised. From the Freighter World Cruises bi-weekly newsletter (I had now switched to this agency in California, also listed on the Internet): "Rickmers-Linie GmbH & CIE Kg., Hamburg is pleased to offer an around the world service on 5 of their old-fashioned general cargo vessels. These ships, 'with masts and beams, still look as a vessel should.' The ms MERIDA, LEON and BIBI and the ms RICKMERS HOUSTON and RICKMERS TIANJIN (German Ownership/Bahamas and Cypriot Registries) are being offered to passengers to board probably in Houston, for an approximate 19-20 week roundtrip, calling about 20 ports throughout the world." Etc. The next paragraph contained even more—and more intriguing—cautions: "scheduled to sail around the world, but . . . not on a set itinerary . . . schedule can change . . . ports can be cancelled or added . . . not necessarily knowing . . . " and the key words in the whole screed: "PASSENGERS MUST BE FLEXIBLE . . . "

Well! Traditionalist that I am—"masts and beams, still look as a vessel should"—this was a very tempting idea. The only drawback on the earlier trip had been that the ship was "containerized", looked like a great blob when sailing, and usually spent about 6 hours in any port. And "19-20 weeks"? That's up to five months! Wow! But I noticed the proliferation of words like "probably", "approximate", "about". There were even more of them in the earlier ads, including the phrase "probable around the world service. "Probable?" My whole idea, nay, my obsession, was to go *Around The World!* No probable about it. I hesitated, talked to FWC, heard things like "the ship was sent back to China", etc. But then the "probablies" began to disappear; the trip took on a more solid state. Obviously, as more ships made the circle, things became more certain.

But time was getting short. I wanted to leave in mid-Spring, May or June, so as not to run into any late winter storms on the

North Atlantic, wanted it to be Summery all the way around, and be back home for the startup of Fall activities. It was already March! For some reason I assumed that everybody and his uncle was dying to take this trip, so it was with trepidation that I e-mailed FWC. Yes, they could book me for "May or June" (talk about flexibility!) on the MV LEON, but it would be an aft-facing cabin. Fine, I replied. Hey, at least I got on!

Vicky Blevins of Salt Spring's UNIGLOBE Travel service was recruited to handle things from then on (a good idea, I discovered: these agents talk the same language, and a good one at your side is a decided plus). There was a rush for visas, health and cancellation insurance, early talk of money-to-go, plane reservations and all the rest, and of course constant communication with FWC. First "flex": could I leave in April? OK. April 10? OK—with hesitation. April 7? No. Too close to the final band concert of the season. "Well, you can always catch the ship at its first port of call, Beaumont, Texas." "Yeah, but . . . " Then the LEON began to lag a bit. The sailing date was back to the 10th, then the 11th, then back to the 9th. Then came "flex" two: would I mind changing *ships?* The LEON was being sent back to China. What other ship? The BIBI—sister ship, virtually identical. When? Same day. If I agreed to change ships, they would upgrade my cabin. Choice of two, one facing starboard, the other facing forward with a "little alcove and a writing desk". Inside a minute, it was "the alcove" and the forward windows. Ladies and gentlemen, this was one of the best decisions Vicki and I ever made! As you know now, it was, as far as I was concerned, the best cabin on the ship! I cannot imagine being in any other location. (See Postlude.)

So it's the BIBI in cabin #5. Now I discover that the Port of Houston has a web site listing all ships expected to arrive. Yes, there is my BIBI, due in on April 9. My unalterable plane tickets are also for April 9, but there is a nice two hour margin there, plenty of time to get to the Port. Then on Sunday the 7th, the web site says BIBI is due in on April 8! Yikes! Can't change plane reservations at this late date. Well, surely they won't *leave* on the 8th—have to load and unload and all that. I'll take a chance. On the morning of the 8th, the web site has dropped the BIBI altogether, meaning, I assume, she has arrived. Afternoon of the 8th, Monday, a call from Uniglobe: BIBI sailing at midnight on the 9th. Whew! Going to be close, but possible. And then the fun starts.

The ferry is right on time, the bus to the airport just fine, a little lunch, that close call at the check in counter, and after a tearful farewell to Ellen I am off right on time. But, by the time I get to Phoenix ... And you know that story.

33

More news from Chief Officer Waldek. The crew, it seems, despite my soliloquy about being at sea, gets as excited as I do about ports of call. They head for the directories and the charts to locate them—just like I do! (But of course, most of these stalwart crewmen have not been off the ship since leaving Japan close to 40 days and 40 nights ago!) "Newport, England"? It's in *Wales*! Just across from Bristol. And Immingham is on the Humber River, quite a bit north of the Thames on England's eastern shore. Some of our cargo is destined for Ko Sichang, Thailand—very close to Bangkok. So, with Hamburg and Antwerp, that's five ports confirmed. I'm afraid both British ports will be too far from my good friend Tony Royse to think about a visit.

We are now 20 miles or so north of Bermuda.

(Clocks ahead again tonight.) I say to Waldek at supper, "Do you know 'peanut butter'?" And he says, "Peanut butter? Sure, I know peanut butter; we no have!" But when Renand comes back into the dining room, I say, "Renand, we *must* have peanut butter!" He says, "We have!", and returns in two minutes with a little jar of smooth peanut butter. "You like?" he asks. ""Yes!" I respond. "Nobody else likes," he says. We talk about peanut butter—on toast, in sandwiches—and, forever more, there is peanut butter on the table (and somebody else *does* like it!). This brand has hydrogenated oil in it, but I'll take it easy. (There are now *19* jars and bottles on the table!)

9.

4/20 Too comfy to get up, so I read for a while, enjoying the pianism of John Arpin, and the counterpoint of the waves. Sullen and overcast out there—"The Grey Seas Under", to cite Farley Mowat's fine book. Realized last night that I really need music not only most of the time, but now in order to fall asleep, which means leaving the player on all night. Ah, well, that's what it's made for—and certainly no cost in electricity. It's the perfect player is my low-cost Wal-Mart purchase. Nothing fancy, called Lenoxx. Just hope it holds out as long as needed. Apparently there are no passenger CD players on the ship. FWC must be advised. I'm not sure I could last this voyage without music.

Off to the bridge.

Looking at the charts and measuring our progress across this vast expanse of paper, I am reminded of Shakespeare's line "Tomorrow, and tomorrow, and tomorrow, creeps in this petty pace from day to day to the last syllable of recorded time." It does seem almost hopeless as we simply crawl across the chart—and the face of the earth. Still, I make it only 5 more days to the Bristol Channel, considerably fewer than if we were running straight to Hamburg.

36°38'N x 62°26'E (at sea)

Haircut day!   (Or "har-kit" as they say in Texas.) I've been cutting my own hair for 30 years or more so this is no problem at all. The "shower" is now "repaired". The Fitter busted the shower head trying to adjust it, but replaced it with the one from his own cabin—no talking him out of it—but there's no difference; it still runs more like a faucet than a spray. But it's wet and it's hot and it does the trick.

"We make barbecue tonight", it being Saturday, but it is raining, so we will get wet for the drill set for 1530, for which I will grab my lifejacket (hanging in the "office") and hasten to the MUSTER STATION (the words are actually painted in English on the deck just aft of the funnel housing.) There is a prescribed list of 20 or more drills that must be carried out periodically, the most important ones, once a month. They cover every possible disaster on the ship from dangerous cargo leakage, to a variety of fire types, to man overboard, to abandon ship—an order which only the captain himself can give. Only a few of them involve me, as a passenger.

Did my deck trek; half an hour or so. Very pleasant with the sea still calm and the ship rising and falling with majestic grace.

Lovely shishkebab for lunch—chunks of beef, bacon, tomatoes, onions, plus the great made-from-scratch French fries. I will surely gain a ton on this trip.

Back in the cabin after the lifeboat drill. Instructional and a bit scary. Seven short rings followed by one long ring on that bloody great alarm bell in the corridor means EVERYBODY TO THE MUSTER STATION. When I get there, having struggled into the bulky lifejacket—taking off glasses to do it—and heading down the stairs and out the A deck stern door, there they all are, the entire crew except for the Master who stands in for the 2nd Officer on the bridge. How did they get there that fast? Many instructions to the crew from Chief Officer Watracz and then we head for our lifeboats. There are two; mine is #1. Renand is watching over me. I stand back, and the boat crew goes to work, actually swinging the huge orange craft out over the side, boarding it and starting the engine! (#2 boat does not have an engine, must be rowed, but no problem: the entire ship's complement would fit in a single boat, which holds 40—disregarding the "bumspots" painted on the seats.) For a moment, I am genuinely afraid that I might have to climb into that boat swinging over the ocean which is quite rough today and is passing us at 18 knots. But no: "How much insurance you got?"

asks Waldek, with a chuckle. The boat is not lowered into the actual water.

Back home again now and settling into my book . . . DAMN, there goes the bell gain—seven shorts and a long. Grab lifejacket, hard hat this time (everybody else has one on), down to A deck to now familiar MUSTER STATION. I travel at great speed, but am still the last one there. No boats this time, more instructions in Polish/English to Tagalog/ English ears, then climb five flights of *outside* stairs!—to the bridge deck where we learn about rocket-propelled line launching. Instructor is of course Waldek who appears to love this job. "When you pull rope make sure rocket is pointed AWAY from you!"

Rain has stopped and soon we will all muster again, this time on the other side of the poop deck for the "Q".

We "make photo"

The weekly barbecue—if possible, that is, if we are at sea—is everybody's favorite time. All aboard gather on the fantail and all eat the same thing—pork chops, chicken, steak, Kielbasa, stuffed squid(!)—in weekly rotation. You *know* this Methodist preacher's kid just loves the Kielbasa and the squid! The crew clusters around the split 50 gallon drum that holds the fire, sitting on bollards and stanchions, while "us officers" share a rough-hewn picnic table under the rippled steel canopy. It is the 32nd birthday of A/B (Able Bodied Seaman) Romeo Melo which adds to the occasion. (There are also O/S's among the crew: Ordinary Seaman—the entrance level.)

Then I sit for a while on a winch housing, just next to the fire, and watch the ship's wake and a rather serious sky. I guess my favorite place on a ship has always been the stern. It seems more heartening to see where you've been than to gaze over the bow at the miles yet to travel. Also, you have left a trail behind, not a permanent one—it disappears all too quickly, but there is great peace in watching the ship's progress from the caboose, as it were.

It is impossible not to become fond of the crew on this ship. They are all, particularly the Filipinos, not just friendly, but eagerly friendly— and they love having their picture taken! Every drill—and every part of every drill, including greasing the cables on the lifeboat davits—must be photographed by the Chief Officer as documentary proof that it actually happened, I suppose, and you'd think the crew would be used to the camera, but just pull out your own and say, imitating the C.O., "We make photo," and the boys instantly fall into a smiling group pose. Quite delightful.

Gazing out at the sea I still cannot believe I am actually here—in the middle of the Atlantic Ocean on a tramp freighter eating barbecue on the poop deck. I am still this Salt Spring Island book cataloger. What am I doing here?

We are just south of Newfoundland—and there is loony Lorne Elliott on the CBC—Radio Canada International short wave.

4/21   Here is the "cold North Atlantic"—with some "bed vawter-r" (bad water) ahead (you have to learn to roll those "r"s if you want to speak Polish) as my friend the "Feeter-r (Fitter)" would say. No more blue skies, or blue water. Mist over all, gray waves breaking. Fortunately we are going with the waves and wind, but the motion of the ship is increasing. Nothing anywhere near alarming yet. Think I'll head down for some peanut butter toast!

Visibility now almost zero. Even the bow is shrouded.

Sea conditions continue to worsen. Ship has pronounced roll and pitch. Rain, fog. But "no biggie". Fell asleep reading on the sofa and now it's almost time for lunch. Not really hungry, but will take my book as I usually either begin or finish alone—these officers are in such a rush to finish and go!

39°05'N x 53°01'W (at sea)

Radar shows heavy weather ahead as does the hydrographic fax, so Ocean Routes, a service that provides advice as to best routes to follow, advises turning south a bit to avoid a storm. I suspect, with an empty ship, we will do so. We are romping along at 20 plus knots, but no matter how huge the ship, the ocean will play with her.

Wow! Ripping along now at 22.5 knots! Must have avoided the storm, as nothing shows on the radar screen. Easy to see why people fall in love with ships and the sea. She is just galloping! Maybe "gracefully galumphing" would be a better term. Nice tail wind and the seas are running with us.

Chocolate ice cream for supper—"because it's Sunday!" Sitting at the table watching "the roll of the sea" through a starboard window, as the ship leans amazingly and returns, seeing first just sky, then a moment later, all sea, then watching a tall bottle of water topple onto the floor . . .

She fairly gambols along, rampaging over and through the waves, throwing a bow wave 40 feet on a side. I think she loves it. Tossing great heaps of blue water at the passing waves—enormous collisions, spray flying everywhere, but she is moving at 20 knots, looking for new challenges. Just not too many, please!

10.

4/22   Sea down, still lumpy, but wind down, sun trying to break through, still rock and roll time. Speed down to 17 knots; no tail wind today and we've swung north to 58°.

Something of an "at sea" routine has developed. Usually wake at 0700 or so, lie abed deciding whether to go down to breakfast. Don't have to, but finally *must* get up! See what the sea and the day look like. Get dressed and—oh, all right—head down for juice and vitamins, then head for the bridge—a five story climb, never take the elevator except with a laundry load—to check course, speed, weather reports, etc., then usually back here to hit the couch, read, drift off for a while with the music playing. But this morning (we are losing an hour every other day now) I say the hell with it and just crawl back into bed with my clothes on and drop off like a stone. Well, I figure, waking two hours later, why not?

Now, I must to the bridge! The noon "fix" awaits, and I must plot our position on my big map.

42°03'N x 44°24'W (at sea)

A bird! Not a flying fish this time—something else, looks like a land bird sitting on the bridge wing rail—but we are 2,000 miles from land! Yes, it's possible, says Waldek, "Had a pigeon on board once—Renand took care of it."

Watching a movie at sea on my little desktop TV; forgetting completely where I am 'til things start rolling onto the floor.

Last look for today at the rambunctious North Atlantic: white horses everywhere, wind up again, but now from the port quarter. Normal for the time of year and lots better than midwinter. We are about halfway across, I figure. Three more days should put us close to the entrance to Bristol Channel.

When Waldek's wife and daughter, Rose, join him in Hamburg and come along to Genoa, it will be their first time "visiting Dad at work". Trust things outside will be a little calmer.

Two weeks ago tonight getting all het up for the trip, preparing to rise at 0530 for the early ferry. Only two weeks!

4/22   Bad night for sleeping! Ship rolling like a barrel. Suddenly occurs to me: *I'm hungry!*   No lunch, not even popcorn, only toast for breakfast, and not much supper, and that was seven hours ago. So down I go to the dining room with peanut butter sandwiches on my mind. Spooky. Most lights turned out, only the pantry lit. Very quiet except for usual ship noises. Wait! A sound! Yep, there's one of the engineers having a snack, bent over the sink. I knock. He chuckles, "Not much here", he says. And lo—peanut butter is gone from the table! Can't find it anywhere. He points to a whole line of condiments stashed in a neat little trough built into the wall under the windows—against their having a smashing good time when the ship rolls. And there it is! Can't find any butter, but grab a few slices of soft white bread (the only kind available right now, but this will change as we provision). I can use "my" popcorn butter (the half pound Renand "loaned" me that day I mixed the first batch). I stick the PB in my pocket and hot foot it up the stairs like a thief in the night. So here I sit, noshing peanut butter sandwiches and listening to John Arpin. The ship continues its rolling, but after a close call when the medicine cabinet almost flew open, I think I have secured everything. I won't try playing solitaire; this afternoon I was doing quite well at it, concentrating on a key move, when BIBI took a roll and the cards just slid away, neatly reshuffling themselves. Well, I was ready for the next game anyway!

4/23   Another rough night, what with the empties rolling around—this ship and my stomach—but got back to sleep about 0200 to be wakened at 0716 by subtle changes in the ship's motion. Never mind—quickly back inside the sack until the morning was brighter. Trouble is, by then, it was irresistibly tempting to get up and look at the sea. This morning, brilliant sunshine streaming in, but as quickly covered by the overcast. Seas seem the same, lumpy, rolling, moving from SW to NE, but a bit quieter perhaps and still pushing us toward Europe.

Oops! Must return the purloined peanut butter. Renand will laugh and say, "Ah, yes." We are now six hours ahead of home and another hour tonight will put us at Greenwich Mean Time. One more hour for British Summer Time and we should stay there until we leave Immingham for Hamburg.

Sun out, barometer rising slightly, seas a bit quieter. When I am on the bridge I read everything in sight: message from Master to Technomar: "Please provide three radio/CD players. Passenger has noticed that brochure promises CD player in every cabin. He has brought CDs, but can't use them." Well, well, well, my word in his ear did the trick!. Message says we will pick them up in Antwerp along with, of course, long lists of parts and supplies and foodstuffs. Good guy. And it pays to be snoopy! Will give my Lenoxx player to Renand, or somebody who would like it.

Moved the arm chair from the office into the "day room"—just exactly fit through the door. Regular living room now. Chicken "loolipops" and "BIBI's BEST FRIES" for lunch.

Sun and blue sky, but still ornery sea.

45°48'N x 35°03'W (at sea)

Am learning a little Polish from Waldek. He is a sketch. We talk about language. Says he, "You can have one hundred words of, let us say, Spanish; that is enough to get along. When we were in Mexico, I have one hundred words and I go to conquer Mexico!" Now I must practice my Polish so I can greet his wife and daughter properly.

Looks like a quieter night.

4/24 Well, I guess I'd better get up! Delicious night! Still rockin' and rollin', but I have discovered the secret of sleeping in spite of it: lie diagonally! Head at upper right, feet at lower left. That way you are automatically partially braced against both pitch and roll. Another tip is not to resist the roll—just sort of go with it. And if you are partly braced already there is much less temptation to fight it, and you won't roll far. Try it; you'll like it. (Mentioned my "secret" to the Captain at breakfast. He nodded, a sly smile on his face, then, "Is even better with "gless of visky fir-r-st!")

Slept soundly until 0430 ("*Don't remind me that I'm getting old; I have a bladder to do that!*"—Katherine Hepburn), then again 'til almost 0800, read for awhile, then nodded off again. The sensation of being rocked in a big cradle is soporific in the extreme unless of course you are rolling all over the place.

40

Mal de Mer : Have not mentioned it for fear of tempting the fates. The 2nd Officer asked me yesterday, "Seasick?" The Captain inquires as to how I'm doing. Hah! I am doing wonderfully! Not a single sign of seasickness to date. And this after days of constant rolling. (I have known seasickness, but either on the good sloop, WOODWIND, during an all night blow, or a small coaster off Newfoundland in an all day gale, so I'm still wary.) Of course there is more and possibly worse to come, but—no, I won't venture any more opinions 'til we are sailing peacefully up the Houston Ship Canal in August or September. I do have some concern however that, after purchasing all those remedies at some considerable cost, I won't get to use any of them!

Good news! "Newport lock"(?) by 1600 on the 26th. Bad news! Something wrong with my camera. On a 36 exposure roll, it just keeps on going—"taking" pictures; I fear the worst.

48°28'N x 25°32' (at sea)

At about 1800 tonight we crossed the good old 49th parallel. (Paris is also on the 49th.) Newport, Wales is at about the 52nd. We are bowling right along, sea much quieter though Ocean Routes says it is expected to kick up again any time.

4/25   I woke at 0714 as usual to find almost no motion to the ship, just a gentle pitch and the occasional minor roll. Back to sleep to wake at almost 1000. Wind and seas up a bit, but still not (yet) the Force 6 or 7 predicted by Ocean Routes. Weather forecasts sent to us are totally unconcerned about sun, rain, cloud, etc., the important things are wind, waves and swells. So what if the sun don't shine? The question is, how much are you going to bounce around? We are considered an "empty" ship or "light" or, officially, "in ballast" so we roll and pitch more than "normal". A laden ship, lower in the water does have similar motion but slower and even more graceful. When we cross the Pacific we will be laden—easier on the cargo and the ship (and us!).
Tomorrow we arrive in Newport.
Looking out the window: endless fascination. Like popcorn and snowflakes, no two waves are alike, no two swells the same. The bow wave changes constantly, its encounters with waves and swells always different. The blue water speeds away from the bow, collides, crashes, falls back, rises and breaks again as the ship pushes through it, all "heedless of wind and wave," jousting its way across unending miles of sea. And no harm is done! We leave a trail of foam and foment, but in short minutes all is as before and the sea goes its merry way, the ship scarcely noticed in its passing. I glance

out the window at this ever-altering maelstrom and find that 5 minutes, 10 minutes later I am still "glancing" out the window. Few people these days are privileged to witness "the play of the waves", and more's the pity. We forget until this experience how tiny we are, and how large the ocean. Endless fascination—and just enough trepidation to make it memorable.

Going around the world "counter-clockwise", i.e., west to east, seems best, I think. The weather is always behind you. The other way, you meet it head on.

11.

50°21'N x 14°35'W (at sea)

Ships! Birds! If my smeller were in better shape, I'll bet I could smell land. We're actually getting there; we really were moving over those "endless" miles of water. Big gulls out to greet us, soaring, swooping—black tips on their wings, long sharp bills—Gannets or Boobies?—the latter sounds good to me. And two ships! Just lights and blips on the radar, but we haven't seen a living thing for 3 or 4 days! Figure we should be at Lundy early tomorrow morning then head up the Bristol Channel to Newport. Just passing Fastnet Rock about 35 miles north.

Getting to be a habit: after supper, head for the bridge for a gam (chat) with Waldek—movies, books, everything. He loves 'em all and has read and seen probably more than I have. At supper each night he brings down a big roll of paper from his watch on the bridge. "What is that?" I ask tonight. "News", he says, "in Polish." "I hope it's better than the news in English," I quip. "Not better", he says, quick as a flash, "but more. Good news is no news!" Very clever fellow.

4/26   Couldn't stay abed after 0730 or so. Today's the day! I rush to the window expecting to see—what? Same old rolling seas and good old British FOG! Waldek still on the bridge when I go up. We are at longitude 5°—pretty close to Greenwich's 0° . Everybody aboard seems excited at the prospect of landfall, even the old salts. I guess crossing the Atlantic is still crossing the Atlantic. Am wearing flannel and fleece these days. Feels good. Only things I may need are more short sleeved shirts when we get to warmer climes. Otherwise I think I packed pretty good, hey, hey!

On the bridge. We have slowed to half speed or less, fog is all around us, and rain. The Captain is here. This is literally a new port for all aboard, so we are tiptoeing into the pilot station with only a small faxed piece of a chart—they didn't give us a proper chart in

42

Houston: didn't know we were coming here. I'm sure the skipper will feel much relieved—literally—when the pilot is aboard. Tides here are 14 meters (up to 46 feet), I am told, so we must enter a lock at high water to get into the inner harbour where we are safe from these rampaging currents. Can't see a thing up here with all this fog, so will descend and read.

Sun! Blue sky! Visibility! But still nothing to see! However, Radio BBC3 is coming in loud and clear. Never heard it before. Splendid! Also "Classical FM", a kind of upbeat classical station—most intriguing. Listening to these announcers, I keep expecting the Monty Python gang to take over any minute.

LAND HO! Over the starboard bow, low hills in the mist.

51°30'N x 5°W (at sea)

WOW! We're just finishing lunch when the Steward pops in all excited and says to the Captain something about a helicopter and points to the stern. We all rush out, and sure enough: there is a huge, yellow RAF Rescue chopper hovering just aft of us and not more than 100 feet up. Terrific clatter and buffeting wind. We watch as it lowers one, then two, then three men onto our stern and then hoists them up again—2 together, once. And off they go with a wave and a radioed thanks to the BIBI. Captain knew nothing about this drill. They just appeared. Great excitement!. (Son Dan, totally unaware of this event, would soon concoct for the website the fantastic tale of "The Famous Helicopter Popcorn Rescue!"[q.v.] Much later, he was flabbergasted to learn of the genuine helicopter visit—but without popcorn!)
We should pick up the pilot at 1600 today and be tied up by 1730. Free day tomorrow, loading on Sunday and Monday, off again on Tuesday for Immingham. There by Thursday, and in Hamburg by Saturday—at least that's the "schedule."

Still waiting off Newport for the channel to clear. Two pilots aboard—very spiffy in "power" uniforms—one Welsh, the other English and they have great fun with that. The Welshman actually sailed on this ship 20 years ago, he says. They are certainly heroic types. Clambering up the flanks of the ship (or down) in any weather, any time of night or day, then just taking over and guiding it to safety. And they are treated like nobility—fed, watered, catered to. An enviable profession. Of interest: names are never used between pilot and Captain or crew. It's, "Captain—how do you do, glad to be aboard." or some such, and from the Captain, "Pilot, welcome aboard, can we get you anything?"

I am formulating a plan—not disclosable at this time—could be one of the great surprises of all time.

Passed Cardiff on the way in—seems a thriving city, 15 minutes by train from Newport, but it doesn't look like I'll get there.

Heading about due west now as we wait. A rain squall is passing ahead of us. Bristol Channel is the estuary of the Severn River, and very muddy water it is. Must be tons of silt and topsoil washing away. Of course, the fierce tidal currents keep it all stirred up. Hey—a sailboat!

We will require three tugs to get us "home" tonight—one fore, two aft so as to hold us back as we wind our way through a very tricky channel and into the narrow lock that maintains the water level in the inner harbour, thus avoiding those tides that would make cargo handling pretty near impossible.

51°30'N x 3°W (Newport)

Tied up next to an enormous yard covered with dozens of stacks of steel plates: our cargo for Thailand. At least we're not at the next yard which is simply great piles of scrap metal. What an ignominious cargo that would be. Still, I suppose somebody's got to tote it somewhere. Our port supervisor here, looks and sounds like Rumpole of the Bailey (Leo Kern—who, I believe, died just about this time). His advice for a telephone: the Seaman's Mission—something new to me. I make ready. Meanwhile, the ship is almost silent and of course has no motion whatsoever. But I do! I'm still going up and down. And forward: to the nearest phone box.

Well, shucks, I sure did try! At about 2145, I set out for the Seaman's Mission which is near the main gate and where I can find a phone. It "closes at 2230" so I figure I have plenty of time. Walk for a good half hour through the scrap metal (including a huge assemblage of retired Pepsi machines) and after several detours and false turns get to the Mission: closed! Rats! But just then a car pulls up and one of our Filipino helmsmen jumps out: he got a ride right from the ship! His quest is for somewhere he can buy a phone card. We head into town, stopping at this or that pub and asking, but no luck. Finally find a phone box, though, and I dial, using the mighty handy Telus international numbers table (What a blessing it is to hear, from almost every place in the world, that nice lady saying, "Welcome to Canada."). Get right through, but nobody is home. More Rats. We start back. Newport has a certain charm in a sort of rundown, waterfront way, but it does have one of four-in-the-world Transporter Bridges—a platform suspended by cables from a high trestle; cars drive onto the platform which is then pulled across the river. There is one in Germany, one in Australia, and the original one in France, I believe.

We amble back to the ship, chatting merrily—he speaks very good English—and stumble up the gangway. I learn that the ship will be here until Tuesday, April 30th. It is now Friday. My fantastic plan might work. A dear friend, Anthony Royse, lives in Broadstairs, Kent. If I hopped a train tomorrow morning I could have a lovely—surprise!—visit with him and his wife and still be back here by Monday night ready to sail on Tuesday. I'll do it! What a kick that'll be!

I am still going up and down!

4/27   Up early; can't sleep. BBC3 playing some Vaughan Williams. grab a bite, check with Captain one last time, then off to see Tony of Kent. This means, according to our Agent, a train from Newport to Paddington Station, London, the "tube" to Victoria Station, and another train to Broadstairs. Hot dog!   A real adventure—and I get to ride on some trains!

The train to London—one every hour!—is fast and smooth and crowded except in 1st class where I mistakenly sit until booted out—and leaves and arrives exactly on time; the underground whisks me to Victoria with a little help from a uniform or two; the train for Broadstairs—one leaving sooner than the original plan—is delightful and has hardly anyone on it, and before I know it I am deposited on the platform in Broadstairs. My friend, Tony, knows nothing of this escapade. To my joy, a map on the wall of the station shows me that his home on Ethel Road is an easy walk from the station, and I am soon standing before the door of a pretty English duplex pushing the doorbell and girding myself for the reaction of this tall fellow whom I haven't seen for almost ten years and who has only the vaguest idea that I have left Canada, let alone that I am standing on his porch.

12.

51°30'N x 1°30'E (Broadstairs)

The door opens amid small dog yips, and there he is! His face is a study; there's a big hug, then, after recovering himself: "Shh—we'll surprise Andy." Andy is Andrea, his petite wife; she sits in the next room, doing a crossword, and when I walk in, she looks up, smiles, and says, "Well, hello Richard!" It is all a marvelous exercise in English understatement.

Tony, a composer, conductor, erstwhile bassoonist, and inveterate collector of recordings and scores, soon ensconces himself in his studio, surrounded by thousands and thousands of musical items of every sort, the latest in compositional and recording technology, and the computer which has allowed us to communicate ever since we stopped sending "boring" (our term for newsy, breezy, occasionally musical) cassettes back and forth. And this is where we spend most of our time during the visit. He is recovering from a stroke and a subsequent fall and has some trouble moving easily about. We relive old times in Oakville, Ontario where he led the orchestra and composed much music for it, including three ballets, A Boiled Suite, and a great deal more. I discover anew his prize-winning Christmas carols and a plethora of wonderful pieces I had no idea existed. "Attention must be paid" to this genius, I conclude, not for the first time.

Broadstairs was the home of Charles Dickens for a while; Bleak House sits right there on the seafront. I take a long walk down "the high street" and discover, at a friendly photo shop, that my camera has been misbehaving badly and the 36 carefully-selected snapshots of sea and ship that should be preserved for posterity simply don't exist. The film never fed itself through sprocket and spool. Bother! I am advised as to what cameral quirks to watch for from now on, and reload the wretched thing. No charge.

I pick up some necessities: huge bars of chocolate (on sale), several packets of butter, a jar of peanut butter to replace that which I have consumed at Tony's home, some writing notebooks, and for Andy, a neat little hyacinth that reminds me of her.

Next day, I bid them a fond farewell, make for the train station, and am soon whizzing across the land again. Tony suggested I take a bus between stations in London—"see something of the city". This I do, climbing to the crowded top deck and taking the last empty seat next to a young fellow, who, seeing the tiny red maple leaf on my lapel, introduces himself: he's from Montreal! We chat until Victoria station looms and I de-bus. I have searched for evidence of small bears at Paddington, and of course, at Victoria, the cloakroom of the Brighton Line and a misplaced handbag. No luck. It shakes one's faith.

51°30'N x 3°W (Newport)

Soon back in Newport where a ferocious wind is buffeting—not unusual for these parts, I am given to understand—and where a cab, driving dangerously on the "wrong side" of the road, plummets recklessly into and out of a dozen roundabouts and finally deposits me at the foot of BIBI's gangway which I mount just in time for supper!

I enter the dining room, flushed with my perfectly-timed and triumphant expedition, to be told that the ship will not be sailing

46

until Friday! *Friday?* This is only Monday. Ah, well. It's all that ruddy steel! There are about 6,000 tons to be loaded. No wonder. So, lots of time to explore the area.

Except that laundry day looms.

4/30 Rain! And the loading of these steel plates moves exceeding slow. There are thousands of these scrap ends still out there!

Apparently the wind just blows constantly off the sea—in Broadstairs and here.

Before anything else, it has to be laundry. I know because my 42 socks—21 pairs of identical dark blue ones—are mostly all in the bag in the closet, instead of in the drawer. So it must be time to take on this new shipboard task. From the Captain's tour I recall that there is a washing machine on this very deck, but I did not see a dryer anyplace. Unless—no, don't tell me!—unless the dryer is that monstrous industrial size hulk back in the stifling corner of the Upper Deck (the Upper Deck is only "upper" in relation to the decks below it: "Lower" and Engine Room; C deck is three stories above the Upper Deck). Sure enough, that is the ship's official dryer!

Actually there is a variety of washing machines on the ship with instructions in Spanish, Polish, Tagalog and, my favorite, in busted English: IF YOU MUST TAKE CLOTH OUT OF MACHINE, BE SURE HAND ARE CLEAN!. But, after some difficulty, some finagling, and some good help from the Fitter, I set the dials, pour in some of the soap power provided by Renand, dump in the 40 socks, et alia (I have the other two on my feet, after all!) and set the C Deck apparatus in motion. Renand has offered to do my laundry but that is definitely not on.

I busy myself about my estate and return an hour later. *Half done!* It's one of these side loaders that swishes around for about 3 seconds, then stops and swishes the opposite way for another 3 seconds, etc. etc. Another hour goes by, and finally . . . but that's just the coloured stuff! We are urged to save water by doing everything together—"Am I blue?", but I figure every three weeks is aqua-fordable for the ship and wait patiently for the second half to finish. then stuff it all in my small backpack and gird my loins (Hah! With what? Everything is crumpled and damp.) and schlep it all to the elevator and down to The Dryer. It's busy! Looks like "laundry day" will be precisely that! But at last, in the sweltering, rackety, and slightly scary dryer room, I dump the load into the enormous maw of this machine (I could climb in myself!) and start the hulking colossus rotating, not without considerable trepidation about what will actually happen to my delicate boxers, let alone those 40 socks!

The rain has stopped and I am anxious to get out and explore this territory. But first I actually meet our "Supercargo"; he is introduced just like that, but, keeping my ears open, I discover he has a name! He is Dirk Meier, German, and he will be with us, or meeting us, in our European ports. A former ship's Master, his job is to arrange for cargos—ordering trucks and stevedores, negotiating with unions, overseeing the loading and lashing of the freight and all the myriad details that make the ship fulfill its mission—making money for Herr Rickmers and the owners. Dirk, speaks excellent English with an accent reminiscent of Victor Borge, though the latter is of course a great Dane.

It was Dirk who first asked Renand for "only 50%" of the usual plateful of food, obviously well aware of the brawny portions usually served up. I told the Steward I'd have the other half.

A fine-looking "coaster" bulk carrier beside us unloading what looks like sand but is probably fertilizer.

Moved my furniture around, getting the sofa out from in front of the windows, so I can more easily look out.

Laundry done! And those $50 "permanent press" pants aren't! I can get along without the creases, but 40 million wrinkles?

Got a ride to the Seamen's Mission with the agent (a representative of the Rickmers Linie, yet another attendant on this princess of the waves), made my phone call to Ellen—always dynamite talking with her, keeping in touch—and the mission van carried me back to the ship just in time to pick up a couple of crewmen setting out for the Mission. The "Missions to Seamen", open to all seafarers (including passengers), "is a Christian Society in the Anglican Church". In 300 ports around the world, it has chaplains who are glad to welcome you to the centre where you can relax in a homey place and use facilities such as a chapel, a small shop, pool table, darts, chess, etc., a lounge with video, newspapers and refreshments, telephones (local and international), and telephone cards, stamps, book exchange. These remarkable entities range from the modest Newport suite of two rooms, to the—expectedly—grander establishments in larger ports. They are often *the* place to go, for seamen far from home. I discovered, to my surprise, that the father of my friend Tony of Broadstairs, an Anglican clergyman, spent a good part of his life as a chaplain to the Missions, in fact, he traveled the country raising funds for the charity. I was much impressed by these amazing places and by the warm and modest chaplains—men and women—who ran them.

Back on the ship, this "seaman", laundry done, home contact made, and 50% supper "et", can relax.

5/1   Bright, sunny day—still windy. Slept like a log. Am leaving Radio 3 on all night. Very pleasant. Hate to miss a minute of that grandest of all radio traditions—24 hour classical music! What a pity that Canada cannot find a way to create such an oasis. BBC now has five radio and television networks with no commercials anywhere! The Royses do pay about 100 pounds a year for a receiving license.

More about these infernal, eternal steel plates. They are, in fact, scrap, the tag ends of the long sheets that emerge from the rolling mill just next door. They are going to Thailand to be used for—who knows? A single plate weighs 3 tons. The cranes lift them three at a time: for 6,000 tons that's 666 lifts! Also on the quay are piles of huge slabs—probably six inches thick and the usual length—12 feet or so—weighing in at 16 tons per. These slabs are not for us; they came in on a ship from Argentina and are even now being trucked—one slab to a truck—to that self-same rolling mill. Some of this steel will, between smelting and rolling and more rolling, probably make 4 or 5 different voyages—each one making money for somebody, each one receiving a probable government "trade" subsidy—before it is shaped into car fenders or ship's hulls: it's a traveling life.

Fork lifts bring the plates to the quayside, then our cranes lift them into the deepest holds (great ballast!). The loading seems to be something of a leisurely matter: the "stevies" "take long breaks, knock off earlier than they should, and start just that little bit later", says Dirk. We are having to decide whether we leave Friday even if all the steel isn't loaded, or stay until it is.

A fairly fierce wind from the east is blowing and has been for many days they say. It is also cold! I am wearing flannel, fleece and windbreaker when I go out.

Learned some more about the famous bridge in town. Known as a transporter bridge or aerial ferry, it was built in 1906 and is one of 4 in the world, the first in France. In 1895 or so the Newport Town Fathers realized they must have a better way to get to the east side of town over the Usk River. Suspension, trestle, and draw bridges were not possible—too high, or obstructing the narrow channel at low tide. A tunnel was too expensive, so they decided on this sort of structure invented by a Frenchman—a traveling gondola. It was closed in 1985 when other bridges were built upstream, but in 1994 was refurbished and opened in 1995 more as a tourist attraction than a working link. Costs 50p for a car, free for walkers, or you can climb the tower and walk across the top—at 362 feet up!

13.

5/2 Beautiful day! Wind gone down, sun coming through, loading continues. I will go and explore the lock and search for another phone.

Lovely walk over to the lock to have a looksee. Sun so warm I just sat down against a bollard and basked. Wonderful. Big ship came through the lock after 3 tugs scurried out after it. Then she was nudged into a berth right across from BIBI.

It looks like we may have two stops in Thailand, near but not in Bangkok, and one in Singapore for sure. Haiphong has been mentioned, but no stop in Jakarta. Good! Indonesia makes me uneasy. The Italian stop is Livorno rather than Genoa. Apparently only 6 heavy pieces to discharge in Immingham so it'll be a fast turnaround. Have been urged to visit York while there, but there may not be time.

Great walk back from the Mission—rainbow in the sky, beautiful sun setting, and it's always fascinating walking along a waterfront. There were the three tugs all snugged up and ready for us tomorrow.

The agent who gave me a ride out, mentioned he had lots of calendars if I'd like one. Calendars just like the one on the bridge. Shows 4 months at a time, has a clever, movable day framer *and* a gorgeous picture of the BIBI at the top (the cover of this book). Who could ask for anything more? *The* souvenir! Rickmers puts out such a calendar every year, but this year it was BIBI's turn to adorn the top panel. What luck! Another piece of good fortune on this trip.

5/3   Exquisite day! Not a cloud, and, oddly, not a whiff of breeze. Observing the loading still going on, I note that among the scrap ends of steel there is the occasional end too scrappy to take along—too curved or warped—so it is just left on the quay to be transported yet again.

This shipping business functions with really three different teams of workmen. 1) The first team has the job of unloading the cargo from truck or train—or another ship—into the transit shed or onto the quay or yard; 2) then, days or weeks later, the ship's crew arrives with the ship and makes it ready to be loaded or unloaded, that is, opening hatches, turning on and lifting the cranes from their beds, then standing by in case of need. 3) Now the stevedores appear on the scene, and actually load or offload the cargo. They operate the cranes and derricks—ours or theirs—and must also "lash" the cargo firmly in place in the holds and 'tweendecks. This is quite a job in itself, entailing rope, chain, and chainsaws, timber balks, and bracing of all sorts. They are very good at this, but still sometimes they slip up. Of course, once the cargo is loaded and lashed it becomes the responsibility of the ship's crew. Sometimes all three of these teams work for different companies; if something goes amiss, let alone adrift, what then? Whose fault?

Holy smokes! A huge ship, the OCEAN JADE came in last night and is unloading "coil"—more steel! Appears to be a general cargo ship like us—4 Stuelcken derricks on deck!

Will I tire of this life? But perhaps it is a "man's life": few women I have ever encountered would pay good money to watch a lock work, or cranes or ships move, or to just walk along the front watching machinery.

Loading done; lunch done; MARINE UNIVERSAL in the lock on her way out.

I take a walk on the desolate plain that once held our week's worth of cargo. A sound interrupts my reverie—a can, a crumpled beer can being blown about by the resuscitated and ever-constant—almost—wind. I am inspired:

> *Across the vast and empty concrete range, once laden with*
> *neatened stacks of monstrous steel-ed plates,*
> *One lonely can, crushed and battered, blows and rattles its*
> *way, in first one direction, then another—*
> *Searching, seeking: Where have all the pallets gone?*
> *It clatters its way toward me; I bend down for a word or two,*
> *but it is off again, this time heading for the great ship*
> *as if to bid a final farewell to its unborn mates resting*
> *deep in her holds.*
> *Oh, disconsolate can! Is it true thy life is finished? Or with*
> *luck will some new incarnation allow thee, too, to make*
> *the long sea voyage to a new land?*

Aha! They are already bringing more steel into the yard for the next ship.

There is a large, framed portrait hanging in a place of prominence in the dining room: a lovely, dark-haired beauty in her twenties or early 30s. It is Bibi! Bibi is the daughter of the first owner of this ship. Her brother is Leon, her sister Merida. All three have identical ships named for them. The family is Mexican. Bibi, it is opined, might be a grandmother now; Merida just married a Mexican man of means, even as we sailed on her sister's ship.

Still here! In Newport! It seemed like we were finished loading around noon, but we have sat here for 5 hours doing nothing. The cranes are bedded down, but hatch #4 is still open. Ah, well—probably paperwork. I wonder if our agent has got away yet.

He had hoped to be home in Middleborough by "tea time"—350 miles.

Well, well, well. Just back from supper! Decided to act the librarian and try to tidy up the videos a bit. What a mess! Some good stuff in there, but half the cases empty and there are dozens of tapes with no cases at all. Matched a few, but many are still orphans. About half of them are Greek, some actually in Greek, some subtitled American stuff. Then Dirk, the Supercargo, came down. We finally actually met. He loves to talk and I learned about his family and children; we began to make elaborate plans for housing and controlling the video collection, for setting up a bicycle rental on board, etc. etc. Some fun. He had told us at supper that, yes, indeed we would be sailing today—at 2200! It's high water then. This would not be the first time I somehow got wind of a totally wrong sailing time. Noon? Where did that come from?

Well, it's 2200 hrs., and I'm waiting. Waiting for the tugs to come beetling out of their berths to pull us out, turn us around and head us into the lock. Wonder if the pilot is aboard. Newport is nice, but a week here was just a bit much.

We're off. The tugs did indeed come and do their stuff. Now we are "unlocked" and I'm beat (such a lot of work!), so I'll watch the going's on from down here in the cabin until I collapse into bed.

14.

5/4   Boiling along at full gallop! So great to have the ship moving again. Boats around us—a sailboat not far off the starboard bow. Must head upstairs to see where we are.

Just coming out of the Bristol Channel to turn on to a heading of 180°—directly south. On our starboard, guarding the Seven Stones rocks, the eponymous light ship rides the flow and just beyond that the Isles of Scilly. To port, Land's End and the Longships lighthouse. The radar screen not only shows the presence of ships, but, if you "target" them, gives their heading in degrees, their speed, their distance from you, and the time it will take to reach them—probably more, too, if you know the language.

Ah, my first shower in a moving ship—no problem as we roll very slightly heading into the English Channel. I count six ships through my forward-looking window. Dirk said at breakfast (well, sometimes I do go down!), "Too bad we are having such nice weather; you need a good storm—just for the experience!" (Alas, we never had onc.) Sometime this afternoon or later we will pass Broadstairs, but too far off to be seen.

Dirk's wish, notwithstanding, absolutely smooth sailing in the Channel. No motion at all, just the familiar and now comforting pulse of the engine. Brilliant sun, blue sky. No ships in sight—not even pirates as we pass Penzance. Will head upstairs to get the noon fix.

49°52'N x 4°47'W (at sea)

When I went up to the bridge Dirk was there and told me that in the "olden" days—i.e., when he was sailing and before GPS—every day at noon all the ship's officers would gather on the bridge with their sextants and on the stroke of 12—counted down by the helmsman—they would each shoot the sun, then consult the proper book, consider the speed of the ship over the last 24 hours, the set and drift of the current, etc., and each come up with the ship's present latitude and longitude. Then they would get together, compare notes and take the average. Now the radar scope with built-in GPS tells us continuously exactly where we are, though signs posted on our bridge warn of some inaccuracies in GPS positioning and urge the use of a backup system as well, though I saw no sextant used on the ship. Dirk misses "the good old days", though he is only 61—just a kid!

Passing the islands of Jersey and Guernsey with Cherbourg, France just visible on the horizon. On the chart: Dieppe, Boulogne, Calais on the right, Southhampton, Isle of Wight, Plymouth leftward, with Dover coming up around 0400. Its Strait is the narrowest point in the Channel. Waldek's watch starts then. "I get to sleep early so to wake up fast," says he, "But when you see hundred ships all around you on radar, you don't need coffee!!" I am invited up at 0400 to "see the fun". Even now ships are all around us—coasters, freighters, tankers, even a few sailboats.

A constant sense of excitement. This is the English Channel! England, France, history, the war, the ships, The Man Who Never Was, D-Day, German fortifications, Dunkerque and the small rescue boats, bombers flying over and back . . .

EMERGENCY! The ship is out of cigarettes! That is, all the ones that can be unsealed have been, and no more duty free cigs can be opened until Tuesday evening—something about customs, and stuff like cigs and booze being bonded. Time to be flexible! Waldek has brought out his pipe; don't know what the Captain is smoking.

Lovely evening, still calm (at least for the ship). Have spotted at least 3 sailboats making passage from England to France. They seem *so* tiny, but still show up well on the radar. They will be sailing most of the night. We are moving at around 17 knots; in this breeze they can't be making more than 4 or so.

Hey! At least eight yachts all in a long, stretched-out row and flying spinnakers! A race of some sort.

5/5   Up at 0400 to see us through the Dover Strait, but just missed it! Captain leaving the bridge after manually steering us through the heavy traffic. (*He* doesn't actually steer the ship; a helmsman does that; he just calls to the helmsman, for example: "Port 5" whereupon the helmsman echoes "Port 5, sir" and the wheel is swung left until a lighted dial over the forward windows reads 5° to port at which time the helmsman calls "Rudder port 5, sir". And when the Captain is satisfied with the new heading, he calls, "'Midships", The helmsman returns "Midships" and swings the little wheel until the arrow on the dial points strait up, and calls "Rudder 'midships, sir". If this is a heading the Captain—or the pilot, when there is one—feels will be held for a bit, he says simply "40"; the man at the wheel echoes "40, sir" and brings the ship, if necessary, to 40° and sings out "40 degrees, sir" and the Captain says, "Steady". This is the drill whenever the ship is "maneuvering", that is, entering or leaving a harbour, or in a potential tricky situation such as this famous Strait, and of course whenever a pilot is aboard. Occasionally, pilot and Captain must stand at the far end of a bridge wing for visibility; then these orders are SHOUTED back and forth to great effect.)

We are between Dover and Calais now, approaching Broadstairs about 12 miles to port. Weather turning rough—rainy, cloudy, even as the sky begins to lighten. Heading right into the seas now and our speed drops by 2 or 3 knots. Dunkerque off to starboard.

Back to bed, but picking up BBC3 again

Crashing through the angry North Sea now, taking the waves head on, spray flying. Water no longer the beautiful blue of the Channel yesterday, but now the colour of split pea soup. Don't' believe I have ever slept so deeply or soundly. The ship's motion, the distant roar of the diesel, even the rush of air through the vents, plus of course the idea of not having anything that needs to be done, or any reason to arise, makes for a marvelous sleep. Am tempted now and then to plan another freighter trip, but would never do that. Don't want to just go someplace—this 'round-the-world trip is *it*. But it is almost as if I have found something I have been seeking all my life. A return to something? A deep need?

Coming out of "Thames", moving into "Humber"—these are weather forecasting areas around Great Britain for ships at sea. Some of them are heard in the Master Singers' classic "Gregorian chant", "Weather Report": Dogger, Fisher, German Bight, Cromarty, Viking, etc. Others are Forties, Fastnet, Shannon, Rockall, Finisterre. The British seem to have an ear for unique and evocative names (hear also, Flanders and Swann, "Slow Train") Waldek,says that once on a smaller ship, heading straight into a gale, they spent 4 days in German Bight—the ship sometimes making no headway at all, but moving astern! He says he now knows that part of the chart by heart.

A heavy-laden coaster passes, heading south, and so low in the water the seas are sweeping her decks and cascading off through the scuppers.

Splendidly appropriate music on Classic FM radio—the old theme from The Onedin Line (actually from Khatchaturian's ballet Spartacus) as the ship turns slightly from north to head into the Humber and begins taking salt water over the bow. Beautiful! AHH! Now spray on my window—400 feet back from the prow and three stories up!

52°57'N x 1°32'E (at sea)

Half speed now as we can't get in for another 3 hours—1830—and the ship is on the "wrong" course (300°) and rolling a good deal—wallowing, we used to call it—crossways to the seas. Oil rigs all over this part of the sea, sometimes can see 3 or 4 at once off to starboard.

I collect more names. We rounded Spurn Head and The Binks, but didn't quite make it to Clee Ness Sound or Pyewipe flats.

As we near the lock, I hear the pilot talking on the radio to Cecelia,, then he mentions Sarah, and then Debbie. A big party ashore? In a way, yes: these are the names of our escorts, the tugboats!

15.

We are finally in the lock at Immingham, a bustling port, one of about a dozen or more up and down the Humber River. When the pilots came aboard at 1830 right on the button, the first thing they said to the Captain was, "It's going to be a tight fit." Yep. BIBI's beam is 26.5 meters; the lock is 27.3 meters wide. Hmm. That's a 40 cm. clearance on each side. But, moving with elegant grace and almost no speed, the tugs got her in. Getting out of the lock and into the harbour will be almost as tricky; then we'll tie up and start loading.

53°30'N x 0° (Immingham)

There. Tied up. Dirk said we would start loading today, and even at 2145 or 2200 we just might. Trucks are lined up on the quay with "things" like huge rotors or something. They've probably been waiting most of the day. Not going to go ashore tonight, even to look for a phone. I'm pooped.

5/6   Gloomy, windy day. Was going to chance a trip to York, but we may sail tonight so won't. Anyway, this is a day when staying inside and cozy is the thing, but I may venture forth to find a phone after lunch. Many, many—dozens and dozens—boxes coming aboard, going in the holds. They will come out in Xingang, China (so we add one more definite port!). As I watch the loading of these boxes, which are stored in the big shed off to the right, I become fascinated, then vastly entertained, by the forklifts doing the runs from shed to shipside. You see, I have this conviction that all entities have their own personalities. A car can be ornery or very well behaved, a wrench downright uncooperative—things like that. I even admire the personalities of popcorn kernels. They are fiercely independent, love to hang back until you turn the popper off—*then* they let go!   My favorites are the real renegades who wait until they are buried in the collecting bowl and then go off—throwing popcorn all over the room. I have been known to talk to and even remonstrate with them! So it only follows that these bustling forklifts—totally separate from their incidental drivers—have their own frisky personas. One in particular beetles through the wide doorway into the darkness of the shed. It is gone for just a few seconds, and then returns bearing on high the 679th wooden box. As it tootles out, it takes a little hop over the threshold "saying" plain as day: "Look at me!   I found a box!" and presents it to the waiting stevies. (Well, I told you you have to be a little crazy to do this!)

Two "heavy pieces" (170 tons) giving a bit of a problem; nobody can figure out where the lifting points are, or where to put the slings. Usually there are indicating marks on the covering or on the device itself, but nobody can find any. Now there are 15 men and one woman standing around trying to decide how to lift this thing.

Such a day! Dismal for weather and dismal watching those 15 guys puzzling over the huge something or other just lying there on the quay. They finally rig slings made of cable so heavy it takes two men to lift the bight at the end, and the shackles are half as tall as a man. They get it all set, then stand around in clumps and just before the lunch break, dismantle the whole thing and give up for the day. "Nobody wanted to take the risk" reports Dirk.

Then the sun comes out and about 1430, I decide to explore for phones. Getting directions from a few folks I find the Seaman's Mission on the other side of the lock, which means walking over the lock gates. I don't particularly like that sort of thing, though I am perfectly safe doing so—people do it all the time and there are railings and even signs pointing the way for pedestrians.

The Mission? Great place! Treat myself to a can of Pringles "crisps" and a Coke, then fall into conversation with the mate of one of those beautiful female tugs—the ANYA. He is glad we aren't sailing tonight (I got the word just before debarking) as he hoped to have more free time on this Bank Holiday (observing May Day). He tells me of a city bus that runs to Grimsby and a seaside place called Cleethorpe. The more I think about it . . . so I board the top deck of the next bus and ride for almost an hour through countryside and town and city and finally: Cleethorpe! It is, of course, holiday time and thousands of English folk are wandering along the front enjoying themselves in the arcades, bingos, fish and chips places—and turning their noses red in the brisk and chilly sea breeze. My, they do like their "seaside places". Don't have sufficient poundage to get me some fish and chips, but I sure am ready for some! Never mind. I catch the right bus back and—lo!—the ship is still there! Make a call home to Ellen with the latest dispatches. Grand to talk to her.

Back on the ship, I feel I have to stop by the kitchen and apologize to Renand for missing supper. But glory be! He has saved it for me! The plate wrapped in Saran, a dish of apricots, and a hunk of cheese. Well, may as well—so I grab it all—plate, dish, silverwear, bread, cheese, peanut butter jar, and start juggling it all up the stairs. Suddenly someone is coming down! It is Chief Officer Waldek. There he stands looking down at red-handed me laden down with all that food. With an impish grin, he says: "Good appetite!" and disappears downward. Such a fine fellow.

5/7   Zowee! Three giant ferries are suddenly here. They entered early this morning with no pilot (i.e., no red and white flag flying from the mast) and no tugs! Obviously they are frequent visitors to this port and need neither. All are loaded with things on wheels—not passengers or their cars, but other things that can be driven or towed off. Huge stern ramps let down and dozens of little cabs or tractors whiz on and pull off low and laden trailers—one holds a railroad car! Then dozens of new automobiles are driven off, and many Mercedes truck cabs. All done at breakneck speed. All three ships are unloading at once.

Meanwhile back at the ranch, they've gotten one of those "heavy lifts" in, now the other one, plus lots and lots of boxes yet. Apparently, somebody (probably the woman) got smart and called the factory where the heavies were made and asked how in tarnation you pick these puppies up? The information was as powerful as the derrick and up they went. They are hoping to finish by noon so we can sail by 1500. Wanna bet?

This is an amazing port: ships constantly moving in and out. Every ship that was here when we arrived is gone and has been replaced at least once. And this is just one port! The Captain suggests there are more ports than cities in England.

Yes! We will sail today—at 2200 tonight! Just too many boxes!

Talking at lunch with Dirk and the Captain. We are loading an entire mill. All told it weighs 7,000 tons. Cost to ship to China, about $40 a ton. That's $280,000! But with about $10,000 in port costs, plus pilot, tugs, crew, provisions, fuel, etc. the company is barely making money, he says. So, Dirk quips, Herr Rickmers is living on what I paid for this trip! Heh heh.

It looks like we'll be in Hamburg by about 0600 on Thursday

5/9. This will be the real beginning of my journey: the first really foreign port where the folks don't speak English, and of course the place where I will be joined by three more passengers. Am I a little nervous at these prospects? Who me?

Think I'll cross the lock again and perhaps spend the rest of my English money.

Suddenly the fog rolls in—so dense the bow of the ship disappears. Will this delay our sailing?

Nope! Away from the quay—and we still float! The ladies STEPHANIE and DEBBIE are paying court, DEBBIE nosing up as if to say, "C'mon, c'mon, let's get this show on the road!" This whole process is a thing of beauty: this enormous ship, moving so slowly and with such grace, the lady tugs crowding around her, urging and nudging.

(There are nine tugs in this distaff fleet.)

It is virtually impossible for a ship this size to enter and leave a lock, especially one this size, without touching—that is, scraping—the concrete walls if only briefly. The Immingham lock hands are aware of this, and walk along beside the ship with big balks of wood on lines, which they keep between the hull and the lock sides—the Fendermen. Very nice service.

In the lock now—we tower over the barely visible Seaman's Mission as the fog thickens again, having thinned a bit earlier on. A sharp lookout on the bridge tonight!

I *am* this ship, and I long to break free from this lock and this quay and this shore and gallop across the sea.

16.

The difference between a coast captain and a deep sea captain, according to Waldek: "When deep sea captain sees coast, he almost has 'accident in pents'; when coastal captain sees deep sea, he almost has 'accident in pents!'"

5/8   Like a pulsating rock, BIBI marches across the now docile North Sea, hell bent for Hamburg—her actual home port—and the, I assume, impatient travelers who long to be doing just what I'm doing and can't wait to get started. No sun today and no wind either and no motion to the ship, just ever onward toward the Elbe. We are probably 150 miles out now—no ships or oil rigs in sight.

54°04'N x 5°27'E (at sea)

We're getting there early! Maybe 25 or 30 hours early. The pilot is coming aboard in less than an hour. Some excitement. The two fitters, father and son, and the electrician, their contracts finished, are leaving the ship in Hamburg to go home to Poland, and several wives and families are coming aboard, plus, of course, the three new passengers, and two new seamen.

Visibility still only about 2 or 3 miles.

Waldek has me in stitches as least once a day. Speaking of his wife's problems getting tickets to Hamburg, he notes that she may not arrive until the 10th, but tomorrow (the 9th), she will "get fire under ess" and get here sooner. He is very sharp; his Polish/English makes him even funnier—and of course he knows it!

Let's go look for the pilot.

Well into the Elbe River now, past Cuxhaven. Many ships, sailboats, para-skiers. Pilots are stationed about 17 miles offshore in a large anchored ship, then are delivered to us in a very fast catamaran. Pilot boats are absolutely the sleekest craft afloat!

The Captain is now making a special point of telling me about—well—everything. I think once he discovered that I spend about as much time on the bridge as he does, he recognized a willing audience. He is quite charming in pointing out landmarks, even to getting out a different chart to do so. I am touched—and very grateful. Still several hours to Hamburg—an enormous port and city—a good distance upriver.

I gaze from my window: this is Germany! Germany is so massively redolent with history, both exemplary and horrifying, that I get very strange urges. I want to ask the pilot, "Where were you . . . ?" Somewhere, just over there, is the Bergen-Belsen concentration camp. Did U-boats traverse this river on their way to . . . ? Here Hitler's voice was heard both in person and on the radio. Nazi flags flew. This is Germany! Will it ever be "just" Germany?

And yet here is Mozart—picked up on German radio.

The Kiel Canal—connecting the North Sea with the Baltic Sea and making Denmark, therefore, an island. Then a wind farm—five giant, three-bladed windmills turning gracefully in the evening breeze. A glimpse of the future. We have changed pilots as we pass the entrance to the Canal. Two pilots on this leg—one for the river, the other for the harbour.

On the radio, the German Youth Orchestra from Berlin: Shostakovich 7, Mahler *Kindertotenlieder*. The music is always the music, but the announcer sounds so amazingly German.

5/9   One month ago today, the harried hurry to the midnight ship—almost the classic story of the dude leaping for the ferry, slipping, falling into the drink, being pulled out and told that if he'd only waited a minute. the ship was just coming in.

A bright, sunny day in Hamburg. We are tied up, portside to, with a lighter already drawn up alongside with *more boxes* to come aboard. We should be here only a couple of days they say, but I'll keep checking.

53°30'N x 10°E (Hamburg)

Dirk is back aboard, having flown over from Immingham. We will sail Saturday, day after tomorrow, at 1700, then Antwerp on Monday.

Today is a church holiday here—*Himmelfahrt,* I believe, or as Dirk put it, "the day Yesus took off". Tsk. It actually means "heavenly journey". So not much work is being done around here except in and on this ship. And most of the movement in the harbour is by little tour boats and—Holy Cow!—a Mississippi River boat! What we are loading here is the rest of the mill for Xingang.

Today is also the 830th anniversary of this port. BIG celebration downtown. Captain recommends I go down. Gorgeous day—almost hot! I may just take the skipper's advice.

Two new crew members and one wife aboard (not Waldek's—today is "fire under ess" day), but no sign of new passengers.

Seven tour boats—all at once.

A monstrous Dutch floating crane nearby; I wonder if it might be the one—or one of the ones—that raised the sunken Russian sub, KURSK.

Hey, I'm back! *Was für ein Tag!* Some day! Dirk gives me a lift to the *Alt Elbe* Tunnel—closed to vehicular traffic on this holiday. Then I just follow the crowds and ride a huge elevator down, down, down, and walk through the tunnel under the Elbe river to the *Landungsbrücken* (Landing Bridges) side where all the fun is, but one of the elevators to lift us up to sea level again is out of order and a long, long line waits for the only other one, so many of us walk up. *EGAD!* Flight after flight of stairs stuck to the curving wall and switching back and forth as we rise up and up. DON'T LOOK DOWN! But there is a net rigged way down there just in case. Then, out of the tunnel building and smack into the biggest birthday party ever! A mammoth carnival (I remember that the Germans *do* love their *"Feiertagen"* (holidays). The *Landungsbrücken* is, or are, a mile long "boardwalk" (though not of boards) hugging the shoreline of the Elbe, connected by short bridges to the shore itself. The walkway is lined with restaurants and shops and today about ten million people enjoying the sun and each other and, on the river side, a solid row of tour boats. water taxis and three "tall ships". More of them are parading up the river along with a British Cruiser, a couple of German Corvettes, a huge freighter (probably got caught in the procession), that Mississippi River boat again and hundreds of small craft, sail and power. Later, a team of water skiers takes off from a barge.

I have no German money to spend and I can't find any place to cash one of my pesky Traveler's cheques, except, I am told, at the *Hauptbahnhof*—the main railway station. Too far to walk, accessible by *S-Bahn*—the elevated train—but I don't have the price of a ticket. Hells bells. So I just walk right up to a stopped train, start my story to tell to the conductor who taps the shoulder of a young woman bystander asks her if she speaks English and points to me. She smiles and nods, and I tell her my story and she tells him and he tells her and she tells me that today, it being a holiday, nobody is collecting tickets, I should get right on in. I do.

Another overwhelming train station, and the *Reisebank* gives me almost 49 Euros (pronounced Oy-rows in Germany, of course) for my $50 Amex cheque. Let me say this about that right now. These are my first Euros. I don't worry about $50 worth of Euros because, you see, I can spend them in Belgium and Italy (and France and Holland, etc. etc.) and I get to thinking about stupid Canada and the stupid United States and the criminal exchange rate that had added 60% to the cost of this trip for me, and the bare fact that *European countries*, which had, for cryin' out loud, "*invented* nationalism!", had somehow managed to get together on their currencies and actually eliminate Marks, and Francs and Lira and (almost) all the rest (except stupid Great Britain) and what a tremendous boon it is to have the same money all over the place (every single European I talked to agreed), and how these two obstinate, short-sighted, unimaginative, ethnocentric, jingoistic countries in North America can't even *talk* about doing it, and I get damn mad. And I'm still mad. In tribute to the recalcitrant North Americans, I visit a "*pissoir*"—and save paying 20 Euro-cents for the privilege!

So when I get back to the party I splurge on a *Bratwurst mit Brötchen* that takes me back 45 years to my stay in Germany as a U.S. Army Neuropsychiatric Technician, and it still tastes absolutely yummy.

The tourist info *Fräulein* had given me a map of the area and I take a look at things to do and see. The first thing I see is the "tall ship" I had been eyeing from afar; it is the Rickmer "RICKMERS"! Now, berthed permanently, a museum and exquisite restaurant (nothing hokey here—real elegance) but still fully rigged and gorgeous to see—which I do, of course. She was built by our man Rickmers or his forebears in 1896 (the company in fact goes back 200 years or more), had a fascinating history under Portuguese and British flags, etc., and finally found her way back to Rickmers which gave her a complete refit, and there she stands! I sit for a long time on the foredeck resting feet and taking the sun, then amble down the quay for a closer look at three other windjammers that have now tied up and are open to the public. They are the KRUZENSTERN from Russia, the MIR from St. Petersburg, and the STATSRAADE LEHMKOHL from Bergen. The THALASSA a smaller square rigger, still being sailed privately, is also in. Later the Captain reports that he had been on the Polish tall ship in 1976 for the big bash in the States.

One of the "amusements" today is, I think, among the nuttiest things I've ever seen human beings subject themselves to. And there is a line-up to do it! It is a big ball inside of which two people sit and are strapped in tight. The ball is suspended by two huge and very stretchy bungee cords which are winched up to full stretch while the ball is held fast—like a huge vertical slingshot; an attendant changes the film in a camera that snaps the hapless couple's "fun" ride. Suddenly the ball is released and it shoots a good hundred feet straight up in the air, still attached, but totally out of control—spinning, dropping, shooting back up again and spinning some more. After several more bounces and spins, it is lowered to the ground for the next victims. *Good grief!* (I can remember from my earlier stay, other wild and imaginative "attractions": motorcycles roaring around inside a steel mesh ball, a huge barrel that spins so when the floor drops away, the riders are stuck to the revolving wall—this back in the fifties.)

Now I climb the embankment along the grounds and find a quiet phone to call Ellen. Wonderful chat. Then make my way back through the tunnel and up the elevator. In my crepuscular German I manage to ask a young fellow if he happens to know the number of a taxi company—no phone books around. *Does he!* He used to work for one! I call and order one up. Then wait. And wait some more. Then, heaving into view, the buslet from Hamburg's Seaman's Mission! Could it run me back to my BIBI? *Jawohl!* And off I go—feeling a bit guilty about the cab, but with all the folks pouring out of that tunnel, I doubt he'll have trouble picking up a fare.

Lots of good luck and good times today; tomorrow I rest.

17.

5/10 Aha! Two new passengers! They are sitting at breakfast when I breeze in. They make as if to rise. I hold up my hand, say, *"Moment, bitte."* and let loose with the phrase I have been rehearsing and which I learned in my Sophomore German class at Ohio Wesleyan University 50 years ago: *"Es freut mich sehr Sie kennen zu lehrnen!"* (It joys me very you know to learn!) Are they impressed? Ho ho, are they impressed! They are the Kments, Hans and Marion from Berlin. His card says "Dr. med Hans Kment". M'god he's a doctor! Will wonders never cease? The one thing that gave us pause about this trip was the total absence of a doctor on the ship; now we have one! So, he's retired. So?

Both these folks look hale and hearty, both seem to be about my age, as the Captain had noted earlier when I asked him about the imminent newcomers, and both speak wonderful English—not always perfectly correct, as I discover, but often more accurate than correct. We chat: they both love good music—have brought along Bruckner and Mahler CDs. We swap "flexibility" stories and things seem to be off to a fine start. The other new fellow will come aboard tomorrow, they say.

Great walk around the "*Kai*" (quay) to an abandoned shed which shows the only likely evidence I've seen of the war: some damage that is not natural on the building, and on the unused quayside.

63

Ship ahead of us is loading cars—dozens of cars—not new cars, old cars, *used* cars—heading for Tunis. Shipping used cars? Are they stolen cars? Nope, I learn from Dirk, there is a big market for used cars in many parts of the world. Who can afford a new one? So off they go—giant, floating used car lots! The jetsam of affluence.

In checking the cargo, I detect some add-ons are going to Shanghai—another definite port! (I write in my notes: "This is all almost *too* interesting and exciting! Am I a total nut?)

Aha—the 4th passenger is arriv-ed! His name is Klaus Bischoff and he is from Aachen, Germany (formerly Aix-la-Chapelle), right on the German/Belgian/Netherlands border. This is his 4th freighter voyage, his second such circumnavigation. In 1999 he took the same trip I was poised to take in 2001 on a Rickmers-Reederei (meaning owned by Rickmers) container ship travelling the opposite way around. During our introductions, I discover that Frau Kment—Marion—is also a physician! Bischoff is a real nut—great guy, speaks excellent English. All of us were originally booked on the LEON. Klaus and I were upgraded, but his cabin is on D deck has about 196 sq. ft. and a window looking to starboard. I got far and away the best deal on the switch.

The Kments brought their bikes.

Watching the loading—they may finish this evening, ahead of sked. Cargo going to Shanghai may be an entire paper mill. One huge box is labelled simply TISSUE MACHINE. (More nose-blowing coming up!) Also. a number of gigantic "chain fairleads" coming aboard—12 tons each.

Waldek's wife (she did arrive!) joins us for lunch with 3 year old Rose. Very pretty lady; very cute little girl,and she talks—to me—hardly at all. But how wondrous it is to hear this tiny little girl speaking Polish! So young to have learned "another language"—and such a complicated one, too. (Well, isn't that what we think?)

A boat just went by called WASSERBOOT—"water boat"? I see. Other cargo resting in a waiting mode on the quay—not for us: one aircraft container loader, 3 mobile microwave transmission towers, neatly telescoped, complete with anemometers and aircraft warning lights, all set to be raised and put into service.

Last box just came aboard—about one foot square and lifted by an enormous 100 foot crane. But we still probably won't sail tonight.

Ship behind us is ABU ZEMINA registered in Alexandria, Egypt, another 'breakbulk" freighter like us. Boxes and more boxes for her, too, plus 25 brand new Mercedes-Benz ambulances bound for Cairo. They are driven onto a platform and lifted one at a time up and into the ship's hold. The drivers cannot forbear when driving so many sleek, fully rigged ambulances and every once in a while we hear a siren go off.

And our electrician was off, too, a long procession of crew and colleagues carrying his 8 or 10 bags. We have a new electrician, quite young, He seems just a tad apprehensive about the whole scene. I, on the other hand, feel like a salty veteran!

Up listening to the CBC's World at Six (at 2330), stealing some peanut butter and bread, and Dirk was there with news: we sail at 0200! I am getting terribly lax and do not plan to be on watch for the event.

5/11   Straightened the books in the library cupboard and found a couple of good reads (really my reason for doing the job). Am nowhere near through the stock of paperbacks I brought along, but I don't want to take any chances.

Dropped the pilot at about 0800. This is a busy shipping lane as we head for Antwerp in, again, fog-shrouded but very calm North Sea.

We passengers all seem to remain in the dining room after eating for a bit of a gam. Klaus telling how on an earlier freighter trip, one large container held only 220 kg worth of matches, while the container itself probably weighed several tons. Another container carried live worms going to Virginia. They arrived safely, and the ship got a thank-you note from the recipient.

There is a pigeon on the bridge wing! Poor fellow looks like he fell asleep after a big night and woke up to find himself surrounded by nothing but water. There he sits, all fluffed up. blinking and weighing his chances of reaching the shore by air. Probably not good. Never mind, Renand will catch him, tame him, feed him and let him go (maybe) in Antwerp or Livorno. Renand is our "Radar O' Reilly". (But that was the last I saw of the bird; maybe he decided to have a go for land—maybe he had a family.)

Waldek came down this morning and knocked on my door—a real surprise. He asked if I could come up to his cabin where we could talk. I went. His wife and daughter were still abed and we sat in his day room. The first thing he said was, "I am leaving ship."

"WHAT?" I was absolutely stunned . He said he is having "big trouble with Captain". He finds that he and the Captain are just not getting along. He is very concerned. This is his first voyage as Chief Officer; he feels he is doing his job well, but has begun to feel unaccepted and unwelcome. On the one hand, he knows he "must" leave the ship, but on the other, realizes this may not auger well for his future career. All of this was a total surprise to me, though I had noticed that communication between the two seemed to be brief and rare. He is determined to leave us in Antwerp unless somebody from Technomar comes there to "negotiate". Even then, he realises he must leave at Livorno. He is in quite a quandary.

Now I begin to see why we hit it off so well: we are very much alike; we are both rather "American"—perhaps an unfortunate trait unless you happen to be in America. We have both had experiences (this is not his first) where a boss or a board of trustees or a teacher appears to be made uneasy by our presence. It is obvious to me that Waldek is probably one of the smartest and most intelligent of our ship's company, and it could well be that he is quick enough, and efficient enough, and generally adept enough to cause some unease, even envy among some. But what do I really know? Waldek says he sees me as "wise man". I say to him that in my experience a person who is sharp and good-natured and imaginative and perhaps a little bold is often seen as a "troublemaker". His response to this is: "YES!" I urge him to talk and discuss and above all to safeguard his future—a career for which he has prepared diligently. He has stopped standing his watches and essentially at this point, resigned from the ship. It occurs to me that this may have been the reason he invited his wife here. I gather too, that he and the Captain were at the moment not speaking! Imagine that! And me—the timid traveller—involved now, if only on the edge. He also told me that if he left in Antwerp, the ship would not be allowed to sail without a Chief Officer—so what does that mean?

The idea of him leaving the ship is a real blow to me. He is a genuine kindred spirit and I have looked greatly forward to many conversations. The voyage would take on a decidedly different cast (literally). But I don't worry yet—somehow things will work out.

18.

53°50'N x 6°29'E (at sea)

Over a really splendid lunch, I was thinking how incredibly lucky I have been on this trip. The Kments are in the Owner's Suite as they would have been on the LEON; Klaus,I believe, is in the cabin corresponding to the one I had reserved on the LEON—the one with the aft-facing window (but his has a starboard window—the ships are not exactly the same). Only I, it seems was grandly upgraded to the absolutely marvellous suite with 3 windows, two looking forward, and a separate popcorn and chart room. My delight in gazing out those "front" windows cannot be imagined.

Then to have not one but *two* doctors aboard is nearly miraculous. And the weather has been perfect—Klaus's first trip

found his ship caught in a genuine hurricane—and in real danger!
I cannot wait to tell it all to Vicky Blevins at Uniglobe on Salt Spring—and to thank her for her good guidance and constant contact with Freighter World Cruises to make this happen. I'm sure she even had something to do with the weather!

We will pick up the Belgian pilot at about 2200 hrs. tonight, then about 8 hours later we should be in Antwerp, according to the chart, a vast and complex port, fraught with locks and sub-channels, etc.

This trip just keeps getting better!

One of the reasons the ship is riding so smoothly is that she is probably close to 10,000 tons heavier now than when we crossed the ocean.

Just looking out the front window over the hatch covers and derricks I am deriving great satisfaction from the fact that this ship is actually taking things to people: steel for whatever, machines to make paper, a thousand boxes of who-knows-what. There is a very good reason why we plow the sea, unlike, say, a cruise ship which seems to have little purpose except temporary diversion for a few thousand people. The pleasure on this ship seems equal or greater, and our ship—*my* ship—is providing a real service.

Was summoned by Waldek, via Renand, this afternoon to watch LORD OF THE RINGS. Waldek and family were ensconced in the darkened and smoke-laden officer's lounge. I hadn't read the book, hadn't seen the movie, didn't really want to, but it's one of his favourites and he has it on a pirated DVD for which he paid $1 in China, so . . . So, the sound is very loud and screechy; it is in English, but with Chinese and Indonesian subtitles. Waldek is explaining it to his daughter and wife in Polish and to me in his marvellous English. The room is hot and fuggy with smoke; he is lighting one cigarette after another and little Rose is bored and fidgeting. I grow just a mite uncomfortable and after about an hour, take my leave. On a ship you don't need to make a reason for leaving—hell, there's no place to go!—so you just say "Excuse me" and go. It is a small place, so privacy and understanding become that much more important.

5/12   I wake before dawn to find us in the lock leading to ten miles of man-made channels and courses that will take us to Antwerp. The river here is tidal and navigable, but unsuitable for docking so the Belgians and the Dutch have constructed this miracle of engineering not unlike the smaller installations at Newport and Immingham. This lock, unlike those, can hold eight ships at a time. We are now waiting for another ship to enter.

The Captain, a fountain of info tonight, says this harbour is connected via canals and channels to all of Europe—Switzerland, "even Poland". I was noticing the words "dyck" and "polder" on the chart— reclaimed land from the sea. He recalls several years ago calling at Rotterdam to find the whole waterfront under a foot of water. Couldn't tell where the quay began! All was water. In 2 days the water had been drained or pumped off, but the Dutch then built a huge flood control gate to prevent this happening again. "Why are Dutch people all so tall?" he asks, with a twinkle. "All the short people sank!"

Hurried up to the bridge in sock feet so as not to miss anything, but am back to put on shoes. Our third pilot since leaving the Channel is coming aboard to guide us to our quay—about ten miles away. I may get a peanut butter sandwich while I'm up . . . . . *Ach*! No bread!

51°15' N x 4°15'E (Antwerp)

Here we are! Antwerp at last!

Ahhh. Shower and sleep in. Still foggy and dismal out there. Will be happy to get out of this North Sea/English Channel-type weather— though we did have a gorgeous day in Hamburg. Will now go on my usual search for a telephone and begin investigating some shopping possibilities.

Sunday today, so nobody works.

Radio: American songs on pop station (Nat King Cole, "Unforgettable"), FM programs in English, BBC 3—90.0 to 92.9 FM, Classic FM 100.0 to 102.9 FM all over the country—or even continent!—amazing and wonderful! Imagine having CBC 2 available all over Canada at roughly the same frequency. What a smashing idea!

Hope the CD players come soon; the Kments are anxious to have at their Bruckner.

At lunch I mention that the Captain had told me earlier that all the new passengers boarding in Hamburg were "about your age". I decide to ask them. Aha: Marion was born June 23, 1934. Close but no cigar. Hans, October 10, 1933—my very year, and Klaus—wait for it!—*July 1, 1933!* We were born on the very same day! But he figures he was born first because Germany is 6 or 7 hours ahead of eastern U.S. So Marion is the young chick and Klaus the old codger by a few hours. I gave him some clothes hangers as an advance birthday present (there were none in his wardrobe either, and when he asked for some, he was presented with one!).

5/13 Good schmooze at breakfast with the good Germans. They all speak English—usually—for my benefit (though they say it gives them practice, and besides, says Marion, "It is the official language of the ship, so we have to!) but I can pretty much follow their *Deutsch*, too. I 'm too shy to exercise my own limping German.

Work started this morning at 0600. It is not loud, in fact almost silent: barges alongside bringing huge rolls of metal sheeting, and great steel stanchions are being removed from the ship. Waldek tells me they support an added layer of cargo in the hold when needed. We don't need them any more so they will either be left here or put back aboard before we leave, and taken to China.

Lots of cargo lying on the quay that seems to be for us—great pipes, huge shafts of steel, bundles of smaller pipes. But who knows? The goal is to sail tomorrow evening or Wednesday morning.

Waldek and family, with Bibi looking on

At lunch today Waldek and family sit very quietly. I don't know what has happened. Did somebody from Technomar arrive? What decisions have been made? Waldek seems to suggest that he will be leaving "tomorrow"; we shake hands and wish each other well; I take a picture of the threesome. I have at this moment no idea what a loss I will feel if he really does leave.

Later we "Four Musketeers" are going to catch the #31 bus into town and see what's shaking. The three of them have fine senses of humour. Klaus is elfin-like and very funny.

Am going down now to help load the cargo.

They are doing fine, actually—the best stevedores yet for my money.

Marion, Hans and I walk to the bus stop and catch the #31 for Antwerp city. (Klaus beat us to it with an earlier bus.) (Pay attention now; this is the only "travelogue" you're going to get.) We get off and walk through the overwhelmingly old part of the city and finally reach the Cathedral of Our Lady. I'm not a cathedral buff, but they are, so I tag along (otherwise, I feel, I will quickly become hopelessly lost—they have been here before). Construction began on this exquisite building in 1352! Imagine! It has "seven naves"—to hold the, then increasing, population. In the 16th century the plan called for *nine* naves which would have made the church about 3 times larger. Big fire in 1533. In 1566, and again in 1581, the church was plundered "during the iconoclastic fury", but refurbished in the 17th century, only to be destroyed internally again during the French Revolution. It was of course renovated, but work is continuous on the building. It is also an art gallery containing two large triptychs by Rubens who lived and worked here in Antwerp.

We sit for a bit in the wondrous sun on a huge plaza, have a bite and a wee dram, and just marvel at this great city

In search of a pillow for Marion, we enter the newer part of town—Yech!—and end up at the Central Railway Station—a veritable cathedral in itself—where our bus—with the same driver!—is waiting just for us.

We alight before the end of the line and walk a windy way to find SUNNY EUROPE, a giant duty-free store selling everything under the sun. The Captain and Chief Engineer are there. I buy a shirt for 7.14 Euros; Hans gets a stash of wine, and Marion finds her pillow; it will all be delivered right to the ship tomorrow morning. We are given a free ride back to the ship by one of the store's vans. Almost all their business is with ships and they publish a snazzy catalogue for broad-ocean browsing.

I don't think I will go adventuring with anyone again. There were two places I would like to have stopped—the Central Library and an Internet Cafe, but, alas, it's not really possible when your companions have other interests. I may catch the bus tomorrow again—very inexpensive. I wondered once again if anyone who hasn't experienced it can realise how absolutely tremendous it is to have *the same money* wherever you go. The Kments love it—and they are experienced world travellers.

5/14   THE STAMP by Klaus Bischoff
"MONDAY: I promised my family I would send them a postcard so I took the bus to the Central Post Office in Antwerp to buy one stamp. I had to take a number, and then I waited more than half an hour to buy one stamp. I put it with my credit card.

"When I got back to the ship I drew a postcard [ed. note: he always makes his own cards], but when I looked for it, the stamp was gone! So tomorrow I will take the bus again to the Central Post Office to buy a stamp.

"TUESDAY: I walked to the bus stop to take the bus to the Post Office, and suddenly realized, I had forgotten to bring the post card, so I had to go back to the ship and take a later bus."

Hans said maybe Klaus could take their post cards and mail them. I joked, are you kidding? He can't hold onto one stamp, let alone three postcards. Marion said wouldn't it be awful if he missed the boat because he was buying one stamp. I said, there he would be, clutching his stamp, on the train to Livorno to meet the ship and Klaus said no, he would stick the stamp on his forehead and let the "post" get him there, and Marion said what if one stamp was not enough, he would arrive with postage due. I said, in that case, maybe we wouldn't accept him and he would be sent back, etc. etc. I said, finally, "Klaus, you will find that stamp in a week or so." And he did. Well, simple minds . . .

19.

HOORAY! Renand just delivered the new stereo, CD/cassette/ radios! They came right on schedule: lovely JVC units with remote control, clock, sleep timer—the works. Ah, bliss!

So, wanting to do something nice for Renand, I gave him the unit I bought in Texas. He was very pleased and said "I will never forget you!"

We sail at midnight tonight, so will call Ellen with the news. Hot dog!

Well, my new friend. Chief Officer Waldemar Watracz is gone! After just one month knowing him, I am very sad. I see the rest of the voyage in a much different light. He seemed like a splendid fellow with a lovely family and a fine career ahead of him. Will he always have trouble fitting? "It is not my century," he said to me once.

His replacement has arrived: a tall fellow with three stripes on his blue uniform (I never saw Waldek in a uniform. Hmmm.); looks like a straight arrow and will not be another Waldek. Alas.

Guess what is coming aboard now. STEEL!

71

And now: containers! 6 or 8 of them will ride on the #4 hatch.

And now: a giant boiler at least 60 feet long dangling from our jumbo derrick.

Omigod! A truck drives up—a 14 wheel heavy-duty "cement pump" truck with extendable tower to carry cement to high or far places. Wha . . . ? Nooo! Not really! Yep! Here come the slings and there goes the truck, disappearing into #3 hold. Better watch out what you drive down here: it may end up in the BIBI! But it looks like the last piece of cargo. Still lots of room; the starboard #5 'tweendecks space is plum empty. What awaits us in Livorno? It is of course something of an art, deciding what cargo goes where, in which of the twenty openable spaces to put what, depending on its weight, size and shape, and where it needs to get off. This is the job of the Chief Officer, who spends much time with his charts and diagrams.

That moment! We are all buttoned up. Hatches closed, cargo loaded and lashed, shore cranes lined up and at rest, their sky-high hooks gently swaying 60 feet off the ground, our own derrick and cranes tucked into their cribs, hooks secured. We are a tight ship, ready for whatever the sea might bring. All the little orange men have departed, slapping each other on the back and laughing: another ship loaded and ready to go. Tomorrow will, of course, bring another, but this one is finished.

After a day filled with rain squalls and wind and bright sun and blue skies, the sun sets over the harbour—a giant orange ball, visibly sinking below the horizon. Let's go!

We passengers are, well, we are passengers on a freighter. We linger after supper, swapping stories in German and English, then, as one, we rise and make our way to the stairway or elevator, bidding good night and "See you tomorrow." as if parting for our own separate dwellings, our own streets and avenues. In actuality, our "homes" are within feet of each other—two of us on E deck, one on D and me on C. We will gather at breakfast (or lunch), meeting and greeting, chatting and eating, then probably go our own ways again 'til the next meal., not often seeing each other between times. A pattern is emerging.

We have, however, planned a "concert" tomorrow at 2000 in the Kment's home to listen to a symphony and sip good wine

(I'm not sure how much *gemütlichkeit* I'll be able to manage; we'll see.)

We're off!

5/15   I wake. The ship has slowed. Sure enough we are just now dropping the pilot—8 hours after sailing. We are quite a way at sea; a very small, but powerful boat leaves an anchored ship to pick him off our ladder. In the distance I count 11 ships at anchor, waiting for space available to enter the port of Antwerp where there are 999 berths! It wasn't just luck that got us in so quickly on Sunday; Rickmers actually "owns" a few berths in strategic ports so they are always available.

And there they are—this time in daylight—the white cliffs of Dover.

50°52'N x 1°04'E (at sea)

After some excellent fish at lunch, we sang songs to each other. Some we all knew—*auf Deutsch*, or in English—items like "East side, West side, all around the town". Marion took part of her medical training in Boston.

The Captain told us that the 3rd Officer also left for home (the Philippines) yesterday; his mother had passed away. So we lost *two* mates yesterday. Too late to replace the 3rd, so the Captain must stand his watches—0800 to 1200 and 2000 to 2400. We will get a new 3rd in Livorno. That's 5 men who have left the ship, but at least the Captain and Steward Renand will be with us to Houston.

Tomorrow we meet the Bay of Biscay, notorious for rough, confused seas.

An event! Bad supper (for me): rice, some yellow stuff, and beef mixed with red things, etc. I have an aversion to red things. But, hey, what's a couple of "bad" suppers in five weeks? Not bad.

There! The first "social evening". The four of us sat quietly and listened to the hour-long Bruckner Symphony #7—the one with the Wagner tubas. Had some wine and cheese and then gabbed for a while as the sun set. Hans, like me, has to get up and peer out of the window every so often to see what is going on. (Nothing is going on, of course: just a lot of water. Still, you never can tell . . .)

We are all remarkably compatible it seems. On Klaus's last trip one of the passengers was, he says, "a Nazi", and they had such differences of opinion that, though they sat next to each other at every meal, they did not speak for more than a month until Klaus sent his neighbour a "diplomatic note". It worked.

It was a nice time, but, I felt my cozy cabin beckoning and was happy to be home again.

5/16   Just entering the Bay of Biscay. Slight increase in ship's motion but nothing to write home about. It will take 18 more hours to cross it, so we'll see what happens. Of course, like Cape Horn, it isn't always rough, just has a bad reputation. Waves rolling across the Atlantic, enter the bay—or bight—and just bounce off the sides and out again, so seas are confused and can come from all sides. And if there is a big storm—well, you can imagine.

So we will pass Bordeaux (50 miles or so off to port), then Cape Finisterre in Spain, then Portugal and finally turn left for Gibraltar and the Med.

46°56'N x 6°56' W (at sea)

Klaus has found in his cabin two "coffee table" books: "Canada and its people" and "A day in the life of Canada" both presented to the BIBI by Environment Canada "as an award for excellent meteorological observations" in 1989 and 1994. My goodness gracious!

Crossing the "dreaded" Bay of Biscay, the wave height diminishes to almost nothing, but the Atlantic swell increases, taking with it the ship.

All right. Now she's beginning to gallop a little. A mist over the sea, the wind picking up and the swell more noticeable. Pop cans are rolling back and forth in my fridge and I stow the popcorn popper so it won't slide off the desk. Spray almost over the bow, but BIBI's saucy flare keeps it where it belongs and shoots it out to the sides. We may get some weather yet.

Thought about walking the deck this afternoon, but no, I guess not. The Captain says we should be in the "Med" for Saturday's barbecue. Ok. It will take us all day tomorrow to pass Spain and Portugal.

Ah, now she's rockin' and rollin'! Things sliding around, even on the bridge. Klaus out on the starboard wing rising and falling probably 20 feet. Have secured the new stereo so it can't fall anywhere. I'm sure that's probably what happened to the audio units in former times. You just have to consider that *everything* can move and *will!* Even the sofa can be locked to the wall, but I took a chance and moved it when I rearranged things and haven't had any trouble so far.

5/17   Now *that* was a night to remember! I knew that when we rounded Cape Finisterre and turned a few degrees south, the seas which we had been meeting on the starboard bow would begin to

74

come at us broadside and we would start some serious rolling. Sure enough! Around 0200 it began. I mean, BIG rolls. Things began to slide and fall (funny, even on a ship we firmly believe "it won't happen to us"). I put the CD player right on the floor, picked up the desk chair that had been thrown over and secured the bedroom door which had slammed shut against its "firmly" fastened preventer. It got worse. I was just getting up to remove the drinking glass from the fiddled "rubber ducky" shelf when WOOMPH!—over we went and everything on the shelf and on the top of the fridge was seemingly picked up and hurled across the room with a shattering of drinking glass—itself neatly whisked virtually off the tips of my fingers as I reached for it. Everything in the medicine satchel spilled niftily across the deck and, figuring it had gone about as far as it could go, I said, "Hell!" and left it all right where it was. Everything else loose was placed on the floor—a pre-emptive strike—and I went back to bed—perchance to sleep. Rolling is funny: it's the "rogue rolls" that do the damage. You get accustomed to the regular pendulum action, then all of a sudden, she just keeps going and you know this is the first BIG one. You launch yourself out of bed, aroused by this unnatural lurch, but knowing that #2 is coming! They always come in pairs. But the arrival of #2 doesn't give you quite enough time to grab whatever it is you're trying to rescue: you are a split second too late and off she goes—WHAM and CRASH! This was the first of two or three such ordeals and every time I thought all things were battened down.

We have no non-skid material for our shelves and table (another oversight besides hangers and plugs and occasional explanations like what to expect in a rolling sea), nor anything to tie something up or back, like the curtain across the front wall of windows. As the ship rolls right, the left hand curtain slides clear across the left window; then the ship rolls to port and the right hand curtain slides across the right window: now I can't see anything! I found a couple of Velcro strips on the curtains and mated them so it was all one curtain now, but at the next roll the whole thing began to slide back and forth on its noisy metal track!

So this morning—clever fellow that I am—I spied a length of lashing line left over and just sitting on the #4 hatch cover. Aha! Just now after breakfast, I walked boldly onto the deck, climbed onto the hatch cover and grabbed that line and another length lying nearby. It now suffices quite nicely to tie back the curtains (a special little hook has been placed in each corner for just this purpose), and to secure the CD player on the desk with bowlines around the handle and the little rail around the shelf above. There was enough left over for a "Siegfried Line" for me, and a length for the Kments if needed.

The Siegfried Line? A Klaus-ism. He reminded us one day of the old English wartime ditty, "We're gonna hang out our washing on the Siegfried Line . . . " (a reference to the heavily fortified but apparently ineffectual defense line built along the French border in Germany in the '30s) and reported that he always carries with him on these trips a "Siegfried Line" on which to hang his laundry—he wears nothing but hand-washable stuff. And now I have one!

I was also fiercely clever in opening my one openable front window without the special wrench needed to do it. The secret lay in a strategic use of my haircutting scissors and the notch in the bronze nut. Oh well, I guess you just had to be there.

We are now well down the coast of Spain approaching Portugal and the longed for left turn east through Gibraltar where the swells will be on our tail where they belong!

Even now the rolling seems to have abated somewhat, or is it just that as the day brightens everything seems less ominous? Very little wind and blue skies—it's just that Atlantic swell and the "Biscay" effect, I think.

Only the guys down for breakfast this morning; Marion "feels a bit queasy when she stands up". Hope it's not the *mal de mer*.

Meanwhile all over the ship the sound of banging and hammering. Maybe the motion loosened up some things, or it's just routine maintenanc—a never-ending task on any ship-especially one 23 years old.

20.

41°N x 10°13'W (at sea)

An absolutely magnificent day! The sky blue with high clouds, the sun crystal bright, the sea a rich, dark blue-green, the bow wave pushy as ever, tossing aside the swell with a mighty playfulness and leaving a wide swath of ice-blue foam.

Only two things mar the day: the incessant swell which makes true relaxation a risky business, and some maintenance work dictated by the insurance underwriters that requires a horrendous grinding racket that is strangely inescapable on the ship. Wherever you are, including the closed-in stairwell, it is coming from *right there*! The Captain apologizes, but feels it must be done, and should be finished in "another 3 or 4 hours".

I am, at this moment, pulling an old Moses trick which began in my Freshman university year. I call it the "To hell with it" compulsion. I have stayed away from the midday meal—just because

I felt like it!—and now I sit here devouring potato chips and chocolate (not a lot) and icy coke. Ahhhh! You see, it's necessary to have a well-balanced life. (Well, I try.)

I climb up and inspect the bridge—the apparent source of this tremendous noise. What they are doing is chipping deck paint. The huge sound which resounds throughout this giant steel drum is caused by a machine like a little street sweeper, only this one has a spinning wire brush that simply abrades the poor deck until there is not a speck of paint or rust left on it. They are working on the outside deck just aft of the bridge—they being the guy with the machine who is wearing ear defenders, heavy boots, coveralls, a tee shirt over his head, face just peering out of the neck hole, but with another cloth wrapped around his head, and all this under a hard hat: not an inch of him can be seen, only two bright eyes that still manage to say hello when you pass by! Another guy has a hammer and his job is to take that hammer and HIT the ship. Any place, particularly around railing posts, etc., he finds a rust or paint blister, he HITS it and maybe goes at it with hammer *and* chisel until it powders away. Being on the ship right now is like being inside a 50 gallon drum with a dozen drilling dentists determined to get in. My flexibility is being strained. But what the heck, for "3 or 4 hours" I can take it.

When they finish denuding a section of deck, it must be painted immediately and sure enough, within hours, not just one but *four* coats—one rust-proof, one white, and two standard brownish-red—have been applied. I gotta say, these crew guys work like the very dickens. I hated to be driven from my nest by the din, so fashioned some earplugs from Kleenex which worked fairly well—but then, of course, I couldn't hear any music!

Speaking of the Captain, it is good to see him and the new Chief getting on very well, eating together, chattering away. The new guy is obviously intent on showing his stuff and looks very good. I think he is a "by-the-book" man who "plays the game", while Waldek marched to his own drummer. I discover as we go along that this Chief and the captain in fact have served together before, on the RICKMERS TIANJIN, and in the haste to find a replacement for Waldek, this fellow was apparently pulled away from a teaching position! No wonder he seems particularly meticulous—and appears to be always very busy. He also talks to himself pretty much all the time. But he doesn't talk to us passengers much—hardly acknowledges our presence.

So I figure about noon tomorrow for Gibraltar. Excellent!

Big fish jumping and playing in the bow wave.

5/18   Wake first at 0530 or so to feel the ship rock steady and headed ESE with the sky just beginning to lighten. Ahhhh—no rolling, almost no motion at all. We are headed for Gibraltar and the Med. Still another day and a half before Livorno. Back to sleep. To be grated and ground awake by the industrious chippers at a little past eight, sun shining almost straight in the front windows—and everything right where I stowed it last night! Nice change. (Did somebody say "3 or 4 hours" of grinding?)

SHOCK!   Question: where is the Rock of Gibraltar (spoken with a hard 'G' around here)? I *know* where it is! I've *always* known where it is! It is right smack in the middle of the Strait of Gibraltar and it is an island! Right? Yeah, they all thought I was crazy too. Wherever did I get this absolutely embedded idea? From the Prudential ads? Nobody ever told me, but I "knew" it as well as I knew my name, and looked eagerly forward to sailing around it as we went through the Strait. What a blow! I was ready to swear that somebody had moved the thing from where it "should" be to the end of that peninsula hanging off Spain over there. Rats! That's ok, I didn't know that Formosa is now Taiwan, either, and I thought the Great Wall of China reached down to Shanghai. Well, hell, you can't know everything! Anyway, it provided some diversionary entertainment at breakfast.

Land(s) ho!   Spain on the left, Morocco on the right, just appearing through the mist, and dead ahead: the Strait of Gibralter—*sans* Rock!. Ships on every hand heading into or out of the Med, all following the traffic control lanes (drive to the right) laid out in every narrow passage—including, by the way, the Strait of Dover.

35°53'N x 6°W (at sea)

First time on the forepeak! Very nice. Klaus loves it up here—sits as far forward on the bow as possible, actually leaning on a spindly rail right out over the prow. I find it a little scary, but he calls it "the monkeybunk" and perches regularly thereon. Even Marion takes a turn now and again. Gorgeous day—sunny and very warm. Mediterranean climate!

And sure enough: there's "the Rock"—in the wrong place! It really has two major peaks and between them an enormous concrete rain-catching slope. It is a British colony, but the Spanish wouldn't give them any water at one point so they had to catch their own.

Across from Gibralter, in Africa, lies Cento which is owned by the Spanish!

Just a popcorn thought:

Funny how a trip like this means different things to different people. Klaus loves the sea and the ship, and loves to stand on the bridge wing, wind tousling his hair, just "digging" the scene. I want to be in the bridge itself, checking course and speed, comparing the chart to the passing scene, and looking for ships. Hans and Marion have discovered the forepeak and seem to enjoy taking the sun there—or aft of the bridge in their deck chairs. They are very cultured people, European in the best sense of the word, have travelled the world, attend, for example, the Bayreuth Festival every year, etc. etc. I feel like something of a rube next to them. Klaus has also travelled widely both with his wife who passed away in 1997, and now by himself. With all his freighter trips, he is a veritable Flying Dutchman.

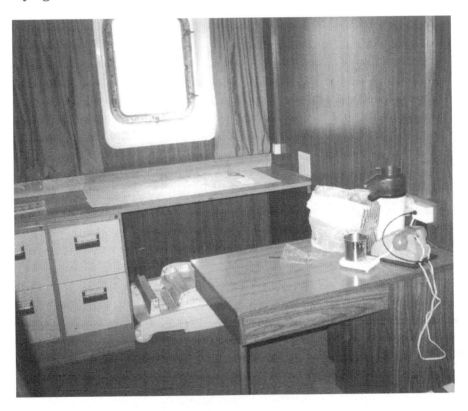

Popcorn thinking place

An emergency drill coming up at about 1530. Then a barbecue on the poop deck—nice to get everybody together. Still grinding paint off somewhere—awful, terrible racket, but they are making good work of it: grinding, chipping, and four coats of paint on very large areas in two days.

So, Africa fades out to the right and Spain to the left as we head northeast for Livorno.

21.

Ah, the barbecue! What fun! Klaus got his camera out tonight, and sure enough, all the Filipino guys instantly and automatically lined up and posed. They are truly delightful—and awesome the way they know this ship and work its giant cranes and derricks (and grind away at its rust and paint! Not a vacation for them!) Steak and chicken tonight, the bones getting the heave-ho over the rail and into the wake. Wine, too, courtesy the Captain.

Laundry in now—may as well get it done. Tomorrow—day 40—I'll give myself a 2nd haircut on the trip. Can't believe it! Spain is still ghosting into view on the port side as we "hug" the shore, going to the west of Majorca and Minorca, over the top of Corsica and into Livorno on Monday.

5/19 Another gorgeous day. Had a haircut and put on my new Sunny Europe shirt. The laundry is someplace on the ship being dried. Got it all washed, took it down to the laundry sweat shop on the Upper Deck only to find that the only dryer on the ship—that huge industrial strength affair—had packed it in. I reported it to the Chief on watch; he called the electrician, who called the steward (Renand), and they both called the Fitter. Still no joy. Apparently some earnest crewman had stuck a great overload of wet coveralls in the thing and burned out a bearing—or something. Damn! Renand simply took the wet stuff, said "I will deliver", and was gone. I was still cheesed. The laundry facilities on the ship leave a lot to be desired. Can't imagine how the Kments will cope. Renand will probably just insist that they let him do it—and he will. He offered to do mine, but I figure that's a bit much with all he has to do. (I discovered later that he was indeed doing the Kment's stuff—but they were paying him for it.)

I mean, we are all "flexible" in this thing, but having to put up with this laundry business is really stretching it. I know we're only passengers and this is only a freighter, but we are not riding for free and perhaps just a touch more thought could be given to our welfare. Not much; just a touch. Interesting: we were all booked on the LEON at first. If we had in fact gone on that ship, our Captain would now have no passengers to not particularly worry about. Hmmm.

We are approaching the Isla Ibiza on the right, the first of a drawn-out chain leading into Livorno.

Radio: passing Ibiza Island: American Western tunes—in English, then an interview with an American country and western singer, speaking English, the host speaking Spanish with a translator.

39°08'N x 1°21'E (at sea)

Hilarious lunch with Klaus reading jokes from his last cruise journal.

Lunch: (l. to r.) me, Klaus, Marion, Hans

It seems the Kments have grandchildren on Ibiza, the island we just passed, but they were unable to raise them on their mobile (cell) phone

Majorca! Tremendous cliffs dropping straight into the sea. A dome of rock hundreds of feet up. Rugged outcroppings. Tallest mountain is 4,740 feet. Island looks from this side like solid cliffs, but over these rocks, unseen from here, lies a flat plain. Island is a bit longer than Salt Spring, but is squared.

Listening to   The Vinyl Cafe on Radio Canada   International—an old show from St. John's. A bit scratchy on the Grundig SW @ 17.87mc. Tuned in as usual for the news, tonight with Chris Skeen—the best news reader on the air.

5/20   Corsica just coming into view to starboard through the haze. We will pass quite close to its northern tip in a couple of hours, then a straight line into Livorno. Funny, of all the places in the world, I have visited both of these. Livorno in 1955 when brother Dave's ship, the USS NEW JERSEY, put in there and partner and I drove our stalwart '47 VW across the Alps from my station in Germany to meet him, then we all entrained for a Roman weekend. It is all as hazy now as the view of the Corsica that hosted a friend and I in August of 1989 when we flew there from Paris to celebrate Napoleon's birthday—he was born there, of course. Not so hazy, that memory, rather stark as a matter of fact.

Chippers at it again—should finish today. A really terrible noise.

Ah—here's the rest of my laundry—the 40 socks. Renand says he has a special "drying room". The rest of the goods came back yesterday but the socks took a little longer. He's a gem! So glad I gave him the stereo. The dryer will take some fixing, I guess, and will require the services of both the Fitter and the Electrician. Will talk to Dirk about this business when he comes aboard in Italy. Hate to bother the Captain—who, in the absence of a Third Officer is standing two watches every day in addition to the usual bale of paperwork.

We have been getting "pirate alerts"—reports of pirate activity in several places, notably now the southern end of the Red Sea and the Strait of Malacca, both of which we must traverse. It is a serious business. Freighter crew members have been killed and injured, once an entire crew kidnapped and left in the middle of a jungle. A special full-colour booklet on how to prepare for, defend against, handle, etc., has been produced for ship captains. I am genuinely apprehensive about this and have thought of how to triple lock myself in the bathroom with all my goodies in case of attack. I'll be very glad to arrive in Singapore. Will not even mention this to Ellen at least until we are safe on the other side.

Not only that, but there may be a special shipment of popcorn waiting in Singapore. I asked Ellen to ship six two-pound bags of the precious stuff care of the Agent, as it looks like it may be harder to find than I imagined. Good old ethnocentrism! (Mine!)

42°57'N x 9°03'E (at sea)

Ah well, a delay. Can't get into our berth until 1800 or so, so there goes my phone call, but will call when I can this evening. We have slowed a bit so instead of 1530 or so, it will be 1730 when we pick up the pilot.

Thoughts while waiting for the corn to pop:

Today I feel overwhelmed and disconsolate. Perhaps the incessant noise—which has stopped for the moment, but mostly the, to me, amazing and depressing level of culture (in the very best sense) to be found in my fellow passengers. They know everything, have visited all the galleries, the great capitals not just of Europe, but the world. And not just "visits", not just fly in, fly out: the Kments journeyed to Shanghai in 1980 when very few people were doing it, and they went there by train! The Trans-Siberian Express! They decided about that time to try to visit every capital city in the world—and they have just about done it. If they can get to Washington, D,C. on this trip, they will almost have accomplished their goal. (Note: They did get there—and Philadelphia, too, after I left the ship in Houston and they sailed on to Newport News, Virginia.)

But I see Canada in a new light—and myself with it. Canada is a newborn, a raw, young, country struggling to "become". We are 135 years old as a country; the Hamburg port is 830 years old—the city more than 1,000! My friends know beauty of every sort, they collect cultures and it is so easy to do. Everything is so close. Italy, France, Spain, just over the border, a moderate car trip away. I am very confused about all this. Why am I living in Canada? Why not Europe some place—any place! I try to imagine how they must see me. They are far too sophisticated to come right out with it, but in their eyes I must surely appear a genuine rube.

And yet isn't there something bright and attractive about a "new" country, a vast and nearly empty, "potential" country where, even though it is centuries "behind", everything is still possible?

And then there is "The War". I am endlessly intrigued by the phenomenon of the Second World War, especially the nature of Germany, the horrible contradictions extant in this nation of major intellectual and artistic and scientific figures, and then Hitler and Goebbels and Goering and all the rest. And the camps. The camps seem to me to illustrate the very worst that the human race is capable of.

And here I am in the company of three authentic Germans! True, they were but 11 or 12 when the war ended, as was I, but . . . Like the FAWLTY TOWERS episode "Don't mention the war!"—I don't. But *they* do—sort of! Today: Goebbels and Goering. Goebbels' daughter is now a secretary living in Munich. They remember listening to the forbidden BBC. They recall a major speech by Goering. But it is strange: they speak of the war as though it were *only* history, something that happened somewhere else—to somebody else. I listen mostly, but am dying to ask, "What about the holocaust? What do you remember? How could it have happened?"

83

These are very intelligent people. What about their parents? "What did *you* do in the war, Daddy?" I am very conflicted about this, too.

Ah! Popping!

Off the coast of Italy—the port of Livorno, maybe five miles away.

More delays. "These Italians!" says the Captain. "Nobody seems to know anything?" "*Dolce farniente!*" (How sweet to do nothing.)

The anchor is down.

44°N x 9°45'E (Livorno)

Well, here we are! And they are loading already—only "six or seven" tons of cargo, they say, so may not get into town, and can't get off the ship. Immigration must clear us first. Then I'll run to find a phone.

Beautiful three-masted "schooner"(?) leaving the harbour as we came in.

I stayed on the bow to watch our crew weigh anchor and then handle the lines to the tug and then to shore. Now, I wait.

Well, RATS! Found a phone booth but couldn't get the damn thing to work for me. Then walked clear around the quay thinking to try the ferry terminal on the other side: FENCED OFF! Tried to "knock up" Klaus to try his cell phone. No luck. Tried the ship's satellite phone and got through, but only to an answering machine. Left a message anyway.

We leave at 0800 tomorrow. They are going to work all night if necessary. So we won't get into town either, and I need some stuff. Rats! Double Rats!! Well, we have to be flexible!

Just did a "reckon" on the next stop. I figure six days should put us in Oman. That's next Sunday. We'll be there a while, since it is there we start *un*loading, so I would think a couple of days anyway. I have no Telus phone code for Oman, so that'll be something, too.

Radio: haven't been able to find a good music station. Lots of junk, half of it American, and a very strong Armed Forces Network station—all in English, carrying National Public Radio stuff.

An impression of Italy: the travelling shore crane squeaks!

22

5/21   Well, made a stab at going ashore for a phone, but very dodgy. "*Pilota*" is coming aboard; we could sail anytime. No phone. Irony: first port where I was issued a shore pass, and had no time to leave the harbour and use it!

We are away after the shortest turnaround yet: 12 hours (Actually, it wasn't the shortest in history; the Captain who Mastered a container ship for a while said that 6 hours was his average port time.) From what I can determine we are now carrying 8,137 tons of cargo, with the 33 huge sections of GRP (plastic) pipe picked up in Livorno: 20 below decks, and the rest riding hatches 2, 3 and 5. These sections are 50 or 60 feet long, 12 feet at least in diameter, and are headed for Viet Nam.

We will pass Elba and Monte Cristo today. Will look for Napoleon and the Count, and by noon tomorrow we'll be at the Strait of Messina between Italy's toe and Sicily.

Many ships in and out of Livorno—a whole fleet of "MOBY" ferries and others—going to Corsica and Sardinia, also a couple of huge cruise ships, plus the usual freighter and tanker traffic, and a military ship of some sort like a tiny aircraft carrier—maybe just for helicopters.

Now passing Elba—too misty to see Bonaparte. Yesterday where he was born; today where he was exiled. I was reminded of the palindrome ABLE WAS I ERE I SAW ELBA, raised the subject at lunch, and discovered that not only do the Germans have palindromes but Hans gave me a jim dandy: *EIN NEGER MIT GAZELLE ZAGT IM REGEN NIE.* Which means, of course: "A Negro with a gazelle never goes out in the rain."

Now comes the island of Pianosa! Unless my memory fails me this is the place where Joseph Heller set his CATCH-22 air base. (By the way, in talking with my sorely missed Waldek much earlier, comparing books we had read, that one came up. In Polish, in which he had read it, it is called PARAGRAPH 22—which of course sort of misses the whole point. I explained the meaning of "catch" to him; he was intrigued.)

Soon the island of Monte Cristo.

That sailing ship that left Livorno as we were entering, just crossed our path under power (not a sausage of wind—the sea like St. Mary's Lake at home). She is Polish, and the Captain had a lively radio conversation with her. We asked how he knew she was Polish and he told us that in fact he had worked on her in 1978, helping to rig her, and then sailed on her final shakedown cruise. Small world indeed! She is not in any way a schooner, but, square rigged on the foremast and fore'n'aft on the main and mizzen, she is, according to the Chief Officer, a barkentine. Beautiful. What a way to see the world. She's probably at least 100 feet overall.

The new Third Officer came aboard last night and is standing his first watch now—much to the relief, I'm sure, of the Captain. Seems just a trifle nervous. Probably doesn't help having the Captain, the Chief, and me popping in on him unexpectedly. But he obviously knows what he's about. He is Tomas Caparal and I mention this because his picture appears in at least two other "journals", one on "Bandit's" web site and one in TravLtips—both written by passengers on the LEON's voyage that just preceded ours. Tomas couldn't have had much time ashore before he was called back to duty with BIBI. A nice enough fellow, bit quiet, except when on watch when he sings pop songs in a high voice.

Can't believe this weather; could be sailing my canoe out here!

And just as I was writing about "no wind", up she came and with her a small sloop doing just fine.

42°42'N x 10°01'E (at sea)

Back from lunch to find, off the starboard bow, Isola de Monte-cristo, her peaks and crags rising from the sea and mists like something from a dream. She is now part of a National Park scheme; there are no signs of habitation, but there she stands, a cloud perched on one end, about as forbidding a place as we've seen—but very dramatic and inspiring.

Wonderful conversation at lunch today—medical. I learn that Alois Alzheimer defined "his disease" during his lifetime of 1892 - 1950's or thereabouts, and lived in Würzburg. These doctors are, of course, a wealth of information on medical breakthroughs—the heart catheter, the cholera vaccine, etc. I also thanked them all for their generosity in speaking English when I am around. They are a truly capital trio.

Supper conversation: fashions. Same everywhere: body piercing, big pants, backwards ball caps, streaking (in German "flitze"). Marion said that when I speak German, I have "no accent". A fine compliment. I only wish I had the nerve to speak it more often.

5/22 Sicily just appearing through the haze off the port bow. Strait of Messina dead ahead. Another sparkling day—calm sea and (let us hope for Herr Rickmers' sake) prosperous voyage. After the Strait and clearing the toe of Italy, a beeline for Suez.

Just in time to the bridge to glimpse the departure astern of Stromboli, an active volcano standing alone in the sea, steam rising from her snout. We will take on a "*Stretto Pilota*" to get us through the two mile wide Strait. Sicily: the home of everybody's favorite crossword puzzle volcano: Etna. Looking out my front window I see we are speeding toward a wall of unbroken mountains. Mountains to the right of us; mountains to the left: somewhere in there is an opening through which we must sneak.

Pilot aboard. (Pilot attire, British: white shirt, tie, black pants, shiny shoes, elegant waterproof, buoyant windbreaker, small black satchel. *Pilota* attire, Italian: ball cap, jeans, T-shirt, flannel shirt—open and untucked.)

Many ferries criss-crossing the Strait, one about every ten minutes. City of Messina spread all along the Strait. Huge tracts of high-rise apartment blocks edging up into the hills.

37°49'N x 15°53'E (at sea)

Lunch topic today: euthanasia. At first, they looked puzzled at my question, then, as usual, Marion figured it out: "Ahh - 'Oy-tan-AH-zee-ah'" Of course; why don't I remember that German pronunciation can alter the entire sound of an "English" word? Another day I mentioned the Toyota Tercel. Puzzled look, then: "Ahh—Tair'-tsel!" Of course. At any rate, we had just got nicely into it, when *right outside the window*, the grinder blasted into action, making further conversation absolutely impossible. We just waved at each other and were about to repair to our respective estates when Renand appeared and I pressed him to perform his mind-boggling card tricks for us in the lounge. He was delighted and for an encore did his "cut-the-rope" trick. It is as much fun watching him do the tricks as it is totally mystifying to behold them. He is the consummate showman.

I say we'll be in Suez tomorrow night—they all say, pooh pooh—two days at least , or maybe three. We shall see.

23.

HOLY SMOKE! We—the four musketeers—just had our long-awaited tour of the engine room! It is an unbearably hot, painfully noisy, and overwhelmingly complicated series of three decks, many rooms, stairs, ladders, enormous, huge, incredible machinery, pipes, dials, control panels, lights, meters and on and on. And these engineers—it was the Second Engineer who guided us through the maze, shouting directions and descriptions—understand everything down there. It is simply

87

indescribable! The engine alone—an Hitachi 15,000 hp eight cylinder diesel—the original power plant in the ship—stands three decks high. At the top, you get a look at the valves and injectors; down one floor a maze of piping and meters, and at the bottom the base of the thing. It is a miracle: running steadily for days, weeks at a time, burning an average 38 tons a day of thick, heavy bunker oil which has to be heated and thinned before being shot into the cylinders.

Machines of every sort surround this monster: machines for heating the oil, for converting sea water to fresh, for incinerating garbage, compressing air, generating heat and air conditioning and electricity, and more, all packed into these spaces and all humming and whirring and roaring away. It is a maelstrom of noise and activity. And in the very, very bottom of the lowest part of the decking sits a Wiper, a Filipino crewman, cleaning the parts of something or other. We were all quite blown away by it all—very close to being terrified, if you want the truth. Absolutely horrendous. And at least four crewmen spend their four hour watches down here twice a day! There is a separate insulated, air conditioned and sound proof control room with a large window looking out into "the works" that can provide a modicum of relief from the cacophonous bedlam without.

I particularly wanted to see and experience the giant propeller shaft driven by those cylinders. And when we got to the very bottom of the ship and moved aft, there it was!. Eighteen inches or so in diameter, spinning at 110 rpm through its bearings, it extends to the furthest reaches of the ship and of course holds the 19 foot propeller, each of its five blades taller than me (there is a spare one on the aft deck). I stood right on top of the shaft, on a little bridge. Not noticeable from this vantage point is the fact that the shaft is not in the very centre of the stern, but is set just a few inches to port in order to counteract the rotation of the propeller that tends to push the stern slightly off course.

Just down the corridor from the main engine room is a separate control room with gauges and levers for controlling the amount of sea water in the ballast tanks. Depending on the amount of cargo and its distribution, the ship must be balanced by adjusting these levels.

I have a new respect for the engineering staff: along with the four engineers, there are three oilers and a wiper. And no wonder the Chief Engineer wears four stripes like the captain and is really the second highest ranking and second most important man on the ship.

5/23 Am sitting in my "high chair"—The Throne: Furniture arrangement #4—in the cabin taking in the sights.)

The Throne (in port)

Just passing below Greece and Crete and above the Libyan bulge. Three more hours to my noon fix. I still think we'll make Suez "today" even if it's midnight tonight.

Bit overcast today, but sun will break through, sea a little choppy, but does not affect our weighty displacement. Don't know whether we're allowed off the ship at Suez—to make a phone call. Probably not. Then three more days to Salalah, Oman.

35°N x 23°18'E (at sea)

Nope. I lose. We're going slower than I thought, and my dead reckoning isn't. We won't get to Suez until tomorrow afternoon. (When I make a mistake, I make a BIG mistake!) We must then anchor in the "roads" and in late evening move inside the approaches when inspectors, pilot, etc. will come aboard and when "baksheesh" is negotiated. The medium of exchange hereabouts is Marlboro cigarettes—cartons of them. The captain must be sure to have on hand dozens of cartons. In seagoing parlance this venerable waterway is now referred to as "the Marlboro Canal"!.

The Suez is "one way" with long convoys of ships starting at either end at the same time—just before dawn. Halfway down, the southbound ships will pull into a large lake and anchor until the northbound convoy passes. We will be through the Canal probably Saturday evening. It will cost us about US$40,000 to make the passage.

Hans's hat blew off yesterday on the forepeak (he caught it), so I carefully told my "hat blew off" joke at supper. (Note 1.) Describing the incident on the bow Marion said "His hat went away with the wind!" Her English is much more charming than if it was "correct".

5/24 Small birds have come to greet us! Black on top, white on the bottom, swallow tail, smaller than a robin, larger than a sparrow. Not sea birds.

Feeling a bit blue lately—seems to be a *very* long trip and a *very* long time to be away from home, and while I like a good routine, the routine here is, let's face it, rather limited. Plus the damn chippers are at it again starting at 0800 this morning. And I now conclude that I should have skipped buying the short wave radio. Only occasionally is it satisfactory, and then, with the constant passage of the ship and the changing of time zones, we lose it all. The Kments are finding the same thing with their borrowed set. Also, it is getting more difficult to find a phone at the right time and I do miss those calls. Ah, well, just a temporary mood, I guess.

34°18'N x 25°09'E (at sea)

Feel much better now. Flounder ("*Flunder*") for lunch—good. Klaus, who loves his newly-discovered word "guff" has made a verb of it—to guff somebody—and is himself a great guffer. He has a wealth of stories from his many travels and seems also to be something of a schlemiel: unfortunate things just seem to happen to him. He runs out of gas in the Australian Outback, has flat tires, loses his wallet—that sort of thing, but he manages to survive in fine style and make a funny story of everything.

The sea has changed colour! No more deep blue; now green. Getting close to Port Said. Also close to Israel. Thinking how long ships have been plying these waters. Ships bringing refugees to Israel, ships "smuggling" arms to the Palestinians. Same water, same charts. Suez. Egypt. Israel. Lebanon. Jordan. Saudi Arabia. We are here!

90

24

HELP! Oh, m'God! The ship has turned into a bazaar! We are tied between two buoys in the channel between Bur Said and Bur Fouad waiting for the "night train"—the convoy—to start through the Canal. No sooner are we in the harbour than little boats begin to pull alongside and men start coming aboard, up the pilot ladder—4, 7, 10, maybe 15 guys. I am on the bridge wondering who in blazes these guys are, but when I go down to supper, I find out. This is S.O.P. for the Suez. They are all "friends of the pilot", and they are selling stuff! The entire corridor leading to my cabin is awash with plates, scarves, wall hangings and other knick-knacky stuff, and any leftover space is occupied by earnest-looking men offering with beseeching eyes and tragic tales, armloads of "product". It is a madhouse. I unlock my door and before I know it a fellow with his hands full of trays and mats is inside my "office", has closed the door behind him and is "giving gifts" to my children. Somewhat stunned, I hesitate just long enough for him to duck back into his corridor warehouse and return with yet more stuff. I make it plain that (a) I am not going to buy anything, and (b) I have to go now and eat supper. I lock the door and make haste away.

He is there when I return, pushing as hard as ever. I'm not good at this sort of thing; I give him $5 for his "seven hungry children" and shovel him and his goods out.

The corridor leading to the mess hall on A deck is loaded with toys, tools, telephones and other gadgetry. A display of shoes is laid out on the poop deck—and so it goes. All the little boats are clustered like suckling pigs along the port flank of the ship. The "friends" must all be off the ship before we leave—and not before time, as the Brits say. And they will make it—well, almost.

It is a busy harbour. A steady parade of green ferries moves back and forth across the channel ahead—perhaps one every five minutes or so. A beautiful old cruise liner pulls out. An exquisite mosque with two towering minarets is on the port—Fouad—side, and of course this whole line of ships tied to buoys awaiting the start of the procession south through the famous Canal. It is sundown now and sure enough from a minaret comes the (electronically amplified) call to prayer: ALLAH AKBAR—audible over the entire scene. The mysterious East is upon us.

Radio: not much FM, but on 101.5 sort of monotonous sound, then—my goodness!—Stanley Myers haunting "Cavatina" from THE DEER HUNTER, and now Michel le Grand's lovely "What are you doing the rest of your life?" A nice surprise in Egypt!

5/25 The procession has begun! Our pilot came aboard at 0345. And lo! our crane has lifted two of the merchant boats right up onto

#5 hatch. Ships are starting to move which means local linesmen must jump onto the huge tethering buoys at either end, free up and fling away the eight or so lines holding us fast, and leap away before they end up in the drink. All of this in the dark! We'll move soon—and so will I—to the bridge!

Beautiful! With admirable precision and timing, 17 or more ships move with elephantine grace in a line nearly 20 miles long: the next southbound convoy to transit the 162 km. of the Suez. At 0415, the first call to prayer sounds eerily over the (mostly) sleeping cities. Again at 0430 and yet again at 0445. At about five the sky begins to lighten in the east and now the pilot guides us between the endless chain of red and green buoys. Ferries are still moving between the ports except of course when the ship parade crosses their path.

Each ship in the Canal must carry special lights for the Canal—one or more aft, some along the sides and in particular a giant flood light mounted on the "monkey bunk" in the bow and pointing forward, all controlled from that panel of switches labeled SUEZ CANAL LIGHTS on the bridge. Looking back down the line, one sees a line of huge "headlights" following along. The ships are spaced about a mile apart. When we reach Great Bitter Lake, we will pull over and anchor to allow the northbound convoy passage—a sort of marine siding. We will be virtually all day making this transit, but think of the alternative: weeks around Africa and the Cape of Good Hope. No wonder this stretch of water is considered strategically invaluable.

Getting into the desert now: one big beach on both sides

Passing the city of Ismailia now, named for the fellow to whom it was first proposed to build this canal. He said OK at first, then backed down: too expensive!

Crows! And tiny donkeys plodding along the bank—with large people on them!

Long lineup for a ferry! Sitting in the hot sun while this procession of pachyderms passes by. But, hey, it's a dry heat!

Entering the Great Bitter Lake now where we will park for a bit. We appear to be toward the end of our convoy. Already ships from the south are moving past us as we divert into the lake. Perfect timing. I put the glasses on them: PUGWASH SENATOR (container), PEGASUS HIGHWAY (cars—the ugliest ships afloat, square and flat and slab-sided), ASIAN MAJESTY (cars), NEDLLOYD EUROPA (container), SEALAND NEW YORK (container), LT UTILE (container),

P & O NEDLLOYD DRAKE (container), LT TRIESTE (container), AL MIRGAB (container), (can't make it out) Deutsche Africaline (container). I give up. Can't see the names and the Middle Eastern flies are driving me nuts. They are pestiferous, invasive, persistent—apparently traits common also to Middle Eastern salesmen! Couple of "real" freighters like us are also in the line.

32°03'N x 39°56'E (Suez Canal)

On our way again—sooner than expected. We seem to be going out of the anchorage with a higher "rank" than before. I sit on my Throne, the best seat in the house: window open to the warm breeze, great view of everything, writing, reading, making notes, munching, sipping.

Ahh. It don't get no better nor this!

No, I guess we are still 16th or so. The Captain says at about 1600 we will leave the Canal. The Red Sea (so-named for periodic red-coloured algae) is next for a couple of days—and pirate country is dead ahead.

Out of the Canal and into the roads—the Gulf of Suez first, then the Red Sea.. One of our cranes lifted the two boats off #5 hatch (four men in each one—they stayed on the ship to operate a mini-bazaar this morning) as we were coming into the city of Suez—a tricky maneuver as we didn't even slow down. But then, the locals are probably used to it; the boats scampered off with no mishaps, probably all set for another ride—and some sales—on a northbound freighter. And their targets are close at hand, lying at anchor.

Big ship wrecked on the beach here. Looks like it's been there for a long time—just too expensive to pull off, I suppose.

Just back from the barbecue. I stayed around awhile to schmooze and hear the Captain sing. And does he sing! Plays the guitar with tremendous verve and confidence and then lets loose with this growly bass voice—BIG!—and with great Polish passion. He began with "What shall we do with a drunken sailor?" (loud and in English), then some gutsy, tragic (of course) Polish songs and on and on for a couple of hours. We were all there and the Chief Engineer really opened up (especially with Marion). We hadn't heard much from him so far. It was a grand evening.

Another perfect day—weather getting hot, hot, hot!—and will get hotter they say. Full moon tonight making a great track across the water. We are still in the Gulf of Suez, that skinny tongue at the top of the Red Sea, and can see strings of lights on both sides. I have both windows open to the warm night breeze and I may leave them that way. We'll be in Oman 4 1/2 days after leaving Suez which puts

93

us in Salalah on May 30. Looks like we may stay a couple of days, though there isn't that much to unload. Then another seven days to Singapore with only a couple of days there.

The Captain sings!

5/26 Ahhh! Long sleep in! Only one or two Middle Eastern flies left from yesterday. I'll get 'em. Red Sea now, no shore in sight, just the accustomed view: horizon to horizon nothing. Other passengers getting uneasy about just when—and how—crosswise or lengthwise—Moses will part this Red Sea. I'm not telling.

25.

24°59'N x 35°35'E (at sea)

Well, a very dull day so far. Klaus is giving tonight a birthday party for his son, Uwe, who is 41 today and who of course is in Germany!

Klaus, I am discovering, is an elderly party animal; he *loves* giving them, going to them, planning them. And he is discovering that I am the exact opposite. What shall we do when "our" birthday comes around in just over a month? He has invited us to his "estate" (the "Spare" cabin on D deck where I would have been on the LEON. Again I grin inwardly at my upgraded luck. The Kments could not be upgraded; they had booked the Owners Suite anyway. I was incredibly lucky!) Klaus has told us that his cabin, whose windows

94

face starboard, was all decorated for Christmas—left over from an earlier inhabitant, so we may end up singing carols. Still I would rather stay right here and muddle along. At supper we talked about, among other things, "mooning". No lack of imagination with this bunch!

So, at "*halb acht uhr*" (7:30 p.m.—1930) I will rise to the occasion and go up to D deck. After that, the excitement of advancing our clocks once again. I will then be 11 hours ahead of Salt Spring. This is Oman time.

Egad! Two parties in two nights! The four of us plus the Captain tonight. A good time was had by all and the captain's true stories were most interesting and amusing. This is his 7th time around the world, plus years with other lines and ships. The best tale was of calling at a port named Bucky in northern Scotland. The pilot came aboard and guided the ship to her berth, and when she was tied up, he took off his pilot's hat, put on another hat and said "I am the port manager, let's look at your papers." When that was done, he turned and said, "I am the customs officer, let's see your cargo manifest" and when that was cleared up, he said, "I am your company agent. Welcome to Bucky!" The Captain said to him, "Won't you stay and have a drink with me?" The fellow then said, "I'm sorry; I must hurry; I am the Mayor of the town and I have a wedding at noon."

We also discovered that we—all of us—love to play table tennis, and we had to admit that we were fairly good at it. The Captain has his own equipment stashed on board, but, alas, there is no table and no place to put one—yet! He has a plan—something about combining two cabins, etc. Says the company will buy him a table any time. Some fun. (We never did see a ping pong table.)

Popping corn thoughts:

I realize I am not a sightseer in the traditional sense. "You *must* see the floating market, the palace,"—the whatever, etc. No, I don't *must* see these things! I don't really want to see these things. Not only that, I am not loaded with spare cash, and don't want to be, and wouldn't spend it if I had it. Well, I suppose it will all work out. Why is it that so many people—not just on this ship—simply take it for granted that everyone is alike? I have, in the past several years, rather delighted in demonstrating that not everyone *is* the same.

I look out the window: it is as though the ship is standing still, there is no motion at all, and the sea is rushing by. It is like standing on the bank of a great mountain stream.

5/27 Aha! Just manufactured a pair of shorts! Actually, I haven't owned a pair of shorts for years, but, on the chance I might need some, I brought along a pair of Khaki pants purchased at a thrift store in Victoria for $1.50 some years ago. What I could do, I thought, was just take my haircutting scissors and cut off the legs: Voila! Shorts! This I just did. Perfect! I only hope they don't start to unravel! And it is definitely shorts weather. Even the Captain is wearing 'em. He dons his uniform only when we are in port, otherwise it is mufti for sure.

Still in the Red Sea. Beautiful sunny day and hot! Calm sea. Must take a walk today.

19°14'N x 39°02'E (at sea)

5/28 Land ho! Reaching now the bottom of the Red Sea, the shores narrowing, islands to the right of us. Favorite hangout of pirates, we hear. Actually a bit more south, apparently around Bab el Mandeb, the narrowest point of the strait, beyond which we make a sharp left turn to head up the coast of Yemen and Oman to Salalah.

Passing the town—formerly a port—of Mocha, one of the largest terminals for coffee export at one time, particularly the thick brew the Arabs seem to like. Our "Moka" coffee house at home is surely named for this village on the Red Sea, or at least the beans that came from here.

Sea is narrowing ever more and in an hour or two the ship will go into "anti-pirate" mode. We have a fire drill scheduled for this afternoon; whether or not to correspond with possible peril, I don't know.

Popcorn thoughts:

I am daily grateful that everybody on the ship speaks English to some extent, but no matter how adept they are, it is always English filtered through Tagalog, Polish or German. I listen through that filter and speak back through it. Does it wear after while? Yes, a little, particularly because virtually all the subtleties of all four languages are lost or much diluted. I'm sure we all miss being able to just let fly with our usual elegant eloquence and not be looking at blank faces. I have had to choose my jokes very carefully—and the German's do, too—some things just can't be translated—at least by us. I often remember Waldek, too, and what a breath of cultured and hilarious air he was on the ship, and I miss him a lot.

Renand brought me some fridge stuff and cookies and I sat him down to teach me his magic card tricks—and the rope trick, and a "can't lose" card game. I pay avid attention, but never succeed in learning any of it to the point of being able to carry it off. Such a likeable guy.

Renand teaches

Hooray! The mystery is solved! How do you reverse—or "flip", as the crew puts it—the Stuelcken derrick? Could not figure it out, but realized it must be able to work both holds from its mounting between #3 and #4. So I watched them do it! Wickedly clever! It is but one example of the cumulative ingenuity of a ship like this. When one thinks of the simple levers and cranes of centuries ago, it is obvious that each generation of new ships incorporates and builds upon the inventions and discoveries of its forebears, until on the BIBI, for instance, there is hardly a square foot of deck space where there isn't some device, or hook, or fitting placed to accommodate something. Those little, carefully-spaced weldings on the hatch covers are in fact there so that iron locks can be fitted to them, locks that then fit exactly into the corners of containers should it be necessary to carry some. (We carry at least one all the time.) There seems to be a fitting, or a tool, or a cable, or line, shackle or hook for every conceivable purpose—and with all the paraphernalia to make it work.

But the flipping of the big derrick had me baffled. Sometimes I would look out and see that it was rigged to serve #3 hatch, that is, with the big hook hanging down the forward side of the beam. Another day, the same giant hook would be on the aft side, ready for #4 hold. What the heck? How dey do dat? Now I know! Shall I explain it? No. Too complicated and besides, you can have fun figuring it out. (Note 2)

In a series of long "tacks" we are turning the corner out of the Red Sea, through the Strait of Bab el Mandeb into the Gulf of Aden and thence the Arabian Sea. To port, Yemen, to starboard Djibouti, Ethiopia, Somalia. No pirates, but we are advised to keep at least 50 miles—100 if possible—off shore. Several ships to-ing and fro-ing through the Strait. The Captain says Thursday morning is Salalah with probably a two day stay.

Fire drill! Muster list says all passengers "STAND BY THE BRIDGE", and instructs the Steward to go to passenger's cabins and take them to the bridge. I go to the bridge. No other passengers are there. Just me and the Captain and a helmsman. Where are they? Why didn't the steward do like he was 'sposed to do? Bet a nickel my colleagues all put on life jackets—aargh! it's 32° out there!—and went to the Muster Station. After about 20 minutes the captain radios the Chief on the poop deck—he is in charge of the drill. "How many passengers do you have down there?" "Three." "Where's the other one?" "Uh - uh - uh -" "Never mind," says the skipper, "he's up here (where he's supposed to be, I'm thinking) but you need to keep track of them." To me he says, "We don't *care* where you are; we just want to *know* where you are."

He says the crew always gets wet during fire drills. For one thing, the hose connections leak and spray them (the new 3rd is in the process of fixing them), but also, as he put it, with a little sigh, "They are not seamen anymore—they don't know which side of ship wind is coming from" so, of course, they turn on the hose, point it straight into the wind and the wind blows it all right back on them. Ah, I love 'em all! Just so we don't have a fire!

98

5/29 Heading directly into the rising sun which pours in my windows and necessitates the drawing of the drapes—so I can keep sleeping. Some clouds in the sky today, the first we've seen in many a day.

As always, to my continuing amazement, the ship just keeps going and going and going, making 16 or 17 knots all night long, I just snooze. That's 130 miles or so without any help from me at all!. Another course change to 72° and we head toward Salalah—a port apparently built and operated by Singapore with local labor and stevedores. By the by, the Captain got away from Suez having had to produce only 40 cartons of Marlboros. Much better than the 75 he once gave to a pilot. Just a way of life hereabouts. We have passed the infamous port of Jeddah, about which the Captain recalls the story of one poor native who, in this fanatically "dry" country, purchased a bottle of whisky from a Dutch tugboat crewman. He was caught in the terminal and summarily hanged right on the spot.

26.

14°01'N x 49°03'E (at sea)

This is day 50 of surely the most wondrous period of my life. It is not unlike any other part—comfortable quarters, good music, books, interesting companions—except that every time I look out the window I am delighted to see that we are moving! Across the sea! And today, the Arabian Sea! And tomorrow we will be in Oman, and next week in Singapore, and then a comparatively "frantic" series of ports to collect more cargo. And one of these days, I will get off the ship in Houston and fly home. I will be willing to do that, but in the mean time, this great steel house of mine just keeps moving like Krapp's punt in the Becket play: "up and down and from side to side" and forward—always forward.

Now that we have passed the Somalian peninsula, a slight swell is felt coming in from down Antarctica way. Nothing to write home about.

Aha! A very nice swell is now a-building. Had to tie back the drapes and rearrange the rolling Coke cans in the fridge. Salalah at seven or eight in the morning.

5/30 Pilot is aboard, shoreline fast approaching. Oman!

17°50'N x 54°E (Salalah)

Tied up in Salalah, a small, obviously newish port, far from anything, and carved out of the desert. Six or seven ships here, mostly containers. Overcast at 0700 but rapidly burning off for another HOT day. Maybe a trip into town—though there is no town in sight anywhere. Here come the C&I folks.

Very hot! In downtown Salalah even hotter. We cadge a ride in with one of the agents and taxi back (we needed passports *and* shore passes to get in and out of the harbour area—the tightest security we've seen yet). I buy some pens and an Arabic book, with everything "backward", for grandsons Jacob and Ben. A plethora of small stores, each with quite limited selection, but a fine bookshop. I duck into a small drug store in the vain hope of finding some special shampoo, and WHAM! About 20 degrees colder inside! Talk about air conditioning! I am the only customer and am watched closely by 3 or 4 clerks. Find myself a bit ill at ease. But find out later that it probably wasn't me; it was my damn shorts! I do notice that on this very hot day, nobody but me is wearing shorts. I probably wouldn't have worn them, but had bumped into the Kments during the morning and they said "We have a ride to town and we are leaving right now!" So off we went. Nobody bothered to tell me that in this Arabic country, in town, and especially on this *religious holiday*, shorts, or any sort of "revealing costume", are strongly discouraged. Well, hell! I felt badly and some irritated that no one had seen fit to pass along this local custom. Damn! So in downtown Salalah I am, as usual, unique! Most of the men I see are wearing the long white *djelaba* and round white cap; a few women are covered by *burqas*, but I do notice a pair of eyes now and then peering out at my fantastic legs. Lucky was I that a local Mullah didn't happen along and do some peering of his own.

Wonderful phone call from the big city to the awakened Ellen. News from home, and sad word of Otto Loewy's death. Telus has no phone code for Oman so there is nothing for it but to try various other methods. None work, so I have my first experience with a "phone card". No idea how the things work, but find a shop—some sort of appliance outlet—where the clerk has, under the counter, a cardboard box of phone cards. We manage a transaction and I buy one worth, I think, $15. But what does that mean? After several attempts at the phone booth which is right in the baking sun—attempts which cause me to run back and forth from the booth to the clerk for further "filtered" instructions, I finally get through. Ellen also gives the tragic popcorn news: to ship six bags (12 lbs.) of Jolly Time White popcorn would run about $144 by air. $34 by surface, but taking four to six weeks thus missing Singapore altogether. Well, the best laid plans . . .The Canada Post lady did ask Ellen, would the corn be popped or unpopped. Will have to continue to keep an eagle eye out wherever we go.

(All this fuffarah about popcorn prompted son Dan to take action of his own. He actually e-mailed the Jolly Time people, told them of my "desperate" situation and approximate location and asked for their assistance. By return e-mail, he was informed that the nearest Jolly Time distribution point was Manilla in the Philippines. Close, but not quite! Now Dan, frustrated and still hearing nothing from me about having found a supply, fell back on his own imagination and inserted onto the web site the following:

"I have contacted the good folks at Jolly Time to see if they can help us get some much needed popcorn to [Dad on the ship]. Picture it a helicopter hovers twenty feet above the deck at the height of a terrible storm during the darkest hour of the night in the South China Sea. A rope ladder is thrown out the side door and a suit from the Jolly Time Popcorn Corporation emerges. He clambers clumsily down on to the pitching deck, taking more time than the helicopter pilot is comfortable with . No sooner does the executive extricate his foot from the last tangled step of the rope ladder, than it rises straight up into the darkness in a deafening tumult of rotor noise and downdraft. The man turns and begins his long, unsteady trek toward the superstructure, fighting for his balance on the narrow cat walk. He pushes forward, the wind buffeting the cargo under his arm, the icy rain like steel pellets lashing against his face. He struggles forward, blind, his frozen, raw hand clasping the case of Jolly Time White like a claw. He is resolute in his mission to deliver the life-affirming snack to Dad, their best customer, who is being attended by the ship's doctor. Days ago, Dad began the slow descent into popcorn withdrawal, known on the high seas as the "J.T.'s". Only the Jolly Time man can help now. It's not too late . . . "

Dan Moses

Of course he had no idea that some weeks before, in the Bristol Channel, a rescue helicopter actually did hover and lower, and all the rest—except for the popcorn. All right, back to the Middle East.

The place is unquestionably Arabian, i.e., desert, sand, palm trees, dust, camels, but on the 10th of this month, not three weeks ago, a cyclone struck and flooded everything, completely washing out a section of the four lane highway leading to the port and shutting it down. We saw the remains: the highway will have to be completely rebuilt in at least one spot. Hard to imagine even one drop of rain falling here, let alone torrents. Couple of "packs" of camels grazing beside the road, looking a bit the worse for wear.

Just watching them unload 6 huge generator units using the big jumbo derrick.: 255,732 lbs.—128 tons—each. The huge derrick moves with such ponderousness as it reaches over the side (we are using our own equipment here; there are no shore cranes) that the ship heels slightly even without a load; with a load, things start to roll and slide in the cabin. This gargantuan tool is operated from a small yellow box with what appear to be two levers, the box connected by a long umbilicus to the machinery, making it possible for the operator to move about the platform and watch his placements, etc.

Heavy lift at Salalah

Still watching the Omani stevedores unloading these huge modules. They are on #4 of 6 now; it has taken them all day to discharge these four and it took exactly one hour to actually *place* #3 on the waiting flatbed truck *after* it was lifted out of the hold and over the side, They now have #4 in hand and almost perfectly in place, and it starts to swing, or twist; then one of them pulls on a guide line and it swings the other way, so the guy on the other side pulls heftily and—so on and so on. So they lift it up a bit and it swings even more; they get it steady, start to lower and it twists. Finally, I can't stand watching this aerial ballet one minute longer and go back to my book. Fifteen minutes later, I peek out—the load is still swinging and twisting. *Aargh!* There doesn't seem to be a crew boss; it's every man for himself. My theory on the swinging is that the enormous dangling weight begins to oscillate like a Foucault pendulum if it stays in one place too long.

According to Klaus, who chatted with a couple of German crewmen from the ship tied to the quay behind us, their ship is full to the gun'ls with ammunition and arms! Apparently the stuff will be offloaded here and transported—where? For whom? Israel? Not likely. Palestine? Hmm. Afghanistan? Pakistan? Iran? Wherever it's going there's a helluva lot of death and destruction in that ship and a helluva lot of money in the pockets of some arms dealer and manufacturer in—where? the U.S.? Canada? Britain? Ah, who cares, right? After all, business is business and "we have the bottom line to think of." My God, when will we ever learn? No tanks, no guns, no landmines, no ammo, equals *no war*. Well, maybe with slingshots and clubs. Few countries at war today have the capability to produce their own weaponry. Few of them can afford to buy the stuff, but buy it they do! Why do we continue to permit the manufacture and sale of devices good only for the destruction of humanity? Only rarely does anyone even ask the question.

Oh, yeah; in the meantime, there's a uniform on the bridge wing with a Kalashnikov at the ready.

27.

Well, something seems to have developed on the quay. They fooled around with the penultimate "package" and the truck for about half an hour—again, I couldn't bear to watch them. I read a bit, played some solitaire and when last I looked the thing was sitting right on the ground! The truck had been pulled away, and our very own Captain was down there talking with somebody. Now, this *is* unusual; the Captain *never* has anything to do with loading and unloading; his job is to get the ship here. Period. But there he is. It is getting dark and there are no lights on this new and still unfinished quay. He finishes and the shore crew starts to melt away toward their vans. The great hunk of cargo is still sitting on the ground; the derrick is dangling; the truck is abandoned. Something tells me we are not going to sail at midnight as originally planned. And there is still another hunk in the hold. Bet a nickel it's noon tomorrow before we get away. I always lose these bets.

I also get the impression that the captain was informing the stevedores—who, I hope, have learned that there is a definite art to discharging cargo—that the day's work is done and their services will not be required tomorrow. I am partly right. As it turns out, there is a regulation against heavy lifts after dark, so they must stop, but the next day - - -

5/31   Well, they're back to have another go! No—oh, I see: it's our own ship's crew down there either showing them how or—no!—they're doing it themselves! No local stevies in sight! The 5th box is on the truck. One to go. Our Chief Officer supervising.

Here's the last one now. I stand in my window looking out; one of our guys holding a line sees me, raises a hand and waves!

Had a look at where they are taking the big boxes—up past the "ammo ship". Clever. The units actually rest on huge crossbeams on the bed of the truck. The truck drives only a short way into the desert, backs in between four big barrels, like oil drums; uses its own hydraulics to lift the beams and module and places them on the barrels. Thus, no cranes needed any more, just another truck to drive under the load, lower it and away they go. Klaus is convinced I'm some kind of nut because I love to "watch the cranes". I do, and I'm fascinated by things like this procedure. So I'm a nut!

Back aboard. Now we seem to have a problem closing one of the #4 hatch covers. All the "suits" are down there, but she doesn't want to budge. Ah, there she goes. And here we go at 0900. Tugs are standing by.

Well, we have made our first delivery! It is a nice feeling to be part (sort of) of providing a real service to people by delivering things that will improve the quality of life—generators, coolers, paper mills, water systems. Another nice thing about freighter travel.

We are "hurrying to Shanghai" (a sort of joke among us four—I don't think we could "hurry" if we wanted to) because we have vital components for the completion of something or other. We have, down in those holds, a crane, a truck, a hundred steel shafts, many mysterious boxes and all kinds of things that will do good stuff—unlike the arms ship parked behind us with the dude and his machine gun.

16°42'N x 54°36'E (at sea)

Roast duck for lunch! Not one of my favorites.

We are absolutely careening and crashing across the Arabian Sea. A stiff breeze and a big swell are coming at us from the SW. Have not seen the sea thrown about like this before. We are rolling to beat the band, but the sky is blue and the sun is shining and the ship is having a grand old time—almost as if she is making up for the 9 hours lost in Salalah. Nobody is going on deck today except for a couple of stalwart Filipinos clambering around on the heaving hatch covers, as cool as if we were in dry-dock, double-locking the lids. We are hanging on, with everything battened down. Somebody up forward is checking the lashings on those ten huge pipe sections riding on #3 hatch. It's a rollicking ride! I learn later that we were catching the tail end of a typhoon that had passed a few days back.

But the flying fish are having a ball (well, it looks that way), darting away from the huge bow wave. Must be a whole squadron of them. They take off from our wave and just skim until they hit another big one—sometimes 40 or 50 or even 100 feet. Think of having all the oceans as your playground!

Oh Lord, save us from an uninhibited, auto-didactic musical captain! Yes, he plays the guitar well, and sings lustily, but he also owns a pretty fancy Casco electronic keyboard with all the bells and whistles (literally!) on which, at the drop of a hint, he will play anything from *Für Elise* to Scot Joplin—and in particular "Lara's Theme" from DOCTOR ZHIVAGO!. In fact he is half a dozen shades beyond Jonathan Edwards (aka Paul Weston), the world's most creative piano player. While the melody is interestingly spaced, the beat goes on—provided by the Casco in any style you can name.. But he also likes an after-dinner whisky, and he *is* the master of this vessel, so when he invites us to his suite for a drink, we tend to go. Another, rather humorous, aspect to the event: while the musical captain was doing his electronic thing, the ship and us were rolling about at probably 35 or 40 degrees, hanging on for dear life and trying to pretend we were at a garden party

But, hey. I paid big Canadian bucks for this trip and am reluctant to spend time breathing left-over cigarette smoke, making inane small talk, and oohing and ahhing at these *soirees musicales*. Yes, we passengers are a ready audience, and I will do my part, but only so far.

Plus, we four already had plans to play a game Klaus bought in Salalah yesterday.

We are still rolling mightily—even more so with the Captain on E deck than down here on C.

Tonight's clock change puts me exactly 12 hours ahead of Ellen, so our watches read the same,

I have packaged the big picture of BIBI from the calendar and will mail it with a letter and some other stuff to Ellen from Singapore. Dan may be able to scan it into the web site and everybody can get a look at "my" ship.

(While I was rolling around down here, writing about calendars and web sites and clock changes, real havoc was taking place out on deck. I knew nothing about it until - - -)

6/1 WOW! HOLY COW! What a night! Rough or what? Everything in the cabin, every pen, every CD, every book, the smallest item was secured, placed on the floor, in a drawer, or stuffed among the sofa cushions. Nothing was loose! Even so, the blasted medicine cabinet in the bathroom, held shut with a spring closure, flew open again and, a micro-second before I could slam it shut, launched my idiot electric beard trimmer (a gift) through space and onto the tile floor with a sickening and fatal crash. And of course everything else in the "secure" cabinet was also catapulted across the room. The only thing in the cabin left to its own devices was Dan's good luck Rubber Ducky, and it still sits cheekily on its shelf having apparently jumped only a few inches. Even the CD player, though tied in place, could and did swing completely clear of the desk, so I put it on the floor, too. The sea plays enormous tricks and one learns—too late, alas, for some items—not to take *any* chances.

Needless to say, not a lot of sleep for this June 1st Saturday, but amazingly, lying diagonally on the bed, one sooner or later falls away into slumber.

But the deck cargo did not fare so well. As I look out my window this morning, down the starboard side of the ship at where those ten big GRP pipes were lashed. I see one section turned completely sideways and another apparently balanced precariously on the rail on the very verge of going over. I wonder if we lost any—and what else may have come adrift.

Conditions have definitely moderated now and as usual the sun is bright, the sky blue. True, the sea and wind always seem more violent at night, but even so, last night took the cake. Now I will set about trying to find all the stuff I stashed last night.

Just up on the bridge. Yes, we lost some of the pipe sections last night—it looks like a good number of them. If there were in fact ten up there, more than half of them may have gone over the side. I watched the crew checking lashings yesterday, but even as we sat in the Captain's cabin, with the sea tossing everything around, those lashings must somehow have let go. Can you imagine the hassle now over the loss? Were the lashings inadequate, the sea too rough, our crew not attentive enough? Lots of fun for the lawyers, but not for the would-be recipients of the piping in Viet Nam who now cannot finish their project,

13°38'N x 60°07'E (at sea)

Well, we lost eight of the ten sections of pipe from #3 hatch. I cannot help but feel a sense of loss, of really the first flaw in the voyage. Yes, insurance will cover it eventually, but somebody goofed somewhere; a mistake was made. We had such a perfect record. We have loaded and unloaded thousands of tons of very expensive machinery and goods with not one error or accident. Until last night. Eight sections of plastic pipe now lie at the bottom of the Arabian Sea *forever!* (They will virtually never deteriorate.)

The two remaining pipe sections

Sitting at the stern after the barbecue watching the last light of the sun as Venus and Mars appear and stars emerge, I still cannot believe that I—*me*—am really here, doing this! Surely it's a dream from which I will awaken shortly and go back to my years of thinking and planning and hoping. But I am actually here! Have been for 53 days! I commented at supper that we would be talking about this trip forever and would probably bore our friends stiff. I do not intend to do that (except perhaps with this book!), but I suspect that I will often think about it and a small smile will appear on my face.

Marion is memorable. I asked the Captain tonight as he lit up a "green package" Marlboro, "What's the difference between the green and the red and the gold packages?" Says he, "Red is regular, gold is 'lite', and green is menthol." Marion, *sotto voce*: "for if you have asthma." And her entire face crinkles in marvelous giggling laughter. She and Hans have been married for 43 years—living, working, travelling together and loving it. They are wonderful pair to watch, have three children, two girls and a boy.

Klaus is a bit more of a real character. He spent some time today "drawing lines" in his notebook so he could get the autograph of every single crew member. He also copies into his own log book, from the ship's log, every detail of our journey: hourly speed, course, air and water temp., etc. etc., and illustrates the log/journal with tiny perfect drawings which are very good. He loves stories—especially of these true "adventures" that seem to happen to him all the time. He is quite lovable if perhaps a bit much sometimes. I wonder what they think of me . . .

28.

6/2   Shower day and once again I thought I was going to run out of drizzle (the time before it actually stopped completely the instant I stopped rinsing), but it was okay. Then decided I'd better put some sort of hem in my new shorts, lest they ravel right off me. (By the way, I saved the rest of pants legs, just in case.) Had a couple of motel sewing kits, so fired up a needle—fortunately one kit contained a threader—with nice khaki thread and went at it. "Basting", I think you call it, but if it holds it'll keep the shorts decent. Didn't have enough khaki for the other leg so used brown instead. Looks ok—better than I thought it would.

Another bright blue sunny day out there. Maybe a deck walk later. The evil swell is down to almost nothing, just enough to remind us that we are, after all, on a ship. Waves only a couple of meters and going our way so altogether a pleasant ride. But we continue to be alone on the sea. At meals it's: "Did you see a ship?" "Nope." "Neither did I." This must not be the main route to Singapore. Our detour to Salalah took us north and off the beaten track. Still the fish fly. But why? And do they fly at night? Always into the wind, it seems, and skip—skip—skipping a hundred or more feet before—blip!—they're gone.

Sunday is still Sunday on the ship. No extra work done by the crew, and it just feels like a day off—even for us Four Musketeers who do nothing anyway!

We are nearing the Equator, but will never reach it—Singapore is about 2° above and that's the closest we'll get. But in a day or two, when we round the tip of Sumatra and enter the Strait of Malacca, I will have gone halfway 'round the world. The "line" is just east of Sri Lanka.

10°46'N x 66°44'E (at sea)

Well, tonight we finally get to play Klaus's "game", the one he bought in Salalah and has been trying to line up ever since. First evening it was the Captain's musicale, second night, the barbecue. He won't tell anybody what it is, but right after supper . . .

Oh, my—such excitement! Klaus bought the "game" for his grandsons (to whom, as he demonstrates, he is THE LION!) and wanted to test it out on us "experts". "*Jeu de Pêche*" it is called and is one of those windup, rotating fish "ponds"—fish open their mouths at intervals and we try to "catch" them with little sticks and magnetic "hooks". For Klaus, we could "hardly contain our tremendous excitement". What a card he is! (I think he bought it for *him*!) He said, "I suppose when I bought this in the store, they thought—What a silly man! " I said, "You—a silly man? Never!"
Looks like Singapore on Saturday—9 days instead of the 7 I thought I heard (but I'm always wrong anyway). Just hope there's a bank open so I can change all my traveler's cheques.

6/3   Ah well, another perfect day—bright sun, wandering white clouds and nothing else as far as the eye can see.
Within an hour or two we will have completed our transit of the Arabian Sea, will move through Eight Degree Channel at the top end of the Maldives, make a slight course adjustment to the SE, and head for the bottom of Sri Lanka—probably the only time we will be in the Indian Ocean. Then we cross the Bay of Bengal, make for the tip of Sumatra and down the Strait of Malacca, hoping to dodge any lurking pirates, and into Singapore. Guess why it's called "Eight Degree Channel". Right!   At the other end of this island chain is "One and a Half Degree Channel". See, this is the sort of invaluable treasure you collect only from nautical charts!

7°43'N x 73°02'E (at sea)

Great progress since yesterday noon! It happens with a following sea and a tail wind. We have already passed the "Eight Degree Channel", and the Maldives and we are now on the "North Indian Ocean" chart. It is always exciting to move onto a new—for me—chart. Sri Lanka can be seen on the chart, though we, of course, see nothing but sea.

Marion has a sore throat but she did see a ship this morning!

Just watched THE TAILOR OF PANAMA from the LeCarrè novel. Fine film! Geoffrey Rush, remembered from SHINE, and a couple of quotes I wrote down: "He who tells the truth will sooner or later be found out." And "[Panama is] a place where a good deed never goes unpunished."

We have a bit of a problem here. The four of us passengers have such a high old time at meals, chatting and laughing—even singing at times—and I suspect that the Captain, sitting alone at the other end of the table is a bit envious. I know the new, young electrician seems to like to "overhear" us and stays around after he finishes. But the Captain is a different story. He really seems sort of bereft. We try to include him as much as we can, but it is difficult. One of the reasons we four get on so well is that we are all the same age—twenty years senior to the Captain. It really does make a difference, even though we are from different countries and cultures; our worlds are not all that far apart.

The Kments are real "football" fans and the World Cup games are starting. I, who care little for such things, said I would try to get the scores on my SW radio. I did so, and at the next meal I presented them thusly: "2 to 1, 1 to nothing, 2 to nothing". They were only briefly amused.

6/4

"On the road to Mandalay
Where the flying fishes play,
And the dawn comes up like thunder
Out of China, 'cross the Bay."

A particularly serious roll (of the ship) woke me at 0600, and in tying back the curtains I peered out the window. WOW! The dawn was indeed coming up like thunder. You could almost hear it! Massive cloud formations with fire behind them causing great Wagnerian chords and fanfares. Clouds piled so high and wide, I feared for the ship heading right toward them. We are getting some spectacular sunsets and dawns these days—and right "out of China 'cross the Bay". Bit of rain in the night; puddles on the hatch covers, but again today, bright sun and white puffy clouds, sea a bit more turbulent perhaps.

5°44'N x 79°55'E (at sea)

Just passing Dondra Head, southern tip of Sri Lanka—12 miles off.

Popcorn thoughts:
One of the great pleasures of this seemingly endless odyssey is that which I experience often in moments of idleness and relaxation. It is the deep contentment I feel when I think of Ellen and the cozy home on Salt Spring, and the friends and neighbors and the activities that go on: cataloguing books, playing the French horn, even the occasional Duty Manager gig at ArtSpring, our local arts centre. As well, the trips into Victoria, seeing and hearing son Dan, who plays horn in the Victoria Symphony, keeping up with the pace of daughter Jennifer and the two grandboys, not to mention Ellen's two lively thirty-somethings, schmoozing with Nana, my favourite mother-in-law, shopping, getting a cone at Macdonald's—all the things I seem to have taken for granted before. I am in no great rush to resume that life, but at the same time, I know it is there, waiting.

I also now have an idea what the remainder of life may be like. I really meant it when I said to Ellen "the rest of my life is yours". Everyone has been so generous and supportive in "allowing" me to make this crazy trip—spend all that money and time, so I will now try to give some of it back. My biggest adventure will have passed—without regret—and I feel I can relax and live a casual un-striving life now and perhaps help others to their "biggest adventures." My only fear is that I will forget about these thoughts and just drift back into the routine. This must not happen.

6/5   It's raining to beat the band, and the fog surrounds us like a "protecting veil". Nice. Sea still the same: lumpy and a bit rolley, but, verily, the rain falleth upon this dusty, sandy ship and washeth away the grit and salt and cleaneth, too, the windows—all free for nothing! The sea is dark gray instead of deep blue. The flying fish won't fly today: too wet!

Ah! A ship looms out of the fog. We are overtaking her, as we do about 90% of those we encounter. Only the "Panamax" container ships, moving at 24 knots or more, can outrun us.

A trip to the bridge confirms many things. We will not overtake that ship: it is moving at almost 25 knots; we are making only about 18. It appeared because the fog lifted a bit but it disappeared again into the next bank. We have crossed the 85th meridian which means that, distance-wise, my trip is half over, and I have traveled—as the crow flies—10,800 miles with the same distance to go, except that our "detours" north to China and south to Panama will add a good many more. And, according to my precise calculations (which are always wrong), we will round Sumatra about 1400 tomorrow, D-Day, the 6th of June, and head down the dreaded Strait of Malacca.

Fog has now lifted a bit, rain lessened but still a gray day, most unusual for this trip, though Klaus says that in Singapore an umbrella should be carried.

As to the trip, we have called seven at ports so far, but there are probably eight or nine more to go, so I suspect that, in terms of time, we are not yet at the halfway point, this being day 56 of a possible 140, or 137, as the LEON spent on her last trip.

29.

5°51'N x 86°55'E (at sea)

After lunch (not very good: "mud" and "insect eggs"—my least favorite types of beef and pasta) yesterday I watched a large bird circle and finally make a landing on our foremast. I reported this to the group, saying we had a hitch-hiker on board, an unticketed passenger. I said the Captain had asked Klaus to speak to the bird about this. Today at lunch Klaus reported that he had in fact spoken with the bird on the bow:

Klaus: Hey, bird, where is your ticket?
Bird: Is this the MV BIBI?
Klaus: Yes. But what about your ticket?
Bird: I don't have a ticket, but for Richard Bradley Moses, I have a letter. [And Klaus produced a "Bird Mail" *Luftpost* letter, sure enough, addressed to me, stamped with a unique stamp featuring Klaus, and properly cancelled. Inside the envelope, a card:]
"Dear Richard,
Congratulations to the half-world turnaround"
[And on the back, a drawing of RBM pointing to a globe and saying:]
"MY GOD, I GOT IT!"

Klaus is indeed a treasure, I will send the card—no, I won't; it might be lost. I will save it here.

Another terrific rainsquall during lunch—water just pours down the outside of the windows and the fog obscures all.

6/6 Possible titles for this opus: "Rotating the Pears," "Conquering the Juice Box," "Hurrying to Shanghai."

Rotating the pears was necessary for awhile as the pears we were given for meals were not yet ripe and too hard. So we took the pears to our cabins, waited for them to ripen (a day or two) and in

112

the meantime more pears arrived—a constant shuffling of pears. Hans and Marion discovered that eating the (ripe) pears with a cookie from the lovely box of LAKELAND BUTTER COOKIES Renand gave us from time to time, was a real treat. Hans said one day, "It's a symphony!" Klaus, not musically inclined, was not impressed. As to the juice boxes, we found it almost impossible to open one without a spray or a leak or a dribble on the white linen tablecloth. We finally decided that a second (air) opening had to be made: conquered!

Having made a verb out of "guff", i.e., "to guff", and a proper noun—"he was a guffer", Klaus seized upon another new word (for him), and, when undecided, would announce, "I am tenterhooking!"

Beautiful day—at last—bright sun, puffy clouds, and chippers at it again! Ship still rolling nicely. I figure once we round the corner of Sumatra, at about 1400, the rolling will cease altogether until we hit the Pacific on our way home. It takes a good long fetch to build up a swell like this and in all the straits and small seas we'll be traversing, there just isn't sufficient distance.

Ships around us now quite frequently—counted four at once yesterday as we move into the "crowded" shipping lanes.

Marion had a bit of a sore throat a few days ago; I started to get a tickle in my own throat and thought, uh oh, but have spent more time in bed the last day or so—after all we *are* losing a whole hour every night now—and I seem to feel better this morning.

6°01'N x 94°09'E (at sea)

Marion still not feeling well, missed lunch for which I had a "double leg" chicken dinner (a favorite back at Swiss Chalet). Our cook, Erlito, does magic things with chicken—and fish. I told him I would call him "Colonel" from now on. He is in his twenties; no idea where he learned his trade, but he is good!

Land ho! One of the islands off the tip of Sumatra to starboard. We'll change course to the south slightly in a while and stop this rolling, though I must say, one gets quite used to it after awhile—say, three days! Group of islands off "Sumatera" (chart name), largest Pulau We, tiny round one to port, Pulau Rondo.

On making popcorn in a rolling ship:
1. Place butter melter (actually one of those things that keeps your coffee warm) back on the desk from the (safe) floor.
2. Turn melter on.
3. Get butter from fridge in day room
4. Take butter to desk

5. Slice off sufficient butter with knife from desk drawer.

6. Place butter in special steel cup, place cup on melter

7. Secure melter by putting cord under telephone

8. Get hot air popper parts out of lower desk "file" drawer.

9. Dump leftover unpopped "old maids" into waste basket

10. Place popper on desk

11. Put popper parts together

12. Secure popper by wrapping cord around telephone.

13. Open desk drawer, get popcorn

14. Fill cup with popcorn

15. Pour popcorn into popper

16. Get salt shaker out of desk drawer.

17. Wait for butter to melt—10 minutes or so.

18. Plug in popper, starting the action

19. Get rolled-down paper grocery bag from under counter, place under spout to catch popped corn

20. Watch popper and melter to make sure they don't take off.

21. When popping starts, stand by to replace any young old maids that fly out

22. When popping is well along, use knife to assist exit of popped corn (low ship's power)

23. When popping is (finally) finished, unplug popper

24. Pur half the butter on the corn

25. Salt lightly

26. Shake bag

27. Pour rest of butter on corn

28. Salt lightly

29. Shake bag

30. Fill butter cup with corn, circulate, pour back

31. Bang cup on the bottom to get all corn out

32. Turn off melter

33. Unsecure melter and place on floor

34. Unsecure and dismantle popper and place in desk drawer

35. Replace salt shaker (borrowed from mess hall) in desk drawer

36. Use tissue to clean off desk top

37. EAT

38. Get Coke from fridge

39. Get towel from bathroom to wipe hands.

114

40. EAT MORE!

Sure enough, we have stopping rolling! Steady as a tank!

A view now of Sumatera itself as we head more southerly down the Strait which is still too wide to see Malaysia to the east, but will narrow considerably by tomorrow. Still looks like Singapore on Saturday morning, though that runs us through the most dangerous stretch at night.

Today is D-Day and I raise the topic at supper. Marion is sure, however, that the invasion took place on June 20, 1944. Not a lot to talk about, of course, as we were all age 11 at the time. But I still would like to dig a little deeper into all this, mention "the camps" for example and see what happens. (I never did.) It is as if they have intentionally, or more likely unintentionally, drawn a scrim over the whole thing and can see it only dimly. It's funny: it all seems closer to *me* and I was thousands of miles away, while they were right smack in the middle of it!

There. I am battened down against possible pirates, and so is the ship. All outer doors locked, gratings lowered over external stairways, a special watch set, bright flood lights hanging over the bows, fire hoses laid out, etc. Both my corridor and bedroom doors are locked and I have taken in my calling card from the outer door and the doormat, so it looks like nobody lives here. Perhaps a bit paranoid, but reports still come in of kidnappings and murders by these nefarious brigands.

6/7   Awakened at 0400—brilliant flashes of lightning—no rain, couldn't hear any thunder, just lightning from all around. Lights on the shores both sides, the pirate lamp swinging over the bows. Otherwise, all quiet. Back to sleep.
    Awake again about eight, several fishing boats scattered about, sky overcast, sea a pancake, no shores in sight. Back to bed.

Up for good now. Same as before. Ship steady as a truck, chippers chipping now and then. All quiet otherwise. Trip to bridge imminent. No pirates.

3°30'N x 100°02'E (at sea)

Six ships off the starboard bow, one of them appears to be a warship of some sort. We are overtaking all of them, except perhaps the warship.

115

Have seen almost no flotsam or jetsam in the waters to date, but here, relatively a lot—planks, cans, paper, etc. Busy place.

Yes—it is a warship. Malaysian or Indonesian, and, up on the bridge a minute ago, she hailed us for ID, registration, cargo, crew, etc. She's carrying a helicopter on her poop deck and looks very sharp. Let's hope she is in fact on "pirate patrol". She's moving slowly now so may be doing just that. May explain the absence of intruders.

Talking with Klaus. I feel a little badly. I gave him Dan's e-ddress with the idea that maybe his son, Uwe, might get a kick out of contacting him. Apparently, Klaus said now, they have exchanged several emms (e-mail messages). I knew about one this noon when Klaus asked me what Uwe may have meant when he reported that Dan had a web site so now Uwe "knew more about Vlady". I told him I had no idea what that meant—Waldek?—Valdy? Don't know how much Dan has put in about Waldek. But Klaus had not mentioned before that they were corresponding and now felt I was being a bit blasé about the whole thing. He was upset. It's straightened out now. I just thought the "kids" would enjoy talking about their dads on the same ship, born the same day, and all. Now I feel badly. Ah, these oversensitive old guys! Latest word is we'll arrive in Singapore at 0300 hours! Excellent! Many things to do: change traveler's cheques, mail photo package to Ellen, phone Ellen, Nana, Dan, look for Internet Cafe, shop for popcorn, chocolate, etc.

30.

The crew, of course, is going ape over the World Cup business. I've been getting scores from the SW and now we are coming into TV range. But I have discovered an English language FM station called "Light and Easy", all American stuff so far, but not unpleasant at all—the Carpenters, etc. Where's it coming from?

Klaus got an emm from Uwe (on his cell phone) just before supper; Uwe got an emm from Dan. I'm trying to keep up with all this . . .

Probably passing Kuala Lumpur and "Melaka", for which this Strait is likely named. It is dark here by 2000, has been since we entered the "tropics." I suspect this is year round as the sun in fact "stays" in about the same position all year. None of this midnight sun as in Hay River, NWT.

Up at 0130 to see us enter the Singapore area, back at 0300: I guess the pilot can take us in by himself—he probably knows the way better, anyway.

Have never seen so many ships at anchor, dozens and dozens. This is perhaps the second largest port in the world. Will put some duds on and look for a phone. Perhaps can make a call or two. I may seem obsessive about this phone business, but my fellow passengers are even more so about finding postcards and stamps and post offices. I had simply told everyone at home, no postcards; I suspected what it would be like trying to facilitate the process. There was almost always a public phone near the ship.

2°N x 103°50'E (Singapore)

Five barges already alongside. This is the third port where we refuel and provision. Our guys are up there adjusting the lashing for the two remaining pipes on #3 hatch.

Singapore, the country/city, is magnificent! Beautiful! Like a big Victoria. And down some of the side streets: the old city. I love just walking the avenues, watching people, noticing the laundry poles sticking 'way out from high-rise apartments, and getting absolutely lost. (Well, I could have done without that I suppose. Left Raffles for the post office to mail the package and, in turning back, somehow got off on the wrong street. Totally at sea! Friendly folks put me right, but that was the first time that had happened—and the last.)

But what a day in the big city! I talk to Ellen and Dan and Nana, find an Internet Café, read all the Yahoo emms, and send a message to my Yahoo e-ddress and to Dan trying to get my thanks to all who have emmed and expressed interest, then shop in an enormous mall called Raffles City, part of the City Hall complex. Explore the whole place—that's where the I.C. was—they even had a Marks and Spencer. The entire city is "in English"—signs, ads, clerks, just everywhere: English! I wonder how the Poles and the Germans, et al, feel about this increasingly ubiquitous foreign language. Am just winding up my chores, but have plenty of time still, and decide to go downstairs and poke around. Little kiosks and beeth (plural of booth), then through an archway and—HOLY SMOKE!—an enormous supermarket! Food like it's goin' outa style!

And there it is: POPCORN!!! One pound bags with Chinese writing all over, but on the back, in a corner: PRODUCT OF USA. I buy six bags, plus some big chocolate bars and other oddments. Take a cab back to the ship alone—the Kments had gone off "culturating"; Klaus, too, was off somewhere—and at the gate, we are allowed to drive right up to the gangway. The Chinese driver, who has a wonderful laugh, has never done this before and is a little nervous. But he gets me right to the ship, collects a nice tip, and has a fine adventure into the bargain.

117

<u>"Chinese" popcorn thoughts:</u>

I'm still not into cathedral and museum-ing. I know it's a flaw in my otherwise perfect character, but there it is. I'm sure the others think of me increasingly as genuinely weird. When I said to someone asking about this trip that I was most interested in the sea and the ship, I was prophesying more than I realized. Why? Why don't I want to see "the sights?" It's damn foolishness, of course. I'll never be here again. The Kments are culture vultures and, like Klaus, have been just everywhere, including Canada. But me? Cancer the crab—loves his house, likes it with him. I want to go around the world because I want to go around the world—to see the world from this ship. I am also, I realized quite quickly, a Timid Traveler, not bold or really adventurous (anymore). But am I having fun yet? Ho ho ho!

A long walk all along our particular quay —about six sheds, each more than a thousand feet long. At least 7 or 8 ships are tied up along here, with room for several more—all of them general cargo vessels like us, all loading up with potatoes, pipes, potassium chloride ("Origin Canada") and everything in between: Anhydrous milk powder, oranges, drilling fluid headed for Indonesia which is, of course, visible from here, and boxes and more boxes. Long walk, but as usual, fascinating.

But where is Klaus? We were all four going to go into town together this morning, but he apparently skipped out ahead of us, and after waiting and searching for almost an hour, we just went.

Just checked around —Klaus not here . He's ok up until midnight, but after that the ship might not be here. A fuel barge is still alongside. One arrived early this morning, then went away and, about 1600, another one came and is still pumping. We actually need two kinds of fuel: bunker oil for the big engine, and regular diesel for the crowd of other machines on board.

No Klaus! At 2115, we now begin to be a little concerned. He is after all quite aged—nearly 69! Did he, in fact, leave the ship? Did anyone actually see him go? I knock on his cabin door; no answer. I inform the Kments—long ago returned; they are a bit concerned, too.

Still no Klaus and it's 2200. The good doctors concur: we should probably let the Captain know and perhaps get a key to his place and just check it out. He is so fond of "adventuring", and with his occasional mishaps, I am getting quite genuinely worried. We get the Captain who gets the Chief and together they discover: *there is no spare key!* So, we can't get in. There is none for my cabin either.

118

I was told this upon boarding, and tried to get one cut in Beaumont, but they were out of blanks, and I've just forgotten it since. But this is not good.

Shuffling about the corridor outside his cabin at 2225, wondering what to do, we see the stairwell door open and the "missing person" suddenly appears! He has been in a pub watching "the football"! We are much relieved and try not to let our anxiety and discomfort show. As Ellen would say, "The brat!"

6/9   The sound of a horn awakens me at almost 0100. Are we moving? No. It is the fuel barge pulling away. But we are still taking cargo into the #5 tweendecks just emptied of steel bulkheading sheets: *boxes!* The decks are illuminated bright as day as they always are in port. The two aft cranes have been coupled up and the double hook shackled on; they have also cleared the two remaining pipe sections from #3 hatch and opened it. The boss loader in #5, right below me, is an animated traffic cop as he instructs the fork lift in the hold where and how to place each box—waving, gesturing, beckoning. He's very good, using the boxes to brace each other and the ship's ribs to hold them in place. There: finished. Now the crane raises the fork lift out of the hold. We may sail yet before morning. Meantime, I sleep.

Up at 0800 to make a call to wonderful daughter Jennifer. Gabbing along with her, and suddenly two cats skedaddle by one chasing the other lickety-split. First animals I've seen in these two month (though come to think of it, there was a lazy lady dog in one of the sheds last evening) and was reminded of Jen's own two cats.
We will sail at 0900; tug is standing by.
I guess they weren't finished loading after all. Work went on, lading (as they say in the crosswords) and discharging (as they say here) until about 0500 this morning. I'm sure that costs the company extra, but we do get to sail in daylight and *see*. And we are, after all, "hurrying to Shanghai!"
We have cargo for Jakarta, but it was decided not to call there—very unpleasant place, I hear—so we'll drop the stuff here and a smaller ship will take it in. Will make for the bridge soon—no, I think I'll just set up my "throne" and watch from here. Music is cool.
Oh. Learned how to make chicken lollipops this morning.

Under weigh! (Which means, of course, the anchor is "weighed" or raised, hence: "Anchors Aweigh".) Sitting in my lovely window: music, popcorn, my crosswords, book, binoculars, a can of Coke and the view of dozens of ships moving or at anchor including

119

the STAR VIRGO, an enormous cruise ship—no: a floating resort hotel. (Information is that Renand's brother is, in fact, part of the crew of that very ship.) It don't get any better 'n' this!

Pilot boat now coming alongside, and there he goes—over the side—stepping carefully onto his home deck as we step on the gas and move on out for Bangkok.

Now we join what seems to be an endless, 24-hour-a-day, parade of ships leaving this busy harbour, with another line coming in. Looking back on Singapore, it seems, from what I observed and the world has discovered, to be in many ways the epitome of civilization, a world centre for commerce and maybe even good thinking. There are laws against the importation of chewing gum(!); littering, I have heard, is almost a jailable offense, and no smoking is allowed in public places. A city that would be nice to come back to.

A big container ship, painted our colour, has pulled in ahead of us. The heck with that—we pull out to pass. Or not. No, I guess she is heading west while we go around Singapore and up the east coast of Malaysia to our next ports of call in Thailand.

Small—70 or 80 foot—fishing boats ply the harbour. Exquisite things! Very high prow, very well kept, sometimes painted in bright colours and patterns. Made of wood and a genuine pleasure to look at—so "yar", so sea-kindly. I immediately want to own one and take it home.

Three great rainsqualls off to starboard. Two cruise ships stopped—maybe waiting for the squalls to pass. We wait for no squall. No, they both have very small ships tied up alongside and other small boats running about. Perhaps it's the Customs & Immigration folks getting a jump start before the ships enter port.

And now it rains.

31.

1°15'N x 104°13'E (at sea)

Fun at lunch (chicken "loolipops"). Learned that Thursday, at least among German sailors, is known as "Seaman's Sunday"—the second Sunday in the week—special treats and so on.

"Threatening" Klaus—after some particularly accurate "guffing"—with one of our truly "serious" steak knives: "See this knife?" I say. Marion says, "No—you say: 'See this knife?'—clutching it halfway up—'up to here it's *fun!*'" Well, maybe you had to be there—but she is so—yes, I'll say it—cute, with her twinkle and her giggle and her quick sense of humour.

120

Tonight we set the clocks *back* an hour! Getting ready for Thailand and Viet Nam, then ahead again for China.

Ho! Gigantic rainsquall, towering thunderheads. Magnificent

6/10 Once again the vast and lonely sea—South China Sea or Gulf of Thailand perhaps—they sort of moosh in together around here—but this time rarely without sight of a boat or ship—the tidy, lovely, high-bowed, gaily painted fishers, or another churning freighter heading in or out of Bangkok. At breakfast (I got hungry) we learned that we will call first at a small island south of Bangkok called Ko Sichang where it may take five or more days to unload all that Newport steel plating, then to another port near Bangkok—quite close—once we can cross the bar or reef that bars deep draft ships, and beyond which lies the city itself. With our draft—9+ meters—we must lighten our load before going in. We may be another 3 or 4 days at the 2nd port. (As usual, I was completely wrong about most of this—where did I hear it then? It must be these language filters.) Klaus has been here before, of course; the Kments have friends nearby and are targeting selected sites to visit. Marion wants to travel "up country" a bit to see "the lying Buddha" with diamonds on his legs. Klaus will probably wander off to old haunts. Me—I want to just wander, catch a bus, make a round trip through the city, find an Internet Cafe for an emm to Ell, perhaps give neighbor Ann a call—just to say I'm in her recently-visited Thailand. The Captain says Thai stevedores sort of take a bit longer to get things done. Not sure I really like these long stays—2 or 3 days is enough. We'll see.

Another perfect day—the sea quiet and helping move us along. Borneo left behind now—ah, memories of those old National Geographics—and the Gulf of Thailand ahead.

The view out my window seems always "the same" but never boring. Water, miles, endless miles, of water—different, yet always the same water: Gulf of Mexico, Atlantic Ocean, Bristol Channel, English Channel, North Sea, Bay of Biscay, Mediterranean Sea, Suez Canal, Red Sea, Arabian Sea, Strait of Malacca, South China Sea—even, back home, Trincomali Channel, the Strait of Georgia, Puget Sound, Strait of Juan de Fuca—and perhaps even Ganges harbor (at very high tide!)—all connected, and this ship could reach any one of them. Ah, water!

8°25'N x 102°36'E (at sea)

121

The view

Fascinating conversation with the Berliners at lunch about The Wall, its rise and fall , and the "error" that finally brought it down. Rumors it seems, were rife in the divided city that something was afoot—something to do with The Wall, perhaps even its demolition. Actually nobody really knew anything, including the high official in the East Berlin government who was being interviewed on television that evening. Question: "Well, when do you think The Wall can come down?" Official's answer: "*Das weiss ich nicht*—(shrug)—*vielleicht jetzt . . .*" (I don't know—maybe now!) And the streets were immediately filled with wall breakers: "He said it! He said it!" And that was the end of The Wall.

<u>More popcorn</u>:

Just occurred to me as I watch the boys down on the deck in their coveralls, hard hats, heavy boots and all, getting ready to paint in the 32° weather: I feel a bit guilty in my air-conditioned cabin just watching them work. I can do this because I have the time and—for lucky me—the money, as do my fellow passengers. We're retired, and living at least partly on pensions. And we may be one of the last generations to be able to do this! My kids? Ellen's kids? Maybe, but the idea of the company pension plan (it even sounds antiquated) seems to be one of those "fringe" benefits that, with a "casual" workforce, many employers have trimmed off, like excess fat on an already thin steak. The first thing to go from my last employer's benefits package (after I left) was the pension plan. Not a day goes by but what I fervently thank those employers down through the years for taking care of me—hell, I didn't think for two seconds about pension plans when I was a young goof—and today's young goofs, like me, probably aren't thinking about it either. And here I am, able to live and travel in relative comfort—and certainly not on the government pensions alone—*and I'm not earning any money!* Fantastic! Of course, the modern trend is not to retire at 65 (a concept, in any case, dreamed up by the U.S. government in the '30s) or at all; just keep on working—at something. Lifetime careers, it seems, have also flown the coop. But here I am, able to take half a year and embark on this fabulous voyage. Lucky me! I predict a great increase in old age "ekeing" in the future.

Took a deck trek, but it got dark by seven and had to stop (not allowed on deck after dark). Climbed to the bridge wing to find Klaus viewing the scene. Nothing quite like it: the bow wave hissing and creaming away as the ship moves as though on rails—smooth as my new granddaughter's bottom. And all around us, boats fishing, their lights making a giant circle. 240 miles or so to Ko Sichang which puts us in there about 0800, though the 2nd officer says 0500 or 0600. He's probably right, since I'm always wrong.

We lost another crewman in Singapore: his contract was up. Delightful guy, used to shake my hand every time we met and the last time said, "I will miss you." Why is that? I have done nothing special, just said hello and joked around a bit. I guess folks just like to be "made over", as my grandmother used to say.

For supper that delicious pork tenderloin and baked potato. Wow! Erlito works absolute miracles in that kitchen—which somehow resembles the kitchen in an old Methodist church, and also has a corner that floods whenever the ship's ballast is a bit off. I wish Ellen could see it—she of the ultra tidy, ultra organized culinary quarters; she would simply not believe it. And he is *The* Cook, feeding the entire crew—Polish and passengers on one side,

Filipinos on the other—somewhat different menus—three meals a day (though breakfast is much less complicated), seven days a week, 52 weeks a year. No days off for this bloke.

32.

6/11 Ship slows, wakes me up. It is 0510. I go to the front window—we're entering an anchorage; shore lights; it is pitch dark. I make out a small boat without lights heading for our bow. Suddenly a bright spotlight flicks on. Our ship's horn blasts—and again. A shout from bridge: "THEY'RE PIRATES!". Couple of our guys go forward. Small boat disappears under our bows. Starting to get light now. Noises forward. I open window to hear. Shouts from below—Tagalog, high-pitched shouts. Boat has moved to our stern on the port side. More shouts. Now I see it moving away at speed, now around to starboard side. Under me on deck one of our guys seems to be guarding a stranger in a pink shirt, ball cap, bare feet. More shouting. Boat is back around to port. Now around to starboard again. I look down. Seems to be four or five guys on board this ship who don't belong here. One uses a small line to climb to A deck. I lock both my doors. Now I see our bosun and Chief Officer on deck. We are dropping anchor and are surrounded by other ships at anchor.

13°10'N x 101°E (Ko Si Chang)

The small boat is here again and goes to other side, in and out. A stranger on deck is totally wet—from an "anti-pirate" fire hose? One of our guys takes a line from somewhere. Can't see—voices coming up. Their boat? Our boat? Their boat, I think. Voices. Not Tagalog! My God—an anchored ship nearby seems to be on fire! Great clouds of something coming from its #1 hold. Small pirate boat that was tied alongside now takes off, several men on board,

0630 I'm fully up and awake now. Harbour surrounded by low mist. Our ship lying quietly at anchor. All seems quiet—but I don't really believe we're out of this yet.

Still at least one alien down there—bare feet, and there's that boat again on this side—somebody on board this ship, secures a line to a stanchion; the small boat takes off! What the heck is going on? Boat now on other side. Voices. Flat Thai accents. Tagalog shouts coming from aft—can't see anything! Two pirates below me now on deck fussing with a box on the wall, now discussing something. I can look right down on them through my open window. They seem very much at ease. What? Are they pirates? Certainly weren't invited

124

aboard. Have they taken over the ship? Seems like it. Where are our officers and crew? What about the radios? *What's happening?*

Should I be getting scared? A little sign over my "throne" window says, ESCAPE WINDOW. Should I? But to where? I close and secure my window. Somebody could "escape" into it as well.

Well, at least our "visitors" do not appear to be armed.

...loaded with guys

0720   Now at my side window looking aft. One of our A/Bs is there and the "guests" have rigged a block and tackle over the side and seem to be bringing things aboard! Fitter is there, too. Apparently the small boat is moored under our stern. "Cookie" with his "I Love Canada" shirt. There's the bosun. They just seem to be watching while the barefoot guys work. A big bag of something coming up, a folded tarp, a huge stereo speaker (*what?*), a "Blue Box" filled with papers and files. The metal grills blocking the stairways from Upper to A deck have been raised!

Another small boat is headed right for us, loaded with guys, around the stern and out of sight. What? Damn!—a ladder being put in place. Here's the other boat again. Must be 20 guys on it! People coming up the ladder!

0735 Just called the captain. He's in his cabin (not on the bridge!). "What's going on", I ask. He says, "Well, we just sit and wait".

A ladder is being pulled aboard.

Called the Kments. Hans says, "We're *going down to breakfast!*" I don't think they have any idea what is happening. *What is happening?*

Now *music* is coming from the poop deck! Another small boat lying off the starboard quarter. More stuff coming aboard—another block and tackle rigged. A small speedboat—"CC Marine"—now puttering around.

Phuket! (actually a Malaysian port north of Singapore) They're going down to breakfast? I'm going down to breakfast! But I leave my Swiss Army watch in the cabin: the pirates are not going to get that, by gum!

I step gingerly into the corridor, carefully locking the door behind me, move silently down the stairs and round the corner leading to the dining room. All quiet. Then I spy Renand standing in his usual place at the end of the corridor. "What's going on?" I whisper. And Renand replies with a big smile: "It's a festival!" and fills me in.

Well, don't that beat all?

These "pirates" are not pirates at all; they are the advance party for this giant festival that is now shaping up on our poop deck, and is apparently *de rigeur* for ships entering Thai waters. "You cannot keep them away," says Renand. "They are business people." But *nobody told us* (even when I asked), and certainly nobody told the Chief Officer who shouted "PIRATES!" from the bridge at 0515!

The merchants bring tents, lights, music systems, and fresh seafood and vegetables—and *girls!* "They arrive at ten," says Renand. "Massage girls—I will reserve one for you and one for Sir Klaus"! He is joking of course. Isn't he?

This sort of "invasion"—a kind of "soft piracy"—is just accepted practice—like the Marlboros at the Canal

The girls arrive even as we are finishing our eggs. Giggling and coy, they peek into the dining room—and flee! The gang of guys on the second boat were, in fact, the stevedores who will unload all that Welsh steel. I did wonder why the "pirate" boat was carrying, on its roof, stacks of plastic patio chairs, and why that first "brigand" was wearing a well-pressed, button-down, pink, oxford cloth shirt!

Now our own crane is bringing aboard a cargo net loaded with stuff for the big sale. Another net is being lifted—full of more stuff, plus three guys!

The ship will not tie up to a pier here, but will unload into the barges that are already alongside waiting for our hatches to open. The barges are also homes and are populated: there's a mother and a child—playing on *their* poop deck!

Things go slowly but smoothly as we are cargoed with the bazaar and the bizarre, and uncargoed of the steel. At 1145 a string of firecrackers goes off—accidentally?—and sends a few people running to the scene. A voice in the corridor: *female!* Fork lifts come by boat and are lifted aboard. The corridors are jammed with merchandise, the poop deck is now totally covered over—a complete snack bar and restaurant, a couple of TVs running—and sound systems going, strings of coloured lights, plus dozens of tables and chairs and displays, racks, boxes, coolers, and, of course, people! What a life! This is their living, I guess, and the boats at dawn were simply reconnoitering and reserving choice locations for selling—saving the spot with a length of colored ribbon.

Wooden beams now go over the rail into the boats. The pilot's ladder is unfurled and laid over the side. It's a circus, a carnival.

At lunch, I beckon to Renand and say to him in a loud aside: "She did not come to my cabin this morning!" Without the slightest hesitation he replies, "She is waiting for you here!" and he gestures toward the kitchen. He disappears and moments later I hear, "Pssst! Sir Moses!" And there he stands, on his arm a lovely Thai lady—obviously in on the joke—smiling broadly. He is having so much fun with all this.

We plan a shore trip—by bouncing speedboat!

33.

Our shoreward jaunt on the BANG BANG BANG speedboat, arranged by our Agent, drops us without ceremony on the deck of a fishboat from which we clamber up a ladder to the cabin roof of another fish boat and from there up another short ladder to the heavy-laden pier which is awash with curious Thai folks, with their bicycles, fish, nets, hibachis, and cars—inching their cautious way through, along the wooden wharf, and into one of which we all pile to be driven to a small building on the very edge of the harbour in which a number of Thai ladies are standing by in a very efficient car rental/taxi/transport/ freight forwarding, etc. etc. operation, and where a ripple of giggles begins when they behold our Klaus who they think, we are told, resembles Colonel Sanders, and who promptly breaks into a paroxysm of flapping wings and cock-a-doodle-dooing which does little to calm these charming and by this time nearly hysterical ladies.

The car and driver, assigned to us for the day, wind their way through the port town of Si Racha and head us in the apparently mandatory direction of The Alligator Farm—an interesting example of what to watch out for: the assumption that all westerners will, of course, want to visit all the obligatory tourist attractions. None of us really wants to visit this "famous place"—but then, we are never asked, and then we are there.

It is, while lovely and well kept, nevertheless a giant zoo where all manner of wild creatures are caged and caught and where literal piles of hapless alligators bask and probably suffer in the noonday sun. We spend money to get in, money to pee, money to eat, and buy souvenirs (well, *they* did) and finally extract ourselves and head off for Pattaya, a sizeable city nearby where the Kments have an old friend from home. On the way, Marion says, "I don't really like alligators."

We deliver the Kments to the outskirts of the city at the friend's place and Our Car takes Klaus and me to beautiful downtown Pattaya. At an Internet Cafe, I send off a passel of emms and then just wander these fascinating streets (Klaus, of course, has gone off on his own toot) sopping up this rather ramshackle country. Everything is almost totally outdoors with just enough roof to keep the rain off. What they do for walls, I don't know; perhaps they just stay open—and "open"—all the time. Some very lovely "resorts", they call them, large hotels with beautiful grounds. One, the Peace Resort, would charge me 600 baht for a single room with pool privileges. That's $15 a night! Everything is priced that way—40 baht to the buck.

I wander into a large, loud carnival. It looks like an old-fashioned affair, with rickety Ferris wheels—probably the very ones we rode on as kids, and now sold to the Thais—and other rides and shooting galleries and a 20-speaker soundstage just getting cranked up. All of it very chintzy. But, hey!, there's a guy selling POPCORN (popped). Does it have salt and butter on it? "*Oh, yes!*", he says. So for 10 baht, I get me a bag. Yikes! Open the bag: one solid chunk of flavorless, yucky fodder. Incredibly inedible! No wonder the "MERRY CHRISTMAS" signs are still up: the popcorn was made for Christmas 1999! Feed it to the birds. Well, bless them for at least trying.

I try a $1 bag of "salted cashews": not only *sans sel* but filled with candy-coated crunchers like those things you get on airplanes. For the birds!

In this carnival in Thailand, a side show features "SIAMESE TWINS!" (get it?).

All over town, great numbers of neat blue pickup trucks fitted out with passenger seats in the canopied boxes. The rig slows at specified spots, you step easily up and in, take a seat and off you go. When you want off you bang on the roof, pay the "cashier", who somehow keeps track of when you got on, and pro rates the ride. No schedule, but one seems to come by about every minute or so. Very efficient, cheap and fast—and, of course, open air. BUS COOPERATIVE says the printing on the door.

Klaus had gone his way about 1600, but later, comparing notes, we discover that we had both been most popular with the distaff side of the population. Friendly winks and ready smiles promise what one comely young thing has printed on a sign she carries: HAPPY HOUR.

Speaking of which, my "happy hour" in the Internet Cafe cost me 50 baht—about $1.25!

Klaus and I meet at the agreed-upon time and place, climb into our waiting car, and head off to pick up the Kments on the way back to the ship. Pattaya, I am told, contains something of a German enclave and we pass a while in an open air, very informal (one wall is missing) pub sort of establishment, before heading home.

This time the pier is not quite so crowded and among a number of high speed water "taxis", one seems to be waiting for us. We BANG BANGETY BANG BANG our way out into the pitch dark anchorage and right to our waiting ship, then a climb up the gangway and—

Oh, my dear!!—I wish you could see this erstwhile drab and workaday ship! It is all party! The coloured lights sparkle, TV sets blare, big band music fills the night, and Thais! Thais everywhere! Even on the gangway. Eating and sleeping in the corridors which even so are draped full of clothing for sale. They are perched on the barges and on their boats tied up to the barges. The ship is lit up as she was when I first beheld her—plus, of course, the strings of Thai lights and the suffusing glow from all the music and jollity, and our crew is loving it. Every single space—on top of the winches, the bollards, the piles of hawsers—every space is filled with something—or somebody. Do they stay all night? Where do they pee? They are such an attractive bunch of people—easy to see why Thailand has the reputation it has. And I do believe that my BIBI herself is smiling!

Two Thais are perched on the back end of a barge tied alongside and are jigging for fish. But more remarkably, the stevedores are continuing to move those wretched steel plates two at a time into the waiting barges.

129

The aroma of rich and spicy Thai food—the real McCoy—wafts into the cabin.

The whole side trip, another adventure which this Terribly Timid Traveler might never have attempted solo. The others plan a trip into Bangkok tomorrow, but I've done with sightseeing hereabouts; I suspect Bangkok would probably be just a larger Pattaya.

Must remember to remind prospective freighter travelers *never, ever* to bring Traveler's Cheques. Spend half my time trying to find a place to cash the damn things and when I do succeed I get only local currency and who needs 2000 baht? I may have to start using bank machines to get smaller amounts. Never again! Take the cash, put it in the ship's safe. (Traveler's Cheques: On a freighter trip, always leave home without them!)

34.

6/12 Wake at 0605 to find the unloading either continuing or starting again. And now I know the answer: the men pee (recycle?) into used water bottles, then toss them overboard; the women—or at least one of them—duck down between the hatch covers. Ahh, rain will be welcome this time!

I try to do some fast figuring about this unloading business—6,000 tons, that's 2,000 pieces, two at a time over the side means about 1,000 loads at five minutes per load, that's 5,000 minutes or about 83 hours which is 3.45 days if they work 24 hours a day. I'm always wrong, of course, but let's see what happens.

Families live on these barges, like those of Germany, the Netherlands, and the like. I understand they rent them from a corporation and, in turn, operate them. These have no engines, so tugs must tow or push them to wherever the work is, But they are brightly and freshly painted and immaculately clean. Grocery boats make regular daily rounds to the barges; the "bargewife" leans over and points while the rolling (literally) store keepers pick, wrap or bag and pass up the produce. Money changes hands, and the "store" chugs off to the next barge.

This great festival/bazaar/flea market, etc. also serves as a mess hall for the stevedores who, it appears, will not leave the ship until the work is done. They have been aboard now for 28 hours—working, eating, sleeping in their suspended hammocks, "living" anywhere they can "hang out". Marion said some slept on the hatch covers last night with their legs hanging over the edge. Women come on board to cook and serve both labor and management (if desired). It's a strange but effective system, but even the Captain was startled when the restaurateurs started climbing aboard at 0500 yesterday.

Well, I "almost" missed the boat in Houston; we "almost" had a "pirate attack", it was obviously time now for an "almost romance". As we are now aware, I love to watch the activity in and about the ship—Klaus's disapproval notwithstanding. This afternoon I became intrigued with the family operation of these barges and watched the near portside one loaded to capacity and made ready for it's voyage to some yonder place. The family on this barge consisted solely of a husband and wife, he, slender and muscular, she—well, at first I thought perhaps I was seeing my first heavyset Thai. No, the "heavyset" was quite specific: she was pregnant, and well along at that. But buttoning up a barge is a two "man" job, and the couple went at it apace under glowering storm clouds. The task consisted of lifting, one at a time, 40 long steel rods that would arch across the barge's open hold, and placing them in holes about every 18 inches: lift and carry nearly the length of the barge, place the ends in the holes, walk back to the end, pick up the next one, and on and on until all 40 were in place. Then two heavy canvas tarps had to be pulled over the arching rods, fifty feet or so at a time and snugged tightly with wedges all along the sides. It was work that would have tired a healthy man, but the stalwart mother-to-be determinedly provided her half of the labor. I watched it all, finding myself turning into a veritable pre-natal cheering section. When the job was done and she rounded the barge's port quarter and appeared on her "back porch", I whistled my real ear-splitter. She looked up immediately and I applauded and gave her two thumbs-up. Her bright smile just lit up the gray afternoon, and she disappeared inside.

It was supper time and I went in to partake, but was back shortly to find the barge casting off, and a (rather strange) "tug" standing by. My lady was now atop her house at the stern, faking down the mooring line, but seemed to know I was there as I snapped her picture. Again that smile. Now the barge began to move, and as it pulled away, she waved, and her voice carried across the distance: "'Bye." The barge moved out and away, but then was pulled around our stern; the tug would pick up another barge on our starboard side. She still stood on the cabin top and when all was ready and the ensemble moved off, she waved again. I like to think that maybe our brief encounter—my "almost romance"—cheered her as much as it did me.

Well, they have been unloading steel plates into barge after barge now for about 36 hours without stopping. Our schedule is moving up: we sail tomorrow night, but only across the Gulf to Laem Chabang where apparently we pick up some cargo. This is all very good news. We actually tie up there so can easily go ashore, and we will be on our way to Viet Nam much sooner than anticipated. The

131

Kments and Klaus were all set to leave tomorrow morning for an overnight in Bangkok, to return, possibly to Laem, on Friday—or something. Anyway, they had to leave this afternoon and will still return to the ship at Laem Chabang. I did not plan to go; Klaus did, but then decided not to.

A vicious wind began to build in the late afternoon—blew one minimal Thai clean off his feet, rice bowl and everything—but the storm itself passed us by.

Rain now and the unloading is shut down, but the fish or squid jiggers are at it again with their light shining down into the evening water, and they are pulling them up at speed!

Ah. Work has begun again.

6/13 48 hours now without stopping—except for the rain shower last evening. Another sunny day, and the beautiful and beautifully seaworthy Thai boats mutter around, tugging, delivering, fishing, just going about their business. And here is the market boat with its floating grocery store nudging up to the barges. Now a—wow!—double-length barge ties up to port. Haven't seen one of these before: separate holds.

And then they are gone! The poop deck is once again just that. Like taking down the circus after the big show: everything unlashed, rolled, wrapped, packaged, netted and lowered back over the side. Those familiar stacks of plastic chairs, tables, poles, canvas, food and drink—and one flat of eggs, on a trip all its own, very carefully lowered to the "pirate" boat hiding under our stern. All those incredible workers, all the smiling faces—gone away to await the next ship, and the next welcome to Thailand.

And by golly, the last of the steel is lifted into the last barge, and out of the barge come two stevedores standing up in the slings and soaring slowly skyward—the final celebratory act in getting rid of that ruddy, rusty steel. Ahhhh. Not bad! A week to load it in Wales, 53 hours for the Thais to get it off! The Captain will have to revise his opinion.

Looks like we weigh anchor at 1400 today for a short cruise across the Gulf on the dirtiest (post party!) ship I've ever seen. A cupcake wrapper among the chains says it all.

Will the thrills never end?

I know we are getting close to sailing so I repair to my A deck "balcony" to watch the tug pick up the last two barges. Standing there, above the Upper, or working, deck, it appears to me there is no one on that deck to loose the barges' lines. I wander down—just in case. Sure enough, the bow line to the first barge is still made fast and a woman (the bargewife) handling the lines is motioning UP UP UP. "*Who me?*" I think. But nobody else is anywhere around, so I lift the heavy hawser off the bollard and let 'er go with a splash. But both bow and stern lines on the last barge are still secured, so I continue forward. Sure enough, on the stern of the barge another woman is waving UP UP UP. So I up!—SPLASH! Now for the bow line. I go forward. The barge is now starting to move. These lines are 'way up on our forward winch deck. I clamber over deck stuff, climb the ladder and find *two* lines. No question this time: UP—SPLASH, then the other goes over with a satisfying splash. The fellow in the first barge had earlier waved at me in my cabin window; now I wave again, he waves, his wife waves. We all wave! And off they go. Very slowly and gracefully, of course.

Now our ship is underway and I beetle up to the bridge where the captain looks at me with a wry smile and says, "I see you put in some overtime." "Yep," says I, "but I won't claim for it."

We are headed for Laem Chabang, a newly-engineered harbourette on the east side of the Gulf and only a few miles away, so since the pilot won't be here until 1500, we just amble along. Still—as usual—it's good to be moving. We have left the island of Ko Si Chang. Laem is now in sight, but we can't enter without a pilot. Cambodia, now Kampuchea, is also in sight.

Again, it occurs to me that I may be crazy (I guess this trip proves it!) because I don't want to be a typical tourist with this seeming compulsion to "see" things, to "go" places. No, I am immeasurably happy and content sitting here with my ship and the sea. I suspected this might be the case, but didn't say much on Salt Spring, while people urged me to see this and go there. Secretly, I thought: I might never leave the ship! As Sir Klaus said the other day, "You are an undefinable person." Yeah, I guess that's me.

Ah, here's the pilot. The agent must have lit a fire under some- body's "ess"—on the bridge a while back, he seemed ready to light something.

We are heading into a man-made concrete bight, very neat, very tidy, very new, but there is nothing here: no ships, no sheds, no cargo! Some small boats and a tug tied up alongside the lengthy quay, a city skyline in the distance, some buildings on the other side of the deserted quay. Mind you, the next bight is the container port, several ships and about a million cars waiting to roll on to a monstrously ugly car carrier.

We are being turned to face out, tugs with their indigenous high pointed bow and sweet swooping sheer, pushing and pulling,

133

but what's to load?. Lovely port here, nicely constructed—same vintage as Salalah, probably, but largely for containers and roll-ons. We are the only general cargo vessel here. Amazing sight: an acreage as large as umpteen football fields, much of it paved with bricks, all nicely marked in lanes, but with nothing on it.

35.

I am just walking across that vast empty space—the cargo we are supposed to load is still not here—and come to sort of administration building/gate house, and there, waiting on the other side is our cargo! Four or five big yellow Caterpillar tractors, and three truckloads of enormous "modules" labeled "PARTS OF HEAT SEPARATOR—DO NOT CRASHING" These items were made in Thailand (by Westinghouse) and are on their way to Owensboro, Kentucky! I doubt the ship will find a port in Kentucky so they'll probably be left in Newport News, Virginia. The "Cats" will get off in Houston.

Anyway, I'm inspecting the cargo and here comes Klaus, He's phoned for a taxi, couldn't find me aboard (I usually jump off as soon as I can to explore the environs, find a phone, or whatever); would I like to go along to town? I'm not sure, but have everything I need so off we go.

The vehicle that arrives is not really a taxi as such, but a "car", more or less (quotes intentional), with driver and friend, which is ours for the roundtrip to Laem Chabang and anything else we might need it for—and all for $10! The driver and his friend take us to the post office (for Klaus's stamp!), then into the midst of what turns out to be a fair-sized city where we seek (a) an Internet Cafe for me, and (b) a travel agency for Klaus. They turn out to be right next door to each other—and also next to a gallery owned by another friend of the driver, and for which the driver probably receives a little something for steering (literally) "tourists" in the right direction. The car will meet us back here at 1900 hrs. and we go our separate ways. I spend an hour in the café for which I pay the nice young man 20 baht—50¢. These places are the best—cool, quiet, clean, friendly, private—and cheap.

Then I begin to wander up the street past a big hotel and come upon the most enormous outdoor market I've ever seen: everything—cooked and uncooked—edible (and—uh—otherwise), and every sort of fresh fish and meat, plus clothing and shoes and—well, just everything! Laem Chabang is not a tourist town. I see not one other white face the entire time—but an awful lot of smiling, curious, interested, and attractive brown ones. The tiny tots are the best: they may well never have seen a mug like mine, and not only that: it is covered with hair!

134

I feel oddly and intriguingly at ease wandering these aisles—me, the Terribly Timid Traveler. These are just people—laughing, talking, buying, selling, and—the first such I have yet seen on the trip—begging: she is blind and older, dressed very prettily with tasteful makeup. She is just standing, with white cane and small bowl—and singing softly. (I had a friend once who called such folks "Ambassadors from God", providing, as they did, an opportunity to be kind.)

I walk around several blocks, then back to the market where I am tempted by some deep-fried chicken—but is it chicken? Decide not to find out—the T.T.T. again!

While I am messing about in the market, Klaus, all unbeknownst to me, has received a call on his cell phone from the Captain back on the ship! He needs our passports immediately—either he had forgotten about this or the Thai officials had boarded early. Klaus tells him he has no idea where I am but he actually rents a scooter and heads back with his passport, only to get another call part way back: never mind, taken care of. And the Kments (and, of course, their passports) are still in Bangkok! Such silliness!

Nearby, I come to a crowd gathered, standing around a man, seated on a box with a loud microphone in hand, and, spread out in front of him on a mat are what appear to be religious articles—joss sticks, candles, etc. He is talking a mile a minute, no idea what he is saying. I might ask one of the young girls in school uniforms—they must be studying English—but, shy me, I don't. An assistant passes around the crowd showing a picture of a young man. Then she goes around selling something out of basket, then around again and sells a few more somethings. People start drifting away. Me too, but I see lights are being put up for the late show, whatever it is. It gets dark here just after seven. Still light, though, at 1810, so I wander away and come upon a wonderful game being played by six young men—late teens, early twenties—on a concrete court obviously built by the city. It is a combination of volleyball and soccer. Played with a net about the size and height of a volleyball net, the rules seem to be about the same as those for volleyball except that you cannot touch the ball (smaller than a volleyball and of plastic like a "whiffleball") with your hands. The serve comes when a player, standing in a prescribed spot at one end of the net, tosses the ball to the server—really pitches it in a high arc—and the server, also on a prescribed spot at centre rear court *kicks* it over the net. But the way he kicks! Over his head! So it WHAMS down across the net—ZIP! It's caught on the head of an opposing player who knocks it up, then kicks it up and WHAM! spikes it over the net where, with luck and great skill, it is stopped by a head or a foot and played back—three kicks and over. You lose the serve when a fault occurs. They spend a lot of time upside down spiking that ball with their feet—over their head, and over the net with lightning speed. Quite wondrous to behold. I am getting such a boot out of the skill and speed of these guys—laughing and applauding—that they "ask" me, with a beckoning gesture, if I would like to join them. Ha! Can you see it? One high kick and I'd be flat on my back and out for the duration, somebody carrying me back to the ship on a board.

Our car meets us at exactly 1900 hrs. and our day is done.

Looking out my window now as I write this. There seems to be something of an impasse on the quay—all the tractors and small bits are loaded, only two huge modules and a couple of long steel shafts remain. There are four guys sitting on top of the first module; the coupled cranes are ready, but nothing is happening. I hope they didn't "crashing" it. Ah, now they are getting the monster in—it weighs 59,600 lbs.—about 30 tons. Hey, I *know* these things!

I'll make some popcorn to ease the strain.

The Kments arrive in a taxi just about now; it is a relief to have them back safely on board.

Even at nearly 2300, I simply cannot leave alone the workings of this ship; *must* go out and "help" them load, and "approve" the new cargo that arrived while we were gone: three more modules labeled "BOILER PARTS" for Shanghai. I give my thumbs up to the Supercargo who laughs and signals that we will be sailing at 0400. Hurrying to Shanghai indeed! I probably won't wait up so tomorrow we'll be on the high seas again: southwest and around Kampuchea to Ho Chi Minh City. Some say we'll arrive late Saturday or early Sunday.

6/14   There is always a reason to get up! My internal "ship's clock" seems to sense when something is afoot. And now, at 0345, it hears voices!

We sail in 15 minutes, and outside on this vast and once again barren quay, the last of the Thai stevedores—two dozen tired, very dirty and disheveled, guys, including a few of those record-breakers from Ko Sichang who were sound asleep in their hammocks when I went up to free the barge lines. A couple of hefty women, the cooks, most likely, are present, overseeing a veritable household of goods and gear deposited in a mound on the quayside: pots, pans, trunks, boxes, propane cylinders, mats, and they are all clumped together below my window waiting for the approaching windowless, paintless, springless, decrepit little bus now putt-putting across the bricks to take them home. There is no way everything and everybody will fit into this buslet. Two bits some of them ride on top. They also must take along all the chains, slings, shackles and cables they used to load us here. Ah—a small pickup truck and a station wagon arrive to assist. I whistle to say goodbye, but can't get their attention.

Now they're "all aboard" and off they go in those whinging, creaking, swaying, smoking machines. The miracle is that they can move at all but there they go in a rickety line across the empty quai..

And all is quiet on the Asian front—well, almost—there is still the sputter of an unmuffled jitney fading away into the dawn's early light.

And now our tugs await. Tomorrow, for sure, it will be, as the Navy has it: "Sweepers, man your brooms; clean sweepdown fore and aft."

Once again, the broad and empty sea, deep green against the blue sky and turning into beautiful sudsy white foam under the constant bow wave. Things in the flexible schedule seem to be tightening up a bit. The Captain says at breakfast: July 1, Masan, Korea, August 2 in Houston! August 2? Wow! A bit short of the "19 to 20" weeks predicted, but a good 16 or 17 anyway. If we have a West Coast U.S. stop it could spin out; if we stop in Hawaii (Hah!) . . . etc. Besides, anything could happen between now and then.

A day and a half to Saigon, a day and half *in* Saigon, says the Skipper.

36.

11°27'N x 101°35'E (at sea)

6/15 Have taken to eating breakfast: 2 squashed fried eggs, toast with peanut butter, OJ. Going easy on lunch—yesterday, one fish (whole). Period.

Popcorning:
Since yesterday's news of possible August 2 arrival in Houston, a subtle difference in my outlook. Before that it seemed the trip would "never end"—at least there was no end in sight. This was good, but also made me a little impatient to get on with it. Now—now that I can "see" the (possible) end, it seems in some part of my mind that the trip is already over—even with seven weeks to go, and I begin to think, Hey, whoa!—not so fast! But I also find myself making plans—to surprise Ellen with an early arrival, to arrange farewell gratuities, etc. Silly—we are barely more than halfway through. I have often pined after the home ground, wanting to resume the old life with a new sense of freedom: "I've done it! Now I can get on with other things." But then, I don't want to rush this affair—not that I could if I wanted to!—but to get everything out of it

137

I can. So the Captain's simple announcement throws my head into a tizzy.

<u>P.S.</u>

I must "rob a bank" soon as I am running low on ready money. There is some pressure from the other three to be "out and about" which I instinctively resist, but some momentous occasions have occurred because I gave in. I find, as do the Kments, that it is possible to spend much money and have little to show for it. The best things, we all agree, are the unexpected serendipities that just happen. They aren't on anybody's tour list. I find, in trying to figure out my reasons for things, that it is *people* that interest, even fascinate, me. Not all that interested in temples, palaces, churches, I would rather watch the stevedores, the barge people, the marketers, the game players—the folks!

We have stopped—to drift awhile until 1400. We cannot berth until the morning (pilot at 0700) so we do not rush to an anchorage. Kments eager to get there—to Saigon—and take a tour. Me, I'm in no hurry. Can't go to the bank on Sunday anyway. We'll probably sail around noon on Monday so there may not be time for anything. OK.

9°N x 107°E (at sea)

Still sitting quietly in the middle of the China Sea and I realize that right over there is Viet Nam, with all its names and places and horrendousness and tragedy. My Lai is just up the shore. Saigon, the Mekong delta—names we grew to know and fear—but were a world away. Now, there they are. All those movies, newsreels, pictures, then the marching, the protests, the names on the wall: Viet Nam.

Two chomps of fresh-made, hot buttered, deliciously crunchy snowy white popcorn, and CLANGETYCLANGETYCLANG—ETY: BOAT DRILL! Down I go. Everybody is there and today both boats are actually lowered into the water since we are not moving. The motor lifeboat's little diesel engine is cranked into action and five crew members (not us!) putter out for a ride.

All goes well except, as Hans says, the ship is not allowed to sink for at least half an hour—that's almost how long it still takes to get a boat down! Not good! It should be SNAP CRACKLEY POP and away we go. Our Filipinos are just grand guys and hard workers but seem not yet perhaps to be "Take charge" folks. Our 2nd and 3rd Officers are Filipino (to save money, I suspect), but there are many things they can't (or don't, or aren't taught to) do like clerical stuff, lists, bills, etc. and the captain has to do it all. Not good, either.

Terrific guys, but are they being used to full advantage? They could, it seems to me, be trained hard so one day they can become Chief Officers and then Masters.

As #2 boat is being lifted aboard (#1 already in chocks) one fellow is fishing off our stern—no opportunity missed.

Boat drill at the Muster Station

Moving again (from about 1830). The Passengers' 'Plaint: "Nobody tells us nothing!"

Dark before seven here and we are far from alone. I just counted the lights of at least 23 fishing boats all around us, some a few miles off, but their bright white, down-pointing, lights—an aid to attracting fish—make it seem that we are in a very populated area.

Fishing boat lights out my window now numbering 42! I guess closer to shore, more boats.

And from the bridge we appear to be in the centre of a great circle of at least 95 boats! Of course, like the solar system, these "planets" are at vastly varying distances from our "sun", some probably as close as a mile or two, others 10 or 11 miles away. But what a night! The sky is crystal clear, with, to me, some unrecognizable constellations—no big dipper that I can find.

6/16 Great red sunrise and the coast of Viet Nam appearing on the horizon. Pilot at 0700.

Hmmm. It seems my "hours" are becoming daylight hours. Hate to go back to sleep now—too much to see, but when the sun sets these days, so do I!

Now the fishing boats appear—some just on the horizon, many close in, some alarmingly near as if to say that no beat up old freighter is going to disrupt their fishing patterns. They seem to be trawling with nets attached to stern and outriggers.

From the chart it appears that Ho Chi Minh City is a good way up the "*Song Sai Gon*"—Saigon River?

Another ship has been calling the pilot station with the same ETA as us—now I see her coming in on our starboard bow—down from Hong Kong, perhaps.

Just sitting on my Throne and peering through one window, I can count 30 fishing boats. Wonder if—or when—*their* fishery will be fished out.

Ship making a big circle—waiting for the pilot, I guess.

Pilots are aboard—one an apprentice. But for some reason we don't go.

Ah, that's the reason: here come the troops—the dudes with the uniforms and the hats and the epaulets—two boats tie up alongside. But there are only four guys! Too many for one boat, I guess. Red flags with gold stars.

Ooh, very fast hydrofoil crossing the channel in front. Huge white statue on hillside near new-looking church. All looks very Christian.

Moving now, dead slow ahead, boats still tied alongside—free ride. Still don't know whether we go up river to H.C.M. City or what.

Aha: had to lower the big derrick—bridges ahead or overhead cables. And the troops are now departing—fast!   I see: the brown shirts get on one boat, the white shirts on the other, briefcases lowered over the side on a line.

Going up the *Song*. What warships went up this river? Was this area bombed?

So, it's up a lazy river to H.C.M.C. Low-lying delta land on both sides, small boats, a village here and there. Long "S" curves. These are the swamps and marshes we saw in the movies and news shots. Miles and miles of dense growth, mountains in the distance. All is quiet now, but 30 years ago . . .

A straight string of large floats reaching out from shore, mooring small boats. The river narrowing. A current, tidal or otherwise, flowing to the sea—against us. Smaller river joining this one. Large house. Big mooring buoys for ships like us. Boats moored on the float strings are homes. Washing hanging out, people. Whistle sounds for another curve to the right like the BC ferries at the curvy Active Pass on the way to the Islands. Another lovely hydrofoil, bow lifted clean out of the water, making at least 40 knots. River seems to split here. Little houses tucked into the banks, a UN flag flying, boats tied on a wharf out front. Fuel boat inching slowly upriver—for the small boats, a floating service station.

A settlement, a long, thin boat as in the jungle. This is primitive living—living right on the edge. What of this huge green ship plowing the muddy water?

At intervals, two white towers reaching above the green.(?)

Perhaps a city ahead, appearing through the haze and around several more curves.

Now, many palm trees, like huge ferns.

Decision: we are offered a tour of area for $42 each. I say no, thank you. Wouldn't mind a taxi downtown, but will hope for a phone that's usable.

Small village church with "swastika's" atop both steeples—perhaps reversed—old Indian sign. Another small town, but not yet any sign of Ho Chi Minh City.

They really do wear those wonderful flying saucer hats.

Fairly good-sized town, but nothing higher than one story. Half of roofs thatched. Irrigation canal/reservoir? Strange patches of bright blue.(?) Ahh, these Asian boats are works of art! I want one.

Getting busier now; a power plant, more boats, barges. Small blue boat crowded with 18 well-dressed people on board including one woman in an orange suit. Going to church?

Well, we're nearing something. Big ship coming our way. Ah, it's the good ship DEVELOPMENT and is carrying cement. Smaller ship, fuel, I think, with trees growing on board. Nice touch.

More ships, tall buildings, a ferry, a shipyard, dry-dock, small Navy cargo ship, and there's the City itself, just coming through the mist.

Big amusement park—huge Ferris wheel, roller coaster.

Dredges hard at work.

Still heading for our berth—turned off the main river, getting closer to downtown. Don't see a quay yet. Hope we're not anchoring out. Water has much vegetation and brush in it. Barges and small boats have "eyes" painted on their bows. Two tough-looking tugs now shadowing us. Laundry out on every boat.

141

37

10°50' x 107°E (Ho Chi Minh City)

Tied up. Had some lunch. Then went in search of a telephone. Found one: cards only. No luck at all. Couldn't even raise a human voice. Cards are it, I guess, even though I have my Telus code. Came back to the ship. Actually got a ride on the back of a "brownshirt's" motor scooter, as somebody once again goofed, and my passport, which I was given minutes before, needed to be stamped again, and a shore pass given me, which I was told I didn't need. I decided to use the ship's satellite phone but it wasn't working! Rats! Must get through to Ellen to know whether she is getting the e-mails. Will keep trying, but not much after midnight her time. (Shore pass says, MOSES RICHARD BARDL.)

Watching the big pipes go—except of course for the eight that lie on the bottom of the Arabian Sea. The stevedores, all dressed in light blue denim shirts and pants, and bright yellow hard hats, seem almost like wind-up toys! They scurry and jump, run and laugh and gabble away, all exactly the same! Or so it appears from my elevated window.

Shortly after we tie up, I encounter "Thanh Hien (Liza)" in the corridor with her two children. She is with the ship chandlery department of Saigon Port. She shakes my hand, asks where I come from, then turns to the kids and says "Canada!". Now she reaches out and tweaks my beard—twice—yea, thrice!, giggling all the while. Can't get over the whiskers. Then she pats my tummy (hmmph!) and departs. Cute as a button!

A small boat puttering past: woman with hat perched in bow; then another filled with watermelons (Yum!), then a load of big pottery elephants—probably lamp stands or something. May be a communist country, but capitalism seems to be alive and well!

Eyes! Dove gray boats—weathered teak?—but perfectly painted, brilliant eyes on the bows. Quite beautiful. I *want* one!

Thunder! Lightning! Rain? Watching the "tug" boat with barges alongside: crew working, bathing, cooking, squatting—squatting is the big thing here.

By jing, here comes the "elephant boat" again—three times past. Lady in bow with hat and lovely, flowing lavender top. A real picture.

At supper, the Vietnamese agent, I think (again: nobody tells us nothin') is there and I ask him about the big eyes on the boats.

"The old folks," he begins, "believe that at sea or in the river, the boat is a fish, too, and by painting big scary eyes on the bow of the boat they make sure that any dangerous monster fish will know that this is a bigger fish! So keep away!" But they are works of art!

Other Viet Namese guys at supper were probably babies—if that—at the time of the war.

All the pipe sections are gone—lined up on the quay, but more cargo comes off tomorrow and into the barges alongside.

Captain says the ship's phone is not working—hasn't worked for four days!—so no chance of calling tonight and may not have a chance tomorrow. Shoot!

The 2nd Officer has taken to saying "My oh my!"

Decide to take a stroll outside—all rain-washed and a bit cooler. Wondered what they were still taking out of #2 tweendecks. Standing at the top of the gangway having a look around, I hear a voice—high-pitched: "Hi - - hello." Where is this coming from? Again: "Hi - - mister!" I look straight down—into the water, and—my goodness gracious! A boat is tucked up in the space between the ship and the quay—no, two boats! The one I'd heard from contains two women and is piled high above the gun'l's with clothing for sale. As I start down the steps, one of them holds up a pair of shorts, the other a knapsack—both with wonderful, questing faces, both ready to choose something else to tempt me. This tiny boat, so fragile against the great wall of the ship, these two smiling women. I just say aloud, "Oh, you are so beautiful!", and of course, they are. Alas, I have no real needs and no Vietnamese money, but when I come back, others are browsing. The other boat is filled with flowers and plants, and is a bit further aft, but these women and their boat, right under the gangway . . . ahh, I want to buy everything and make them smile. How long will they stay? The boat has no cover, no room to sleep, hardly room to sit.

I go down a bit later to see if I can get a picture. They are gone.

They are truly beautiful people in this part of the world. Thai, Vietnamese, Filipinos: delicate, lovely people.

Just figured something out. The barges in Thailand, and now the tug waiting below, all have areas as part of their "houses" that are roofed over, but are far too low to stand up in. Why? What is this for? Now I think I know: it's certainly "squattable", and is for stringing hammocks and sleeping. Sure it's open air, but so what—it never cools off here, Probably cooler sleeping there than anywhere else on boat or house. And they have canvas curtains you can roll right down "in case there's a change in the weather."

143

Well now: comes down the river *two* Mississippi River type "party' boats—all lit up; the first sporting what looks like a broad mouth and—of course—blinking eyes. Big sign: TAU BEN NGHE - TOURIST SHIP RESTAURANT (in English) and the whole ship is made to look like a big fish. Here comes #2—ahh, music on this one—two separate musicks! Three decks, all full. Both boats look full. I have to remind myself this is not Centre Island in Toronto, but Viet Nam!

Has been raining lightly for a while. Hope it doesn't spoil the Deutsche trio's outing to downtown Saigon. They should be back anytime—may be back already.

Whoops! Here comes yet another lit up party boat.

6/17 It's only 0630! (These early hours are killing me! Some vacation!) It looks like we could sail any time. Ship all buttoned up, barge alongside buttoned up, but still there. Probably waiting for me to drop her lines! Had hoped to make a quick trip to town for bank and phone, but . . .

Whoa—there's a new one! A thatched roof—two guys standing on top—is motoring up the river—no boat visible, just "roof". And here come two more roofs!

Well, there goes my big plan: we sail at 0900. Hong Kong, here we come.

On our way, now being turned around to head downstream. Directly across from the cargo quay what could pass for a movie set: tropical village along the shore, palms, thatch, chickens, dogs, laundry, boats . . .

Tried the new "Chinese" popcorn from Singapore, again. Doesn't appear to be as good as the other stuff—many old maids.

Just occurred to me: not a single sail—as in sailboat—have I seen.

Radio: 2 FM stations here, one you would swear is a North American "easy listening" outfit, but the songs are all Vietnamese. The other seems to be all talk.

One of the places visited yesterday by the trio was a "Museum of War Remnants in Viet Nam". And I'll admit my ethnocentrism was showing. I had, I guess, never really put it all together. When the U.S. pulled out, the Viet Cong effectively won the war, and took over South Viet Nam. Saigon was renamed Ho Chi Minh City, the red flag flies everywhere—and I mean *everywhere*—from every boat of any size, from tiny houses in the middle of the

144

jungle, etc. and if it is not a Communist country, it is certainly strongly Socialist. The tour guide yesterday (a Vietnamese who spoke German!) was fond of spouting the party line ("the puppet regime of South Viet Nam", etc.).

At lunch we had a good talk about the war here; the Museum flyer is quite graphic in it's pictures and text (would have made great grist for the protest mill during the war), but a bit too much for Marion in the actual displays.

They did notice a certain esprit with the people—moving forward, planning a future, more so than appears to be the case with, say, the Thais. What I noticed, forgetting that this is nearly a Communist country, is that the spirit of entrepreneurial, go-get-'em capitalism is thriving and the place seems to be sort of aggressively alive, the moreso with its hundreds of scooters whizzing and buzzing all over the place.

Well, we are at sea again, Viet Nam disappearing off to port. Captain says a day and a half to Hong Kong, then a day and a half there. Longer in Shanghai, he thinks, and he will try to arrange a trip to the Great Wall. That's what he said! (This was another wonky idea of the captain. The Great Wall is hundreds of miles from Shanghai; he meant, I think, from Tianjin.)

6/18 Hong Kong—1800 tomorrow. For some reason it got out that we would be there at noon today. I didn't think so (but I'm always wrong anyway). Once again, we had to ask the captain, who sits at breakfast at the other end of the table and usually says nothing. He must know his passengers are eaten up with curiosity about—well about everything, especially ETAs and lengths of stay, etc., but he doesn't communicate, often gets things wrong, and gets himself in repeated binds because he waits until the last minute (we are, e.g., signing customs declaration forms at 0400!). If he has too much work to do, why not delegate some of it? He has three assistants (mates) to help him. The new Chief Officer (1st mate) is turning out to be quite "interesting". He appears—or seems to like to appear—frantically busy all the time, talks to himself constantly and is always in a great hurry. What one discovers is that people, even "exalted" ship captains, are just people; they are not perfect, they make mistakes—and they do try. Our captain does go out of his way to arrange transportation, shore trips, etc. Nice.

Chippers at it again

And then there's the ship's phone—still busted? If so, more than a week, if it's fixed, why not tell us? I know we passengers ride along at our own risk and behest, but surely there is the matter of simple courtesy. He is obviously a lonely man. He could have our fullest attention any time by just giving us the information he has in his head, and gladly gives us—*if we ask!*

14°48'N x 111°36' E (at sea)

Late news:	Hong Kong	6/19 - 1800
	Shangai	6/23 2-3 days
	Xingang (Tianjin)	
	Masan, Korea 7/1	
	Japan	one week stay
	Houston	8/2

Have been writing in this journal, and got up to stretch. A little rain is falling. The ship just plows ahead on a course of 34° and a flock of those big birds with black wingtips has joined us— swooping and soaring. Where do they come from?

More birds and a full arc rainbow in the east.

Later news: We're early for Hong Kong so must stop for a while tomorrow (and drift). Pilot at 0100 Thursday. We'll anchor about at 0300 (again, we must anchor out as there is no quay space there, so the pilot will guide us to the right spot in the crowded anchorage and depart) and at 0700 unloading will begin. Then we shall sail at maybe 2000 Thursday evening. So we get the whole day in Hong Kong. Great! I have much to do.

6/19   Now we are stopped, drifting, while the infernal chippers continue with the task of scraping and painting the decks. Almost finished, and they have added bright yellow "paths" for the pilots to follow after coming aboard. (They stayed "bright yellow" for about two days.)
Beautiful sunny day; we are close to Hong Kong but it is not yet visible.

20°48'X 114°03' (at sea)

Aha! We move! It is almost dark, but it feels good to be on our way. About 5 1/2 hours sailing to pilot pickup.

6/20   Awakened by the ship's slowing at 0200. We are standing off Hong Kong which appears to rise from the sea like a classical Chinese painting: towering mountains reach up through the hanging mists, and banks of high-rise buildings glow and twinkle suffusing the clouds with a mystic light. It is absolutely enchanting.

38.

22°N x 113°E (Hong Kong)

Now we are at anchor off the Island of Hong Kong, near buoy
A41. It is raining.

(In investigating money changing, I come across the
following: for one Canadian dollar I can obtain, should I choose to,
833,333 Turkish lira.)

And here's a bit about our stalwart pilots and the rules they
work under. International regulations govern the type and placement
of pilot ladders on ships, and it's a fair job to set one up. First there
must be a set of metal steps leading up to and hooked over the
ship's rail, then metal railings must be secured on either side of the
steps. Next, long and hefty lines are threaded through the tops of the
railing poles and dropped over the side as an auxiliary safety
measure. The ladder itself is made of heavy line with rungs of
composition rubber with longer battens every six feet or so. It is
heavy and takes two men at least to heft it up and over. The ladder
must not touch the water, but must stop 2 or 3 feet short. A special
life ring with light and whistle attached is placed adjacent to the
steps and, at night, a floodlight is suspended over the side. It is up
to the pilot which side of the ship he wishes to board—depending on
wind and wave, etc.—so the whole rig (there is only one) is moved
from side to side. It is mandatory that an officer meet the pilot at the
rail, and a good one will inspect the ladder after the crew sets it up
and before the pilot comes near. He does this, finally, by standing on
the top rung and jumping up and down a few times. If he ends up in
the drink, he knows the ladder's placement left something to be
desired. (This never happened!)

Aaargh! Pouring rain! Squally, windy—cats and dogs. It will
pass, I think, but certainly the most inclement weather yet on this
trip. Barges all in place, hatches open. Nothing happening. *Rain!*

So, off we go this morning—damn the threatening weather!
Down the gangway and onto the prow of a bouncing baby launch
which takes us, swooshing and WHOOMPHING to the Star Ferry
terminal in the Kowloon section of Hong Kong. Just getting on and
off one of these little boats is an exercise in derring-do! We arrange
to meet back at the Terminal at 1900 for the bounce back to the
ship, and start out—at first all together, but in less than five
minutes we have split up, Klaus heading off to who-knows-where,
the Kments crossing a busy road in the direction of banks and

stores, and me? Well, therein lies a tale. It turns out we have been walking around the back of the Kowloon Cultural Center. Ahead of me now, a door is open. It says STAGE ENTRANCE and inside I can see a row of bass fiddle cases. Hot dog! An orchestra! Maybe a rehearsal! Manifestly unable to resist any such door, I say, aloud, to no one in particular, "I have to go in there!", and so saying, sashay right on through the door. (I'm a "crasher" from way back—except for parties.)

A nice Chinese lady is minding the desk. I mutter something in English; she mumbles something in Chinese which sounds like it might be "philharmonic?" and I say "YES!", and just at that moment two guys come through the door, both Western, one of them with lips a-buzz—warming up his embouchure.

"Aha", I say, "a brass player!"

"Yeah," he says, "trumpet"—and in we all go.

The rehearsal will start in 45 minutes, so I wander onto the stage, peek at the horn stands to see what they are playing (the Shostakovich First Symphony, the Beethoven Violin Concerto, and an overture), then duck out and head for a bank.

A lovely young Chinese woman is   extremely   patient as I cash the rest of the damn Traveler's Cheques, add some credit card cash, then ask her for a fcw Chinese yuan, and the rest in U.S. funds, but in denominations: 50 ones, 20 fives, 20 tens, etc. She is a princess.

(I will insert here the story of the Kments which I heard later. After crossing the busy street, they first went into a shop, made their selection, handed over their only credit card and were told it was maxed out. What? Something wrong, but there was nothing for it, and they hied off to a bank machine where they stuck the card in the wrong slot and the machine ate it. Here they were in Hong Kong, with no money and no credit card! By the merest slice of good fortune—this had never happened before—the local ship's agent had come over with us on the Bouncing Betty and had given each of us his business card "just in case". Well here was truly a "case". They called him; he appeared in short order, tendered them a generous loan, and they were saved. I said, "Next time, stick with me!" But they were smart enough to purchase new glasses in this city—known widely for its excellent ocular workmanship and low prices. They were delighted with the quality of their purchase—and they should know, having been eye doctors.)

Back in the hall, I call Ellen, full of excitement and news, then sneak—no, stride boldly up the public, but roped-off, staircase in the magnificent hall (it would have been better to be carrying a clipboard—no one ever stops a clipboard) and into the hall itself, being now as invisible as possible. They are playing the first movement of the Shostakovich: it is the Hong Kong Philharmonic,

Samuel Wong conducting! I notice that three of the five horn players are Western, so, when their break comes, I climb cheekily onto the stage, chat with the 4th player, have a word with a clarinet player, then amble backstage looking for more hornists, then back into the hall. At last, a fellow approaches, asking if he can help. They must have wondered who this grizzled geek was wandering around through their orchestra. I say no thank you, and agree to eclipse myself. But what a kick! I am ready for more adventure anyway.

Grab the venerable Star Ferry over to Hong Kong Island—another fascinating look at the folks, none of whom seem particularly interested in me, but they are a panorama of faces and slender figures—almost never saw a fat Chinese—and, from the ferry going over, see my only authentic Junk in a harbour that once was jammed with them—and this one is taking tourists—a genuine slow boat in China.

Wander about the huge waterfront buildings, part mall, part offices, and find a real Internet Café—a small restaurant with one terminal over in the corner—free, but occupied. So I inquire as to the best bus to take to see a bit of the city, and hop onto a #8P for a long ride along the harbour, through forests of immense high rise apartment buildings—40 stories high at least, and just dozens of them as close together as physically possible. Millions must live in them. The route ends at a fine, airy indoor mall where I wander to my heart's content, find another Internet source, buy butter and, wonder of wonders, catch the correct bus back to the Terminal, and the ferry back to Kowloon.

I still have time, so decide to catch a Kowloon bus and see some of that part of Hong Kong: the business district sports hundreds of enormous signs hanging out over the street, but the bus goes on and on; I take in the people and the scene—and my watch! Not yet at the turnaround point and time is getting short to make the return trip, so I hop off, but have to walk several blocks before I can even cross this hectic avenue on a bridge; bus comes along after just a wee bit of panic: me—traipsing around Kowloon, hopping busses! But the Cultural Centre finally heaves into view and, as I de-bus, I hear music: a lovely, informal, free concert is going on in the lobby—some traditional Chinese instruments mixing it up with more familiar types.

We are all in our places at the boat landing at 1855. Great crowds of people around, enjoying the frontage as we jump again into the bouncing launch and in 25 minutes under a lowering sky and a gone sun, reach the ship. To our astonishment, we discover the gangway pulled completely up and a huge barge directly under where we would "normally" re-board the BIBI. Hanging on for dear life as our tender bucks and rolls in the chop, we fill the dark night with shouts and whistles to try get some attention on deck.

Ultimately our shouts reach—no surprise to me—Albert and Romeo, who always seem to be handy when "extra" duty is required. The barge crew (by totally ignoring us) has made it clear *they* aren't about to move, and the only solution, if we expect to reach our cozy beds—that seem to beckon even more urgently now as it begins to rain—is to "boldly go", and step from the rolling, pitching deck of the bouncing boat to the rising and falling deck of the barge, make our way—carrying packages and umbrellas—over her bow and around her perimeter, taking good care first to see and then avoid lines, cleats, bollards, drums, etc., to the side against the ship where that precious gangway waits—still three or four feet up and too high. Klaus struggles mightily and makes it up, but Marion—a stalwart soul in any situation—balks. I holler into the night, "IT'S GOT TO BE LOWER!" And lower it comes so the rest of us can slowly and creakily (us, not the gangway) ascend to that blessed deck above. Again I think of Ellen. She too is a stalwart soul, but, had she opted to share this adventure, this may have been her Waterloo. Of course, I underestimate women's resources and gumption—men are wont to do this constantly. I was furious with this whole episode but, after scorching a page in my journal, swallowed the rest of my rage in the interest of "flexibility", put the new butter in the fridge, and whipped up a furious mess of popcorn.

Ahh, popcorn: the ultimate comfort food! And no further mention is made by anyone—including El Capitan—of our latest adventure.

6/21   First day of summer and absolutely teeming with rain! Coming through my leaky window, puddling up in the open holds of the waiting barges (our own hatches are closed), washing away accumulated dirt and salt and soot—and Thai pee. Will probably clear up by morning—just a passing squall, but it's ever so nice to be cozied up in my little home.

The rain falls in blowing sheets through the beams of our flood lights outside, while inside, the drops appear at the bottom of the window, run into the little trough on the sill, overflow across the sill and run down the wall where the carpet soaks them up very nicely. I try, over the course of the trip, half a dozen methods of stanching the flow, with no real success. No big deal.

The rain runs in rivers down the long walkways from the bow of the ship, along the rails, around the stanchions and bollards, seeking a scupper to escape to the sea.

A lone tug goes silently by, ships are always dropping and weighing anchors in this tumultuous port.

I will try again to sleep, but as always on this trip, excitement either reigns or looms. Alas!

Morning now with bright sun and clouds over the hills surrounding us. Barges ready or arriving. These barges each sport a huge derrick so they can unload themselves if necessary. Tugs deliver the barges, one at a time, help get them tied up, then come back for them later. We now have five barges snugged up on our flanks. I should say barges and powered cargo ships—same size but without the derrick. Again, they are home for families, and one has a dog on board.

Been noting some container-laden barges anchored off to port. Just barges. Now, heaving into view a large container ship, which anchors close to the barges—they were waiting for that ship! And now, just as the anchor is dropped, a tug appears to bring them all together. Talk about organization!

We sail at 1600 for Shanghai where we will remain for two days.

39.

I find myself very often standing at my window just watching the harbour. Always something moving, passing, loading, unloading—always something, and before I have a chance to wonder why I'm doing this, I realize that if I lived near a harbour—and I have—I would spend much time standing and just watching. Ships fascinate me—their slow and deliberate grace, amid the "play of the waves", as Debussy put it—as do the activities of the men and women who live by the sea. Of course, I'd watch trains, too, but the sea and ships are something special. Will I, when this trip is finished, say "That's enough of ships and the sea?" Not likely. More, it will be that every ship, every glimpse of the sea will remind me of this window and the harbours we have watched together.

Excuse me, I must go again to the window.

Radio 4: Chinese and English hosts—all classics, arts news. Very nice. FM 98.2—Call letters: "RTHK"

Underway. An amusement park on the eastern tip of Hong Kong Island—two roller coasters clinging to the hills, tea house of pink and orange at sea level. Looks inviting.

The Captain tells us at supper that the MV LEON is arriving in Hong Kong tonight! How about that? Don't know where she's coming from or how long she has been in the area, but we came that close!

Marion has taught me how to get the peel off an orange with virtually no fuss, just a sharp paring knife. She suggested I open an

151

"Orange Opening School" on Salt Spring. Why not? I've never seen anybody strip an orange like that, and peeling the things has always put me off buying and eating them.

It is Marion's birthday on Sunday; she wants to have a party, and is giving the crew lots of liquid refreshment, which they will love. Klaus, the party animal, is thinking of having "our" party ashore when we reach Masan. They all know of my aversion to parties and have found a place I can hide out until it's over—the paint locker under the bow. I'm tempted.

6/22 Long walk around the deck. Still trying to find a sort of hook on which to hang the story of this trip. Maybe it's just not a hanging offense.

119°N x 124°E (at sea)

By my admittedly very dead reckoning, we are sitting now on the Tropic of Cancer (*Salut!,* Henry Miller!) in the Taiwan Strait. Taiwan is too far off to see, maybe 25 miles or so, but this is the place where Kennedy had all the fuss about "Formoser (sic) and the Pescadores— Formosa now Taiwan, of course.

Today at lunch, the topic of hunger, as we good-naturedley grouse about the seemingly limitless servings of watermelon being placed before us. Marion, it was noticed by our astute steward, was not eating hers, so, suddenly, when the rest of us got a chunk of "*wassermelonen*", *she* got a big juicy apple, or a rotatable pear, or even an openable orange. What's going on here? She swears she didn't say a word to Renand, but we had great fun. Just to watch her giggle, I accused her of batting her eyelashes at him. I was rewarded.

Then Klaus asked me if I'd ever been *really* hungry. Answer: no. Well, he has, and so had Hans—the sort of post war hunger where the rinds were eaten. Hans still has an aversion to potatoes—that's all they had to eat for a while—and bad ones, at that. Again, I got the urge to delve a little deeper into the whole war business, but refrained. Was Klaus just recalling those sad days, or perhaps subtly making the point that I had never experienced them?

I asked Renand when the watermelons came aboard. "Singapore," he said. "Half a million of them?" says Hans. Answers Renand, quick as a wink: "Two tons," and laughs in that endearing way he has.

Fire drill! We just stand by on the bridge. Coming down afterward following Eric Velarde, the 2nd Officer, who is carrying some long, rolled up thing. "Whaddya got?" I ask. "This is the stitcher," he replies. "The stitcher?" I repeat. He makes a motion.

"Ah, the *stretcher!*" I say. "Yes, the stretcher," he says, "Oh, my!"—his latest expression. He's a peach.

We are sailing along the Fujian coast, the very area from which those four (at least) ramshackle boatloads of people set out for our B.C. shores a few summers ago. Imagine *their* journey!

480 miles to Shanghai—about 28 hours which gets us in about 2000 tomorrow. Captain says nine out of ten times they bring us in at night, so we may wake Monday morning to find the ship tied up. For how long? Only "informational dentistry" (pulling teeth for news) will help us.

6/23   A serene and peaceful night, the ship again moving with the seas and wind, taking on the gentlest rise and fall, the small beginnings of a tiny roll—just enough to turn it into a giant cradle and make it impossible not to fall asleep.

Clear blue sky, bright sun as we cross the East China Sea and make for China's largest city (not counting Hong Kong).

Today is Marion's birthday and as a gift to her we three have vowed not to mention watermelon all day!

30°N x 123°11' (at sea)

Marion's birthday lunch (the inevitable party comes tonight). Klaus drew her a wonderful card depicting a downtown Saigon scene: umpteen motorbikes carrying everything from lumber to entire families and enormous packages, and also made her one of his now famous "*Sonnaugen*" (sun eyes), flowers from wire and his supply of "*Die Zeit*" newspapers. Lovely. I am going to make a great bowl of popcorn for tonight's party—a surprise. (Nobody knows I've got popcorn aboard—at least I think they don't know.)

It being Sunday, we had "*Eis*"—chocolate chip ice cream, and Klaus produced a small bag of "*Handjes*"—little cookies made only in Antwerp by a company "born" in the same year as Marion—1934!

For lunch itself, my favorite French fries and something else deep fried and crisp. I tried a piece: very good! Finished the plate, then asked, "What is that?" "Octopus!", said Marion. A new taste for this reluctant gourmand.

We seem to be much closer to Shanghai than I thought (of course!)—favourable winds, seas and current, I guess. This little swell coming up now is probably happening because we are out of the lee of Taiwan and not yet behind Japan and the fetch is very long from the SW.

153

OK. I have made four loads of popcorn (one of which I—uh—ate); borrowed a big aluminum bowl from the kitchen along with five soup bowls and some paper napkins, and I am ready for the big surprise at the party. Of course, they may all hate popcorn . . .

Now we—the ship, that is—must anchor for the night: Fog! Nothing to be seen out my window, but the radar shows 40 ships out there anchored. Ah, there's one—and another. But nobody ain't goin' no place. I figured as much when I saw the Chief going forward—he heads the bow gang for anchoring, tying up, etc.

6/24 "I went to a marvelous party!" And now I'm back—at 0045!

Pensive at the party—Marion's.

Up in the Kment's owner's suite with its separate living or day room. Marion had invited the Captain, the Chief Engineer (a wonderful Polish character), the Electrician and the Fitter. They all came! I took my popcorn which went over famously (especially with the Electrician), wine was provided, dishes of peanuts were laid out, etc. Then, suddenly, Renand appeared bearing beautiful trays of chicken "loolipops", bacon-rolled sausages, grapes, cheese, and olives on sticks, all set in beds of lettuce with wedged tomatoes around the edges. It surely was a table fit for a king—or a queen! They really are a priceless treasure, those kitchen guys. We oohed and aahed, and then I heard Renand, standing just out of sight in the doorway, ask Marion: "How old are you?" I thought, uh oh, but we all laughed and Marion said "68". 'Oh, good!" said Renand, "I got it right!" And in he came bearing a large frosted cake bedecked with 'HAPPY 68TH BIRTHDAY' We love that guy to pieces!

Then we just talked and talked about art and music and ships and countries and Poland and Russia and on and on and I got a medal for staying so long at the party.

See, my problem is that while I dread the thought of a party (I know, I know—we'll talk), once in a while, having forced myself to attend, and in spite of myself, I have a good time and manage somehow to help others have a good time. But still . . .

Pilot will be here at 0900, then perhaps 5 hours on the river to the Rickmers pier in Shanghai.

Oh, my! Still fog. But we seem to be alone on a great sea. Other ships could easily be seen last night, but not a one this morning. Maybe they have gone in. Hooray: there's one and it is moving!

Yes! We are moving. Took the emptied and cleaned popcorn pan and bowls back to Renand and thanked him again for all his efforts for the party. On the way back up, heard the drums going: there is a full drum kit in the crew's lounge. Don't know who plays, but every once in a while—BOOM, biddedy BOOM.

Sometimes I really love this old ship. Cool enough in the cabin this morning to put on my fleece. Yummy! Haven't had it on for many a week. I can shut off the incoming always-cooled air coming through the overhead vent, but the Kments and Klaus can't—the device is jammed or stuck. And there were times when we were genuinely chilled in our cabins. In one of my scrounges around the ship, I chanced upon a vacant, but unlocked cabin, and found in it a lovely heavy wool blanket which I nicked. When Klaus seemed really to be suffering from the chill, I presented it to him—and promptly found another to liberate. Marion was occasionally quite unhappy being constantly air-conditioned. The AC was left on, the Captain told us, because it takes so long to cool the ship when hot weather happens.

There goes the pilot ladder.

And this is (about to be) Shanghai, the place to which we have been "hurrying"! And as we move through the brownish water and fog, it is, again, nice to know that somebody is waiting for us—for this ship to arrive, to bring needed materiel for some important project. We will also load cargo here and may stay for 4 days, said the Chief Engineer last evening.

Pilots (2) are aboard. Huge white ship with PILOTS on the side is anchored out here from which small fast boats deliver and pick up the necessary guests.

Ahh. the excitement of entering a port (even though I can't see anything, from my throne), John Eliot Gardner on the tune box, my book, crossword puzzles—it just don't get *any* better than this—have I mentioned that before? About 5 hours now up the river to the berth permanently waiting for Rickmers ships. Sun trying to break through and burn away some of the fog. (It will not succeed. This is not fog, it is smog and, like our berth, seems to be a permanent fixture in these large Chinese cities. Masks are worn by some residents hereabouts. We may be well out to sea before we see the sun again.)

Have not been mentioning the books I am reading—they will total 30 by voyage's end—but am on my second one by Robert Kroetsch with whom I have some acquaintance. He is a certified nut, but what a talent, what characters, what bizarre, wondrous, and wise tales he spins A true original. Must communicate with him again.

Still waiting for the first glimpse of Red China, the infamous Red China—Mao, the Little Red Book and all the rest.

Passing what is, I think, the first sea-going tug I've seen, the kind Farley Mowat writes about in THE GREY SEAS UNDER. It's all muscle!

At last, off to port, low-lying land through the fog. Fishing boats abound, outriggers, nets, lines, boats in groups—sometimes five at a time.

Now about to leave the great Yangtze and turn left into the Huangpu River which actually flows through central Shanghai and where our berth is located. Second Officer Eric says the fog is always here, and it certainly is hanging on today. Visibility may be half a mile. Another hour on this narrow stream and we should be tied up.The Yangtze at this point is very wide indeed; can't even see the other side through the fog.
Several Chinese Naval ships tied up to starboard.

Well, this is where those boat peoples' boats came from, I'll bet. Look at 'em! Dozens of them tied up in rafts—probably sell for a song—a quick engine overhaul and they're off across the broad Pacific, packed to the gun'ls with hopeful emigrants having laid out maybe $15,000 U.S. for a chance in the "new world". How many will never get there? No shortage here of "refugee" craft. Rather gives me the creeps. In Port Alberni, just "up island" from us at home, I toured one of the boats—a former freezer/packer—that had made the three month passage with more than 100 hapless seafarers virtually stacked on board like the erstwhile cargo. Truly frightening.

40.

32°N x 121°E (Shanghai)

Tied up. Beautiful quay with huge red mobile shore cranes and already the stevedores are here, the fork lifts rumble—though our last line is not yet secured! And it's cooler here!

Well now ain't that   a kick in the head? (Remember "flexibility"?) Instead of four days here, we get 19 hours! Cargo didn't arrive. But how could the company have been so wrong? Our Captain seemed quite stunned by this cargolessness. Klaus plans to go into town tonight anyway, don't know about the Kments. I'll go along. I want to see at least something of the place. Supercargo (he is German) told Klaus that the freight business is 'way down since 9/11—"100 container ships idle in Singapore".

So we grab a quick cab amid a jungle of container trucks—lines of them, streets full of them, all heading in or out of this very area. A madcap dash to inner Shanghai—the big statue of Chairman Mao, the "Tourist Tunnel" under the Huangpu. the Peace Hotel where for about $15 I e-mail everybody I can think of, then take a hike along the river, a giant promenade with a million people, lights and booths selling stuff, then a stroll up what we heard was "Nanking" Street (actually Nanjing), major shopping area, taking it all in, and suddenly, there is McDonalds! Me eat at McDonald's in Shanghai? Well, only a large fries—tasted exactly the same! But there doesn't seem to be a big call for them—have to be made up for me. Never mind; supper! Then to meet the gang back at the Peace Hotel for another insane taxi ride to the ship. In China, there is no "highway code"; the only rule for driving seems to be GO! Never mind that scooter, that truck, that bus, those cars, those *people*: GO!   Keep the horn going, and the faster you can burn out your brakes, the quicker you get new ones—about a week, I'd say. It is

157

astounding that there are not more crashes, though I did see one right in front of the Peace Hotel.

On our way to the "Friendship Store", a sort of tourist emporium of (pricey) Chinese goods, to change money, a cute little older lady sidles up to Marion and tries to interest her in whatever she is selling. What I notice is the collection of aprons around her neck. I immediately want one for Ellen, but have no money at the moment. Later, with a fistful of Chinese yuan, I hurry back to the spot: she is gone! I walk up the street and down, and suddenly, there she is! I wave at her from across the street, then go to her, look at all her aprons, and buy the brightest, most flamboyant one she has. I probably should bargain a bit, but, not being good at that sort of thing, I pay her price and give her the change as well. She is ecstatic, grabs my hand, thanks me. The apron will probably fade and frazzle and not last long—but her smile will, and Ellen will get a kick out of it. (I was strictly warned not to bring back "more stuff".)

While waiting for the troops at the Peace, I wander around and, in a large hotel restaurant discover "The Old Jazz Band." What a treat! Average age of these gents, about 70 (really old!); they play absolutely "cubic" "jazz" which would probably not make it onto the CBC, but the old guys are havin' a ball—and the rapt audience eats it up. There is a "menu" posted telling us what we might request from them. One number is called "MY HEART   LEFT SAN FRANCISCO"! What a find!

Coming back, and entering the ship's "house", I encounter "The Corridor of Sleeping Stevedores"! There they are, half a dozen exhausted Chinese dudes just flaked out along the wall, "steady blowin' zees", as a friend once put it.

6/25 Something wakes me—sounds like our engine starting, our horn blowing. Lo—the sun shineth, the fog is gone—there is the city. Blue sky overhead (but not for long!) and our ship all buttoned up for travel. Sailing? Early? Now "hurrying to Xingang"? But all is quiet on the Eastern front except Albert and friends are flipping the Stuelcken derrick to work out of #4 hold.

We're off. First being turned around by the tugs and disrupting the entire river's traffic flow—dozens of barges in a steady parade, just meters apart, some of them almost touching, many carrying sand or gravel and so heavy-laden that the river laps clean over the side and up against the coaming, and each one flying the bright flag of Red China—some of them *two* flags

Back in the Yangtze now with some further news: 90% chance we will, after calling Xingang, *return* to Shanghai for the tardy cargo! And perhaps remain there "a week or so". So, it looks like that "schedule" is in a cocked hat—no Korea on July 1 for sure, and the rest extended by a week or more. At least 2 days to Xingang, 2 days back, then figure a week more in Shanghai.

32°N x 122°26'E (at sea)

Pilot gone—but not without some difficulty. Very rough seas out here and, even in the lee of the ship, pretty bouncy. Very small pickup boat, probably *too* small for these seas, but then it has only a few hundred yards to go back to the anchored PILOTS ship. It all works out—they're probably quite used to it.

My mood is disconsolate. I know I must be flexible, but this round trip back to Shanghai—I hate retracing steps!—will delay the trip by about a week I should think. I had, I realize now, begun to count on Houston by 8/2 and maybe even being home to surprise Dan on the 5th when his Victoria Symphony plays its annual barge concert. I haven't mentioned this 8/2 date to Ell; part of the plan—still—is to make "*ein überraschung*"—a surprise. At first I was mildly shocked at the 8/2 return date, then got used to it, and started to plan for it. Too, I really don't want the "opportunity" of another visit to Shanghai. I don't care if it's in" exotic" China, it is just another huge city with thousands of people talking on cell phones—though not nearly as many as in Hong Kong—and driving insanely in Volkswagens (almost every car in Shanghai is a VW) through overcrowded streets. I may not even go into town again. Well, we'll see. I'm just having a bit of trouble adjusting to this new "wrinkle" in time.

The River—even 'way out here—makes the sea a muddy brown, but we are approaching the line of demarcation. It is not a gradual thing; the water is brown, then suddenly it is green. You can see the line coming. BUMP! There it is!

It's a real Nor'easter blowing out here—small boats making heavy weather of it. Even the ship is pitching nicely as it bombs through the seas.

Now fog. Now rain. A terrific day to be cozy in the cabin.

Weary of the routine! Tired of Klaus and his "guffing". Tired of watching Hans "fix" his salad—oodles of salt, pepper, then oil, then vinegar—then, later, two glasses of orange juice after the meal—so much orange juice is being consumed at every meal that we ran out once and will probably run out again. I like a glass of OJ for breakfast—but there ain't none!

159

Also tired of "sort of liking" the food sometimes, and then having to eat it "in public" and occasionally "justify" my tastes—or lack of same. A bit weary, too, of trying to think of something to say or talk about, and sitting in the same place every time.

Oh stop it! What a fussbudget!

So, I'm staying home tonight! Got some leftover chicken lollipops, grapes, popcorn, coke. Ahhh! And music, of course!

These big waves may be coming through between Korea and Japan.

Hey, maybe dinner and a movie tonight! Yes!

Later Klaus drops by to lay out the plans for "our" party. Don't know where we'll be.

41.

6/26 'Way off to starboard, a liner—big, white, but being towed by a tug with another close behind. Hmmm. Possibly heading for breakup in some Chinese yard. I am inspired:

In slow and stately cortege.
The aged princess moves across the Yellow Sea
For Dalien, Yantai Qingdao
Where breaker's torches, cutters, cranes await her
*   coming.*
Engines stilled, their spaces oddly cool, all
*   unmanned,*
While up ahead some tiny craft tugs, insolent and
*   unrespecting, a half-mile hawser.*
She resists the pull toward her ignominious end,
And cannot let go her echoes: voices, laughter,
*   music, decades of parties, galas, gaiety—*
White-clad officers, black-tied passengers .
Now her decks are empty, her staterooms, row on
*   row, bereft of baggage, trunk and expectations.*
From here, the graceful lady, all in white, hides
*   with shame the tears of rust that drape her*
*   stain-ed sides.*
Farewell, bringer of joy, beholder of dreams
*   and drama.*
You live forever in ten thousand hearts, and even
*   as you caress these waves one last time, ten*
*   thousand smiles remember you and what you*
*   gave.*

6/26 MV BIBI,
Yellow Sea

My mother's birthday today; she would be 99.

Seas down now, sun bright, several ships around.

36°N x 122°53E (at sea)

Calm day, uncalm tummy, so sleeping more. Klaus and I on the bridge wing tonight watching very Oriental, "Zenny", sunset. Huge Chinese red ball dropping lower and lower between sudden islands.

Pilot boat at 0500 tomorrow; we should be berthed by 0700. Klaus very anxious to get to Beijing, the Wall, etc. perhaps to fly back to Shanghai to meet us. Not me, the TTT rides again.

6/27   At 0440, nearing Xingang—a "small village"—Captain says, but many ships lying at anchor—I count 23 without even trying. Foggy, rainy morning, just getting light. We move through the pack; pilot soon.

Oooh. a BIG TUG is bringing the pilot this time. It snuggles right up alongside, rubbing shoulders with us, and there he is! My goodness: he's Chinese!

Interesting: 40 or 50 ships waiting to go in. Some—Captain says—will wait a week or two, but here we go, straight on in without even stopping. Some ships have priority: regular berths, critical cargo, pre-scheduling, etc. Our agent or Supercargo says 15 hours here.

39°N x 116°E (Xingang)

Tied up, after two nifty tugs hooted and hollered at each other—the echoes over the sleeping port seconds apart—and there, just across the quay is the MV LEON! She looks even sadder than I remember from Houston—needs a paint job real bad, but probably won't ever get one: she is nearing the end of her circumnavigational life with Rickmers. But she still very obviously works well and inside is every bit as spiffy as BIBI. I will try to go and see. Klaus showed a certain lapse of tact in joking about the unfortunate appearance of our sister ship; the captain said nothing. You just don't do that. She is still a lady, after all.

And "TIANJIN XINGANG", as this port is called on the chart, appears to be no "small village". There is actually another large city on our side of this channel. Xingang, the small village, is on the other side. Very confusing, but this is obviously the port for China's third largest city, Tianjin. We can see large buildings in the distance, dozens of port cranes and a very busy harbour.

161

But looking at LEON across the way, I think there but for pure happenstance go I—in a rear-facing, much smaller cabin on a ship that really does look like a "tramp" steamer—and no Renand, the steward! But how odd to have these two sister ships in the same port at the same time—twice! Looking over at her gives an idea of what we look like—size, shape, rigging, etc. Big handsome boat! Her Plimsoll lines show she is nearly empty.

The bird of choice here seems to be the swallow—dipping and swooping.

A crew of 15 or so men with "natural brush" brooms is sweeping the harbour grounds, raising clouds of dust and seemingly just pushing the dirt around a bit. The Chinese are ingenious at finding jobs for their millions. During our visit to Shanghai, in the Peace Hotel washroom, an attendant not only welcomed me and pointed out an empty cubicle, but then later turned on the water tap for me! I suspect we may see more of this anon.

Don't know how long we'll be here. Klaus is gone to his Wall, the Kments want to go into Tianjin. I may go along. One of our number told us there was a Wal-Mart there. (We never found it.)

Here we go! Tianjin, here we come!

My God! Absolutely impossible to describe the traffic and the driving. For every 7 million people, 2 traffic lights. I could just see Ellen in this traffic—*riding*, never mind driving! What it's like is a giant roller skating rink: hundreds (thousands!) of people (trucks, busses, cars, vans, bicycles, motor scooters), all moving in and around each other—but nobody gets hit! Driving rules: never make eye contact—peripheral driving is the key. Be absolutely inscrutable! Never get angry. Don't hesitate for a second. GO!

Had to change our money: in the bank, an abacus beside every teller and that's where the total comes from, not from the computer it sits next to.

Bike paths? Forget it! Entire separate roads on each side of the main street for the ten thousand bikes passing every minute.

No popcorn to be found here, but 5,000 other seeds, nuts, herbs, tiny animals, etc., etc. Ate at McDonalds. Sorry. Food is exactly the same, but for sure not a lot of people there—at lunch time, too—don't think they're making much money, but have Arches all over the place. Marion thinks they could do a lot better if their menu included McRice!

Large and lovely "art mart". Wonderful for wandering. I come across a fellow selling the "Great Chinese Linking Rings Trick." Perfect for Renand. I am told I must actually purchase a set before being told how it's done. I do, and I learn!

162

We decide to take a calming walk along the river before leaving town for the hair-raising jaunt back to the ship, but just as we start out, there, in the middle of the road on a broad parkway, speaking of hair, is an open-air barbershop; 15 chairs: no waiting! Both Hans and Marion get a cut, sitting on high stools, wrapped in sheets—all to the enormous delight of the students in this barber college. I pass, having just cut my own mop a few days before. Though I can tell they would love to have at the beard. Photos are taken, the barbers surrounding us, smiling. It is probably the hit of the year for these young people. So nifty they are. And no charge for the cuts!

Tianjin barber college "faculty" with clients (and me).

Then roaring back to the ship in our Chinese more-or-less car—the driver is with us all day, speaks not a word of English, but obviously manages behind the wheel. Sitting in the front passenger seat on the way in, I attempted to make use of the seat belt, but was "told" it doesn't work! Our lives are in the balance on these Chinese trips—I'm not kidding—and suddenly from the back seat Marion begins to sing "Cherry pink and apple blossom white . . . " no doubt convincing the driver once and for all that he has a car full of lunatics.

On the way out (not literally, we hope) we pass blocks and blocks of buildings that are, to our eyes, simply uninhabitable, but on closer viewing, not so. People live everywhere. But these are no

163

"slums". On the streets are the residents themselves: neat, clean, well-dressed, lovely, slender, elegant people. How do they do it?

Back in our port city, some of the most atrocious roads I've ever beheld. Originally concrete but now—forget the pot holes!—huge chunks of roadway just gone. I fear that up here off the beaten tourist track, we are seeing the real urban China: disheveled, badly run down, infra-structure just barely making it, and of course millions and millions of people.

At home we see that the MV LEON is gone, and we did want to get aboard the ship we almost took. Oh, well . . .

There seems to be a perpetual blanket of fog (smog?) over this whole area. The sun never appeared today, but this evening made a brief appearance through the thick layer of whatever it is—not to warm but just to be seen—like the moon.

We sail tomorrow at 1530; next stop—again—Shanghai.

6/28 1000 Wonderful sleep! Up at 0830. Something cooking outside. Aha: The Big Lift. Jumbo derrick needed, special enormous tackle—shackles so huge one man can barely move them. Then here comes the module—up and out and over, but—what's this? No truck anyplace! Suddenly: big, long truck glides into place, big van whizzes in and 25 guys are instantly on the scene, all dressed in clean blue overalls. This in addition to the 12 or so more men in orange, a dozen supervisors, observers with video and still cameras, 12 or so people watching from the ship's rail—and of course those 15 sweepers who are still around. This, is an actual count, by the way. Jobs for everyone!

From here on, according to our Supercargo (a somewhat jaded young German fellow) "it's a Muppet show!" Nobody seems to be in charge of this assemblage of willing workers. Timber balks are taken off a truck, then put back on again. The enormous load comes down, then goes back up, men in blue (and two ladies in high heels) run about, 12 of them carrying one big timber, measuring, eyeing, shifting blocks, and, above all, shouting. Another gang is at the bow repairing a container (of ours) that got ripped open last night by an errant hook. Supercargo is fulminating and quarterbacking the whole affair, but only muttering from the sidelines. Not his job at this point. Three more of these "heavies" to go. He's not betting on a 1530 departure.

Meanwhile, the ship is listing nicely to port with the weight of the derrick and the load.

Supercargo also says a day and a half in Shanghai when we get back. A week here? Not likely.

Well, 1530, and we ain't sailed!

Unloading appears to be done; no more men in blue, though some men in orange are still aboard. Jumbo still unsettled, cranes 4 & 5 hanging free. And still we are tied to Xingang's meager sun and abundant smog.

We are a virtually empty ship now—drawing only about 5 meters (we draw around 9 when loaded). Asked S.C.. about Japanese stops. Hitachi, for one, he thinks. But first Shanghai, then Masan.

The sweepers are back, now with a big hose. This whole place is covered in red dust—sweeping actually does little good. Let's see what the hose can do.

Here is what the holdup is: no truck to take the last heavy lift. Eric ("Oh, my") said "something broke" so now we wait. Jumbo is all bridled up to the lift from #3 hold, the stevies are sleeping, the crew is all aboard, but no truck! I'll bet the S.C. is chortling now. He was always skeptical we'd be out by 1530. But then we probably would have been save for the broken doodah.

They are lifting the "module" out of the hold—but still no truck! (Isn't this exciting?) Oh, so slowly it rises. The sleeping stevies awake from atop their boxes. The load now starts to move across the ship. Ever so slowly. But to where?

Truck arrives. Lowering starts. Seemingly no problems. But now the fun begins. The slings are loosed from the 110 ton load and the laden truck departs. But now these giant slings must be removed from the derrick's hook. Four slings—much too heavy for men to carry. Shore crane is brought into action. Slings are to be stored in a big 10x10 foot steel box. Box is not where it can receive slings. No fork lift around. Sixteen men push the box about 30 feet. Idea! Get the shore crane to move the box by attaching the box to the hook. Tiny length of line produced, slung over the hook. Hook goes up, line just runs over it and drops to the ground: only one end was attached, box does not move. Quickly a loop is thrown over the hook—up goes the hook. As soon as the line feels weight, it again slithers over the hook and drops. Hook comes down, line again wound around the hook, hook goes up, lifts end of box about 3 feet, line slips, drops box with enormous CLANG. Another try, and crane actually moves box 10 or 15 feet. As slings are lowered, the 20 or so men (fewer than before!) scatter and scurry as the huge slings swing and writhe. Shackles are reassembled—one man with the pin, the other with the bight. Meanwhile, a brown shirted guy is hosing down the quay. Several of us on the ship have been a most appreciative audience.

1930 and we're away!

42.

6/29 A bright but hazy day—and the day before my Ellen's birthday, Will try with might and main to reach her from Shanghai when we arrive tomorrow—may have to be 0100 if I can find a phone. Figure we should be berthed about 1630 if we go straight in but could be much later. Five hours up the river, of course.

28°N x 122°47'E (at sea)

Hooray! No more fog—or haze, or smog, or whatever. Clear, sunny, blue day. Fog will probably envelop us as we approach Shanghai though.

Tonight we "make barbecue".

Spare ribs, steak for BBQ. Lovely sunset, bit chilly on the poop. Capt. says LEON is anchored off Xingang for maybe two weeks until her next destination is decided. Yikes! Shortage of cargo, or what?

We'll anchor off Shanghai; pilot comes aboard at 0200 (7/1); we'll be berthed at about 0700 for minimum 2 days. The three of us will head into the Peace Hotel for e-mailing, and I can still phone Ellen on her birthday—7/1, 1300 for me; 6/30, 2200 for her. It will be both our birthdays simultaneously!

A little John Arpin tinkling on the box. Nice. Korea on July 4th. If the skipper's previous sked holds; that puts us in Houston on August 5, but I'm sure there will be more delays. I figure 8/9 to make it exactly 4 months.

6/30 Well, Happy Birthday, dear Ellen! Though, for you, your day is still seven hours away.

Rain and fog greet us again as we near Shanghai. We wonder about Klaus wandering around the Great Wall, Beijing, flying back to Shanghai tomorrow morning, not really sure if the ship is going to be there. He is certainly a fool for travel and adventure! Good for him!

At noon we are at the anchoring point! Capt. must have meant two in the afternoon for the pilot, or maybe not. We will probably anchor in an hour or so, but to wait 14 hours for the pilot? Hmmm.

Ocean is all brown again—the Yangtze pouring the good soil of China into the sea. Frankly I'll be somewhat guiltily glad to see the last of today's China—a gargantuan and cumbersome country filled with millions and millions of people either desperate to find work, housing, sun—or just resigned to the way it is—no wonder there were nearly 60 people "helping" to unload our ship, sweep the ground, etc. It's one way to ease the unemployment situation. Looking forward to Korea. Don't know quite why. Certainly a different sort of civilization. Then there is Japan—*really* looking forward to that.

31°30'N x 121°30' (at sea—at anchor)

Ahh. Nice snooze on the forward winch deck. Absolutely quiet up there—can't even hear the grinders. Just the slap and tickle of the ripples against the anchored hull. Put my deck chair cushion on a faked-down hawser, read for a while, then just dozed off. First near quiet I've "heard" in almost 3 months. Now it is an hour and a half until Ell's birthday, but she doesn't know it, as she is asleep.

Yes, it *will* be 0200 when the pilot comes on.

The group is trying to find the World Cup final. TV is fine here, 6 or 7 channels, but no game! Supposed to start at 1900. I'll watch it if it comes on. Germany vs. Brazil. Hans and Marion are both ardent fans, but feel the winner will be Brazil. (As it was.) Never could get the game at 1900 or so, but learned the next day that the whole thing was run at 2300 hrs.! Bummer.

7/1   Happy birthday to me! (And Klaus!)

32°N x 121°E (Shanghai)

Well, here we are, back in Shanghai in nearly the same berth as before. And today I am—gasp!—69! Don't like that. Far too close to unbelievable, inadmissible, slightly frightening, *70*. Not so good. Slept through the whole entire 5 hour entry to the port, the docking, the whole schmeer. Been here, done that.

Now they free up the cranes, open the hatches and get ready for the cargo—but what is it? Quay is full of stuff, but all covered with tarps.

Again a blanket of smog over all. Endemic to Chinese cities? More L.A.s?

Chinese stevies hang big cargo nets over the side of the ship when they are working. Protection of ship? Prevention of loss overboard—including stevies? Nice idea.

Pipes! A cargo of pipes! Small (1 foot diameter) steel pipes. They are lifted seven at a time using a hydra-headed cluster of hooks, and will fill both #5 tween decks right to the top.

167

The other birthday boy is back! Full of stories and adventures, ready for more guffing and busy organizing "our" party for tonight. He encountered much fog at the Wall, got sore feet in Beijing, but had a wonderful time. We are all glad to see him safe and sound. The three of us will grab a cab for the Peace Hotel at 1000 while Klaus recuperates (he was literally shaking with fatigue at breakfast and made a comment that perhaps he was not as young as he used to be) and return in late afternoon. I look forward to talking with Ell yesterday on her birthday.

At lunch the Kments gave each of us a tiny jade turtle in one of those exquisite little boxes. The turtle in China is the symbol of long life. I was much moved and will treasure it always.

7/2   (In the wee hours.) Oh, my dear! I'm just a bit tipsy after the big party. Lots to report—trip to Shanghai and the evening that just ended. Whew. Great relief. More tomorrow—or later today!

An hour walking all over the port looking for a phone. Couple of hot leads, but in the end: *nada.* Can't explain to the somewhat suspicious Chinese the concept of "collect call", and when they hear "Canada" it's all over.

Still reeling a bit from the bash last evening. Have never had so much really good fun at a party. Can't possibly write it all, but subjects were: Chief Engineer's gall stones, his forthcoming surgery, his dislike of A) Japanese (years ago in Kobe he was, apparently, repeatedly asked to leave one restaurant after another with "Japanese only, Japanese only!", experiences he has never gotten over), B) pain, C) smoke, i.e., from cigarettes. We tried to make the him feel "better" by suggesting that (1) from Hans, "there's really nothing to a gall bladder operation, just this huge RIPPING GASH up your middle", (2) from the rest of us, "there are many fine surgeons around, many of them Japanese who smoke!". His wonderful Polish exuberance and characteristic gesticulations kept us in stitches—as it were. Have never seen the Captain, who had not slept in 48 hours (not that unusual for these captains), laugh so hard. We will lose this Engineer soon; his contract was up several weeks ago, but he must await a replacement. The 2nd Engineer has also finished his contract and will fly out today.

I popped up about six loads of corn and gave a big plastic bagful to the crew on my special day and I guess they liked it; they "demanded" I come over to their lounge for thanks, congratulations, handshakes all around, and a lusty rendition (they were watching a porno flick at the time!) of Happy Birthday, with guitar accompaniment. They are a very special bunch. Also gave Renand his new magic trick.

Latest shipping news: we sail from here at 0200 tomorrow, reach Masan, Korea in 24 hours or less, go from there to Yokohama, Japan, then perhaps Kobe, and one other port, probably Hitachi. We are scheduled to leave Japan on July 11, arrive Panama July 29, and Houston (still) on August 2. After I get off, the ship will visit New Orleans, Newport News, VA, then off to Europe all over again. So the time we lost going to and from Shanghai, we'll make up with shorter than expected calls in Japan.

Poor LEON. Turned around to bring cargo from the U.S. to China, now lying at ignominious anchor in the smog off Xingang, awaiting a destination. Was thinking about her and the paint job she'll probably never get. The newest Rickmers general cargo ship—almost 100 feet longer than BIBI and LEON and equipped for virtually any sort of cargo, is now, we hear, already in service—with eight more of her sister ships to come.

Now, of course, my plan is to surprise everybody at home with an early arrival—no announcement, just show up, make the Symphony Splash, and give them all a big wowser.

Captain said at the party that Dan had sent him a fax noting my birthday and hoping there might be a modest observance and maybe a cake; he was sending this because, he said, he was afraid I would not tell anybody about it. He was right, of course, but little did the lad know that with the crew and passenger lists posted in every corridor—a list that includes dates of birth—the entire ship was quickly aware of the impending date. And when Klaus appeared with the exact same birth date, well . . . so much for secrecy!

Ah, Klaus gave me a wonderful hand-made card (the scooters in Saigon) and a little foldout painting of The Great Wall. I wrapped my brand new map of Texas in a sheet of Chinese newspaper and presented it to him with a little speech about being unsure why I had bought the thing, but when I realized he was such a collector, it became obvious why.

We discovered at the party that Marion had never seen Mr. Bean. The Chief has CD ROMs full of him so this evening is the Bean scene. Everybody knows Mr. Bean! In Poland he is called Mr. Fallash, or something like that.

43.

Trip into Shanghai yesterday. We have traveled to and from the big city four times now and every time the route, the fare, and the time taken have been different. Fares have been 60, 70, and yesterday's cake-taker: 80+ yuan!

So, yesterday, we get to the harbour gate which opens on an *extremely* busy highway—2 lanes each way. Almost non-stop lines of huge container trucks, busses, cars, motorcycles, all travelling at speed—fast and furious. Your life is in danger just getting close enough to the road to watch out for and whistle up a taxi. LOOK OUT—here comes one! He's in the inside lane but I whistle shrilly anyway, expecting him to ease over to the curb as soon as he can and we'll run for it. Nope. He hears me and **STOPS!!** Right in the middle of the road! Brakes screech, horns blare, the entire street comes to a teeth-grinding halt. Instantly we should have run, not walked, back inside the gate to hide behind something.

But foolishly we hie off through the slowly recovering traffic and pile in. Off he goes. I think my best theory, looking back, is that this is his first day on the road as a driver (let alone a cab driver!). He speaks almost no English, has no idea where the Peace Hotel, the giant TV tower, the Bund or even Nanjing Road (perhaps *the* street in Shanghai) are—even with the pictures we show him. Perhaps he has never been to downtown Shanghai before. He strips the gears, rides the brake, leans on the horn, and gives every indication that he has no idea where he is going or how he got where he is. He takes us through every major road and bridge construction site in eastern China, constant, dense and heavy traffic which produces great clouds of odoriferous exhaust, all of this over highways with enormous caverns in the pavement. Time is passing; we seem to be getting no closer to our goal, and we begin surreptitiously to count our money: have we enough between us to pay this tyro! Finally, as the meter and our impatience mount, he pulls up beside another cab and asks the way to the Peace Hotel. The light changes before clarity is achieved, but at last we begin to spot familiar landmarks and ask to be put out (hell, we are already put out!) *THE NEXT TIME HE CAN SAFELY PULL **OFF** THE ROAD!* This he manages, is paid with all the yuan we have, and leaves untipped. I have an idea he is still grinding and honking around Shanghai with no idea how to get home. Poor fellow. Or, with luck, he has taken up paper-hanging.

We get our business done; it is starting to drizzle; I am sauntering down Nanjing Street when I hear English being spoken! I search and find two young people who turn out to be art students and who love to speak English. They have an exhibit in a nearby building, would I care to see it? Yes! Up we go. They are very talented, he in a traditional Chinese style—his "four seasons" panels I would be proud to have in my home; she is more modern, but still very good. I have little money to help with their cause—a trip to New York for another exhibition, but we have a grand talk and part with handshakes and best wishes.

At 1630 we three meet at our old friend the Peace Hotel, hail a cab, gird our loins, take a deep breath, and present the driver with a card on which is written the name of the ship and its "address". He speaks not a word, but goes straight to his work. We follow an entirely new route—very interesting sections of the city, light traffic (even at rush hour), no construction, smooth, well-paved streets, and suddenly we are there! He comes at the gate from another direction completely and drives right in! 54 yuan! Amazing.

The three Germans have gone in again today—determined to view the city from the TV tower (a kind of CN Tower). I don't think they'll see much through the smog. I stayed home.

So far, every trip I've decided not to go on has been something of disappointment to those who went: fog at The Wall, crowds at the Tourist Tunnel, etc. I pretty much trust my instincts now, and another day in the city does not really appeal.

A shore crane has hoisted a (new) man in a cage; up, up, up adjacent to one of those doomed light-weight derricks of which four are mounted on the Stuelcken towers. He has climbed even higher onto the railing of the platform, has fired up a welder's torch and is going to—what? I know the captain wants those derricks taken off and the company has okayed it, but is this maybe the beginning of the end for them? Much hardware and cabling attached. Can they really do this?

(Good grief! Huge container ship being turned *right there.* Where will they put her? Behind us, I guess. Ha! There goes a barge laden with laundry!)

Now another shore crane, a beautiful Chinese red, has moved onto the scene—loud siren every time it moves on its track.

Well, they're doin' it. Cutting torch, loosened cables, lowered boom, more cutting, pulling, lifting; the derrick is comin' off.

Yep. They did it—2 derricks gone. The forward port one did not want to go! Cut some, pull, cut some more, pull some more, lift, cut—and finally she broke free. Well, 23 years on this good ship, part of the family as it were, and unceremoniously we cut her loose. Sad. 'Course she probably hasn't been used for 20 years, but still, she stood tall, and enhanced the look of the ship. Now for the other two derricks. Not an easy job. Wonder what will happen to these four gallant and graceful ladies now.

Wonder, also, how many miles of pipes were loaded. 50 foot lengths, 30 foot lengths—3 holds and two tween decks filled. What? Here's more! These are small, 4" or so, 50 feet long. These stevies are wonderfully efficient. Smart!

Oooh, the ignominy of it: they are cutting the stripped-off derricks into pieces! Can't take down the other two—no time. But still more pipes!

7/3   Now oozing our way out through the Shanghai smog and brown water, out of the Yangtze River and into the aptly named Yellow Sea. Fog is so thick I can hardly see the missing derricks! I believe we need to spring forward another hour before arriving in Masan.

It was Mr. Bean last night till almost midnight—much of which I had not seen. I suspect they chop these things unmercifully to make the half hour shows we see on the CBC. Marion was quite delighted; Klaus uproariously so.

Am assuming this morning that the pilot came at 0200 and is still aboard. I was sound asleep. If he is with us, he should be over the rail in half an hour or so. Can you imagine what ships did before radar? In weather like this, there could be a ship 500 yards ahead and we wouldn't be any the wiser. As it is, our path is laid out for us clear as daylight, and with a bit of course-tweaking and a blast of the horn now and then, we are safe as in a church. But my windows are all smooshed up again—mix of salt spray, grime, greasy fog and rain: yuck! One of them I can open and clean, the other, next to it, needs me to lean out and toss a couple of glasses of water against it, and it is clean as whistle.

Am still bent on surprising Ell totally. She's due for a "Moses Surprise". Have started preparing her for a long period without communication. It'll be a bit longer than she imagines, but by only a couple of days. I was thinking that maybe even the summertime non-stop Bowen Queen ferry to Salt Spring will be possible. Terrific—and my snack bar friend might even provide the traditional free hot dog!

Pilots are gone—onto a tiny motor boat that suddenly—after several long blasts on our horn—found us and appeared out of the impenetrable fog. No radar on these small craft. Over the side they went with the ladder not even completely installed—no handrails or anything—and—whisht!—the boat was gone. Now we head off at 85° to Masan, Taehan (South Korea), very near Pusan on the SE side of the peninsula. Picking up speed now.

Sun breaks through, though fog still lies on the sea. Fog? Urban smoosh, more likely!

31°25'N x 123°31'E (at sea)

Slept most of the day. I think we are all a little overextended by our Chinese sojourns. Klaus is uncharacteristically quiet. Tired? Not feeling well? But so am I. My gut is still behaving strangely—almost as though I was on a liquid diet. Have given up fruit for the nonce, bad experiences in the past, but so far nothing seems to make a difference. Not even popcorn! No other problems or symptoms, no aches or pains. Perhaps a slight improvement over last week, but still not "normal".

Weather a bit stormy with some pitching and rolling. Ironic since this is our shortest passage so far.

Just did a calculation. We make about 432 miles a day (24 hours), 18 days across the Pacific, 7,776 miles. Yikes!

Dope from the bridge: it is about 420 miles from Shanghai to Masan. We are covering about 17 miles in an hour. We have 17 hours to go, so 1100 tomorrow should see us tied up. But, hey, what do I know?

We have an interesting situation right now with the Chief Officer, a somewhat aloof man, constantly very busy, tending to ignore us four. Klaus is upset by this behaviour, and we have mentioned this in several of our meal time conversations—including one about THE CAINE MUTINY where Captain Queeg, who behaved strangely, was increasingly ignored, suspected and tacitly accused by his "disloyal" officers who found his behaviour bizarre, even dangerous, so shunned him, and finally mutinied, replacing him in the teeth of a booming gale. An officer who behaves in a manner we—*as supernumerary passengers on a working freighter*—find "strange"—may well be doing as he sees fit for the good of the ship. Are we reacting a bit like the officers on the CAINE?

I just talked with this same Chief on the bridge and asked him "how far is the horizon?"—something I had been curious about for some time. I got a full and thorough explanation, with blackboard calculations—even the variant known as the "Fata Morgana (mirage) effect". He was very forthcoming and willing to share—even if he wasn't back-slapping and joke-cracking. His answer: it depends, of course, on how high above the sea you are; on the bridge, perhaps 10 to 12 miles away. No Captain Queeg here.

More Mr. Bean tonight—the final 2 CD ROMs,

Last of Bean—and probably not too soon. Silly laugh-track all the way through—and really not some of the better Beans.

Renand at supper, knowing I liked to read, said he had some magazines I might enjoy. I sounded interested. He went away and shortly returned with an old Reader's Digest and an even older

National Geographic. I oohed and aaahed a bit, and in mid-evening there was a knock on my door and in he came with 16 more Geographics and a pile of RDs. In another trip to the cabin he brought more soap—bar and laundry (I already had about six boxes.)—and a can of Pringles chips which he had noticed I like. He is a dear man. Chips were perfect, as supper was, for me—a rare occasion—not to my taste.

Midday in Masan tomorow, 2 days loading, then off again.

44.

7/4   The fourth of July! More than thirty years since I celebrated it. Canada's "fourth" is, of course, the first, and my kids, now grown up and on their own, still believe the whole country shuts down for Dad's birthday! Well, maybe they don't.

First look at Korea, through the mist. Ships—car carriers mostly—anchored offshore. Sharply defined peaks and high hills reaching above the mist to port and forward as well. Masan at the top end of a long bay. And yet another ugly, ugly car carrier waiting to be filled with Hyundais and Daewoos and KAI s (there are at least six Korean car manufacturers), heading around the world.

Almost in. Passed Naval Base; more than a dozen warships, flocked together, and a submarine heading out to sea. Just a few days ago, there was a shooting incident involving North Korea. Connection? Overgrown children with their deadly toys.

Here we are: good-sized city, many tall buildings, more naval ships. Lovely harbour, tall hills all around. Sort of a mini-Hong Kong. Water sort of a bronze colour. Tugs approaching. I love tugs; I definitely want to be a tug driver!

Notice on the bridge board: we are carrying only 3,667 tons of cargo now. Looks like lots more on the quay. At lunch the Captain (again) turned a smiling thumbs down on a visit to Hawaii. We have been teasing him steadily—leaving travel brochures (in Chinese) by his plate, and inventing all sorts of plots to get him to stop there: we need more watermelon; I have a big date with a young lady there, etc. etc. We even tried to talk the delightful electrician into falling off a ladder so we could head to Oahu for emergency medical treatment. No go. But now we hear there is a chance of stopping at Long Beach, California!   All right! "People who speak English!" I think. Well, I'm almost right.

34°30'N x 129°30'E (Masan)

174

We are here! Pilot and tugs gone, city across the bay. Hey, this is MASH country, also Hyundai. My three Ponies may have left this very port.

Had a look over Pier 4, found a telephone and quite by chance was able, by pressing every button in sight, and finally a red spot over the Emergency Number, to dial the Telus code and hear those sweet words "Welcome to Canada". Hooray! The others went into Masan as soon as we tied up; they figure to go to Pusan tomorrow. I may make a trip into Masan, then, and spend the day snooping and Internetting—and trying to find some popcorn! Am listening now to some classical Korean music (I think) on the radio. Strangely attractive.

Something has happened—is happening—amongst the four of us passengers. Don't know what. Things quite cool. Klaus untypically quiet, not "guffing". I'll ask Marion—or all three. Feel like I may have offended somehow. Of course, living this close to total strangers is bound to be a bit of a strain, but it could be my independent thrust which is maybe getting stronger. I want to wander around, check the cargo coming on, see about a telephone, just sit and watch the ship at work; they prefer a quick cab into town for sightseeing. I am just a guy riding on a ship and going wherever it takes me. More and more, I see this ship not as a means to an end, not just as transportation from one place to another (you may have heard this before), but as a fascinating entity in itself, and my kick is experiencing the workings of that entity and its crew. What I *do not* need is another huge, crowded, city. Masan looks to be well over a million—big enough. Well, we'll see. I just feel badly that I may have offended somebody in some way.

This Korean music bears a striking resemblance to our Canadian First Nations music—even the language sounds similar.

High drama on the quay tonight! (Why is it *this* sort of thing I enjoy?) Two heavy lifts—45 and 100 tons—a second hand gas turbine generator and the rotor that fits inside. Cost: about $13 million. Talked to the young factory rep who came from Seoul to oversee the loading. Very nice guy—has been to Nee - ah - GAH - ra. Falls.

Fascinating—to me—to watch them plan, invent, improvise, a way to lift 100 tons off a truck and into the ship. Never goes as planned; something always just a little amiss, but they won't do the final lift until everything is perfect—and I have yet to see a mishap. #5 hatch, right below me, has taken in a load of raw steel "logs" each one weighing 1,000 lbs. Each crane-load handles maybe 8 of the 6" x 6" x 10' logs. That's four tons per load—as much as two good-sized cars. Actually, all the logs together which must weigh 60 tons or more won't make much difference to the ship.

Across the harbour the city of Masan sparkles and gleams like Christmas. Rather looking forward to a trip in tomorrow—even though rain is predicted.

Haven't talked to the others yet—they returned after the supper hour and I was "busy" watching cranes. I believe this the prettiest port yet.

7/5   Pouring rain! Typhoon warnings. Nobody working. Probably delay our "sked". Will watch the weather, maybe go into Masan this p.m. Trio spent most of their time there yesterday buying stamps and looking for postcards with no success until somehow they ended up at a convent, told the Mother Superior of their plight and she fetched some "postcards" of the nunnery!   Apparently they had a marvelous chat and now feel they have a "direct wire" to heaven! Hans took US $20 in yesterday and changed it for 23,520 Won! Lovely coin worth 500 Won—about 45¢ or so.

Lunch time. Rain easing. A beautiful ship just tucked in ahead of us: LOVE LETTER out of Dubrovnik. Ship names are truly wonderful. I thought at one time of keeping track of all we encountered, but it soon became apparent that hundreds and hundreds would have to be noted.

Well, dad blame it: I go! Rain has stopped so I gird my loins (I seem to do a lot of that), don my rain gear just in case and meander to the gate where, right across the street the #39 bus is due in not more than an hour—actually much less. 700 won (59¢) take me "downtown"—wherever that might be (See, I'm gathering courage as this trip proceeds.). So when the business section, hotels, intersections, etc. look right, I leap from the bus to find myself completely surrounded by Koreans! (I never saw another western face.) And signs. Asians are great on signs; not one of them makes the slightest sense to me. But as it happens I am smack dab in front of what looks like a major department store. First things first: Internet. A shop that caters to the video game player—rows of games to sit down and play at—has a friendly English-speaking manager who actually closes his office and walks me down the street, into a building and almost up to the second floor where, sure enough, there are four rooms full of computers. Not much English here, including the monitor screens, but, hey, I'm an old hand at this by now and soon I am checking my mail on Yahoo. After about half an hour, the desk lady comes over and says something. No idea what. I go on answering emms and having a ball. After about an hour, she comes back with two guys and they all say things. The gestures and the words "Internet" and "you're out" and finally "twenty minutes" give me to believe I have overstayed my welcome. I am nearly finished, I reply, so hastily sign off and pay the nice lady what she asks for, 1000 won—85¢—and am on my way when it hits me that the one thing I have really gone there to do I have not done: write to Ellen! I skulk back and plead for just one more. Interlinguistically, the guy indicates, "Well, all right." And I hastily bat out my favorite things to Ell. I am wondering what the big deal here is; I am the only one in the place; there are plenty of spare machines. When the lights start to go out I realize they are *closing*—at 1530! Amazing. Even the smallest hole-in-the wall cafés in Laem Chabang were "OPEN 24 HOURS A DAY"! They refuse further payment and are, I'm sure, glad to see my retreating hat.

Now I had better—it is now really raining *Katzen u. Hunden* and a brisk wind has sprung up—find the stop where my #39 will pick me up. I cross a street filled with—hooray!—civilized and orderly traffic and there's the spot right across the from the big store. I have a hunch I should go in there, but good grief, it is a typhoon out here! OK, I say: Go! And I go back across the street, this time on a handy overpass, and enter the store. It is a veritable wonderland of elegant retail marketing. Lovely Korean ladies at every counter, bowing and greeting, and a directory that lists FRESH FOOD. Well! Having had good luck with these midtown lower level super markets, I head on down. And once again, I can not believe my eyes: an immense, beautiful super market—acres of foods of every description. More Koreans bowing and greeting—wonderful custom. I just laugh out loud. Astonishing! Everything from Campbell's Chicken Noodle Soup to live King crabs, and even a McDonalds. And to top it off, right where it should be: **POPCORN!**

I buy two 2 lb. bags, a bag of chips and a trio of CRUNKY chocolate bars (almost inedible, but the name is worth the price.) Have a chocolate shake and catch the good old #39 (how fond I have already become of this lifeline to the ship) and am soon back home without a mishap. Now that's what I call an outing—and all for just over $10. Korea: a civilized country: you can get change on the bus!

45.

While whipping up the popcorn:

Tip for future travelers of any stripe on any conveyance: Be sure you make the trip *your* trip. It may be difficult, with other passengers eager to share their knowledge and experience and excitement, but take from them what you think you need and use it the way *you* want to. It is too easy to get distracted, talked into side trips—expensive or not (it is *time* here that is the precious

177

commodity)—that you don't really want to take, but for which you feel a sort of "responsibility". No! Aside from common courtesy and politeness, you have no responsibility for their trip. The cost is too high, the time too short; this may well be a once in a lifetime event: it is *your* event.

At least 15 small ships have come into the shelter of this fine harbour, hiding from the typhoon that is expected about midnight. We won't get the brunt of it when it passes to the south, but harbour authorities have advised that we put out more dock lines fore and aft. We already have 6 and 6, but will add another two at each end. Boy! It's blowin' pretty good out there now. If there were large ships at anchor in the harbour, they would probably have to put out to sea; nothing worse than a big tanker dragging her anchor and fetching up at the foot of some high-rise.

Still raining! Ship's crew, stevies, us—all sitting and waiting. Supercargo says only eight hours of loading left, but when? Remember that first sked? Korea on July 1st? New sked says we must leave Japan by July 11th. That's only four days there if we leave here tomorrow. Possible? Does the delay make Long Beach more, or less, likely? Little info forthcoming unless we ask, and SC is the best man. This one is Polish, but speaks very good English and seems a bit more outgoing. Our contentment and curiosity are *not* a priority here, understood. Still, at a meal, sharing knowledge and information might make for quite a popular activity.
Captain's birthday tomorrow—he'll be 47.
Rats! This is the kind of blustery weather I love to drive around in! Tool on out to the point, see what the sea is up to, feel the warmth and security of a cozy car as the wind and rain buffet us about. Still, this nifty cabin is not a bad substitute.

Decision made: everybody back to work. Rain has stopped, still some wind but union says Go. Latest re: Japan. Kobe by 0800 Tuesday, then Osaka, then Yokohama and Hitachi. No word yet on Long Beach.
Me: I take bus ride this p.m. The #39 of course.

Holy doodle! as old sailing buddy Len Irvine would say! I've never been really scared on a city bus route before. I grab the old familiar #39, after calling Ell, and ride it into town again, but don't get off; just go to the end of the line—way out into the villages—about an hour's ride. Then back in again, and through, and past the ship and down the coast—misty, but a very pleasant ride right along the water: ships anchored out, the usual waterfront

178

activities and sights, and all is well until we get to a small fishing village—good, wide tarmac roads so far right on through the village. The bus keeps truckin' along although it looks to me like the road just ends. Nope, it just narrows way down to a skinny concrete, chopped up single lane affair that apparently heads straight up into the woods! I almost say aloud to the driver (I am the only passenger left on the bus): "My God—you're not going up there!" But he does, and it gets steeper and curvier and my heart is in my mouth, my white knuckles gripping the seat as I peer over the lack of shoulder to the sea and the rocks below. Doesn't stop him! On we go, meeting cars and passing cars on wide spots and up and up and around and down and into the next village where the road gets real again for a few yards, then swoops up a long hill and pulls into a parking lot with a lovely lookout and park setting: his turnaround spot. I get out, mosey around a bit and then we are off again, and this time he takes a different route through the smallest village: over the hill and onto an even worse and tinier road—hardly any road at all in spots. Houses virtually on the road, real farm country (with a magpie or two here and there!). Nobody waiting at the bus stops so down we go to meet that few yards of good road, before wheeling up into the wilderness-type eyes-closed "path". This is a 40 foot, big city bus we are talking about here! Driver is whistling away, passes a slow car with its flashers on—no doubt terrified of going any faster—and then we're down and gliding along the coast highway. Some ride! Two hours for a buck eighty.

Back at the ship, great boxes and two cranes (*sans* their booms) are going aboard.

7/7   Early. SUN! Still some haze about but sun shines brightly and we are loading again against a 1400 departure. Yes, we will call at Long Beach. Great! This will extend the trip by a couple of days and will also break up the long haul to Panama. The Captain's enthusiasm seems somewhat restrained at this piece of news.

Last box heaved aboard, stevies head for home in their very nice, quite new cars, cranes are bedded, and we prepare to sail. Climate here best yet—warm, breezy, not too muggy. Even in the rain it is warm. Lovely setting here—this pretty harbour nestled among the hills. Very "western" place—no bikes, few scooters, everybody seems to drive a late model Hyundai or Daewoo. No Japanese cars to be seen. A BMW place downtown, but have yet to see one—or a Mercedes, for that matter. No American cars either. And no "junk" on the road, as in China. Cars are not large: Hyundai Sonata about the biggest I've seen (looks good!), but all seem spiffy and shiny. A well-to-do country, I'd say. And the written language

179

does remind me of our aboriginal pictograms. Wonder if there's a connection. Must investigate Korean history. I think these stevies are well-paid. Very strong union. And I learned that the Hyundai plants are now unionized as well—organizing was banned for a while, causing me to stop buying Hyundais.

Underway. Very hazy, hard to see much except the whole fleet of warships now absent. Every one—gone. Perhaps off to the "front". It appears that they might have been assembling, rather than being based here.

Little nap, there. Still foggy out, sea a bit choppy but doesn't affect us. We are a little heavier now, which helps. 26 hours to Kobe, Japan. "We make barbecue tonight", for the Captain's birthday party.

Ahhh. With any luck, the last party of the voyage! (What a poop I am!) Though the wonderful Marion has decided that the ship should be a "party training camp" for me. Tonight's is still going on down there, but it gets a bit tiresome after while. The Captain did tell a fine story. Some years ago he was Master of a container ship running between Europe and North America. On one trip their first stop was to be Halifax. It was April and icebergs were not an uncommon sight. The six passengers were very interested and asked the captain to tell them when the ship was to pass an iceberg, as they wanted both to see it and to "make photos". At about 0400 one morning the Captain was on the bridge and noticed on the radar what looked like a large iceberg. He waited a while to confirm it—no lights, the right size, and all. He had made previous arrangements with the steward that he, the captain, would tell the steward of the iceberg and the steward would wake the passengers. So, good as his word, he woke the steward, who, as it happens, had been partying until 0300 and was now very fast asleep. The steward roused himself as best he could, donned his white jacket and proceeded, some-what woozily, to knock on the doors of the passengers. They, in turn, roused themselves (all on the same corridor) and when they were assembled, the steward said simply: "Ice cream!" There was some consternation, but two of the passengers got dressed and repaired to the dining room. An hour or so later at about 0500, the captain sent the A/B on his fire watch rounds and—lo!—there were the two passengers sitting in the dimlit mess room. "What are you doing here?" the A/B asked. "The steward invited us down for ice cream", one trusting passenger replied.
I must say that when the captain or Renand tells us a joke or a funny story, their telling of it is at least half the fun—and there is no way to duplicate that.

180

Now it rains again, but perhaps it will clear away the fog. One route to Kobe from Masan is to the north of Kitakyushu, through the strait between Honshu and Kyushu Islands, up the inland sea past Hiroshima, and into Kobe, Osaka, etc. But a pilot is required almost the whole way—at great cost—$3,000! So the captain has opted, given the fact that we don't have to be in Kobe until 0800 Tuesday morning, to run south, all the way around Kyushu, up the Pacific coast and then into Kobe. Yes, it will take about 12 hours more, use up 18 or 19 tons of fuel, but even at $2,000, will still save Herr Rickmers a thousand or so. That's what a captain does! So we'll be in Kobe at about 1800 tomorrow.

We will be in Long Beach on July 24, but "for only a few hours", then head for Panama for Aug. 1 and Houston probably the 4th or 5th. Well, I'll miss Dan's Splash bash but won't have to sweat trying to make it in time.

7/8   What a treat! Crystal clear weather. Not a fog or a smog or a mist or a haze in sight, and the first sighting of Japan off to port: very high cloud-capped mountain with low-lying rugged shoreline around it. Have no idea where we are in our rounding of Kyushu, but will find out.

Still trouble with the gut—mine. Don't think it's the fruit. My diet, of course, is as usual rotten—mostly meat. almost no veggies, except potatoes and popcorn. Drinking 6 to 8 glasses a day, about half of that water. No other symptoms. Will consult with Ellen ASAP.

Today is day 90 of the trip. This is possible? I can't believe it.

Bit of excitement last evening as we eat barbecue on the poop deck. A ship appears off to starboard, headed generally across our path. It comes nearer and nearer and doesn't change course, nor do we, and we watch, at first with interest, and then—especially the captain, who is sitting with us—with the beginnings of concern. Both ships still bowling along. Suddenly the captain jumps up and heads for the bridge where the Chief Officer is on watch, we hope. We are still waiting for the blast of somebody's whistle, but the ships are less than a mile apart now and still making full knots. Then BIBI starts to turn away in an obvious "hard port rudder" maneuver and the other ship which may or may not have (a) seen us, or (b) changed her own course, crosses behind us.

There ensues a brief discussion of collisions at sea (y'heard the one about the aircraft carrier and the lighthouse?). I think probably the Chief had already started the evasive action when the Captain arrived. Actually, too, I believe we were the burdened vessel as the other was approaching from the right—or is that only with car traffic?

We remarked on what a memorable birthday *that* would have been for the Captain: "Oh, yes, I recall my 47th—that's when we crashed into that ship in the East China Sea!"

Weather is so fickle; we are now heading into rain squalls while the sun shines merrily on.

46.

31°19'N x 131°43'E (at sea)

At about 1030 today we rounded the foot of Kyushu and headed north again, past Kyushu and Shikoku which puts us right out in the Pacific Ocean with its long fetch to California and its resulting swells. Since we are headed pretty much across the seas there is considerable rolling going on with the usual sounds of things sliding and falling and slamming. Soon, everything battenable is secured and the only thing to do is walk carefully from handhold to handhold. (Which reminds me: in China someplace I was watching the translated names on trucks going by and one company was named HENG ON. I thought it most apropos of driving in China.)

But it's a beautiful sunny day. With this long trip around the edge of Japan, it will be late tonight when we tie up in Kobe. As long as we are loadable at 0800 tomorrow we will be fine. Marion decided to "live in her room" for lunch—a "little tummy trouble", says Hans. Hmmm. It's interesting but none of us has been seasick at all—and I don't think that's Marion's problem now.

A Big Mama roll of the ship sent a pile of CDs to the floor, scattered my stack of Renand's magazines across the office (they were already on the floor!), and lifted the radio right off the desk, again suspending it in midair by its lashing line. Now we are slowed right down and seem to have changed heading from north to south (?). Better run up to the bridge and find out what's what—just in case they need some help.

No problem. We're running early so we'll drift for a few hours, engine stopped. Definitely an easier movement to the ship. We'll "waste a little time" says the Chief.

Nope. Take it all back. Ship has—of course!—drifted directly broadside to the swell and the roll is worse than ever. I think the bridge better put at least a little way on here to keep our head to the swell. (Moments later:) Yes! Ship is moving very slowly, heading up and into the swell. Swell! You do understand that it ain't the comfort

182

of the passengers at stake here; it's the welfare of those millions of dollars worth of cargo down there!

Renand cleaning the bathroom—he has to: I have nothing to clean it with! We chat. He works an average of 15 hours a day, every day, for a year. (His contract.) He serves the officers' and passengers' meals, cooks sometimes at breakfast, cleans the cabins of passengers and officers, does the Captain's laundry and ironing, delivers orders for Slop Chest purchases, etc., etc., etc. He gets no days off, no vacation (evenings in port, he can go ashore when there is time). For these tasks he earns $276 a month—$3,312 per year (US). His contract stipulates "open overtime", i.e., unlimited overtime when required. The way this works is that he must work more than 20 hours overtime per week before he gets paid for any overtime—and then it is only for the hours over the 20. But the allotment for overtime for this ship is limited and he is now owed for at least 20 hours from last month. He gets the same salary whether or not there are passengers to take care of. We four are the first passengers on the BIBI since he began his contract in October of 2001. Some ships pay the steward extra for passengers. He will of course receive "tips" from the four of us when we leave the ship—$2 per day is suggested by the literature, but none of us can really swing that. I will give him $120 when I go; the Kments will, I hope, be able to improve on that. To get this position—the lowest paid on the ship—he had to work for a year in the personnel placement office in the Philippines as a sort of "man Friday"—*without pay*. He has two brothers on ships as well, has done many things, but still prefers the sea.

7/9   Awakened at 0325. Pitch dark. Ship moving slowly. Crew setting up pilot ladder. Lights around us in the distance.

Awakened at 0615. Pilot ladder still up. Ship moving very slowly through viscous sea. Rain. Vague land shapes in distance. No real land to be seen. We seem to be waiting. For pilot? I thought he was coming at 0400. Someone said the pilot would be with us for 3 hours. We load in less than 2 hours. Is pilot here? Why are we moving so slowly? Shall I rise and find out? ("Do I dare to eat a peach?")

Ah, a city comes into view—waterfront cranes (always the first things you see), ships at anchor. And we *are* waiting for the pilot.

Now we are stopped. Chief Officer goes again to the ladder to greet the pilot. But no pilot! And no pilot boat in sight. Bosun now also on deck. He looks up at my window; we wave. Super chap. Aha! small fast boat appears off port bow. Pilot?

Hmmm. *Two* small fast boats—one says PILOT, the other is orange. Pilot gets off PILOT boat, another guy comes down to the deck, gets aboard orange boat. *Two* pilots? Customs guy? Hmm. Mysteries of the sea. I obviously slept through something; must stop that!

City of Kobe spread out along the shore as far as the eye can see. Sky overcast, but weather balmy, no rain. We move at "top speed" (this is top harbour speed which is 5 or 6 knots slower than open sea top speed).

I am looking at Japan! Culprit of Pearl Harbour, victim of the A-bombs. Did ships leave Kobe on that "surprise" mission to Hawaii? Did the Enola Gay fly over Kobe to present "Little Boy" to the awakening city of Hiroshima on that August morning? This is that "land of the rising sun" I heard so much about as a pre-teen. We passed Bungo Strait during the night—mentioned in several epic war films.

35°N x135°E (Kobe)

We are tied up. A small motor boat carried the first of our lines to shore and a spiffy little truck dragged it to the bollard—never mind trying to wrestle these hawsers—bigger around than my leg—by hand. Classy! I suspect that Kobe and Osaka are essentially the same large port—looks that way on the chart, so this one stop may suffice for both. It begins to rain as our cargo arrives—not only on the quay but on barges on the sea side of the ship.

Some distance off the port bow we have a well-equipped amusement park—huge Ferris wheel, great roller coaster with two loops, etc., and dead ahead the elevated tracks of an LRT. In the distance the "Big Ben" chimes are heard—a bit late for 0800—5 minutes, to be exact—and only ringing three times. Hmm. Perhaps speaking in Japanese.

On the quay, the stevedores are lined up doing morning exercises.

Some amazing loading going on. Shackles—the biggest I've seen yet—far too big for men to carry, and slings that require a second crane to hook them to our Jumbo.

Kobe: The Automatic City! Quick trip to *Sonnamiya* (downtown) on the "el"—tickets at a machine, train with no driver (like Vancouver), bank virtually all automated—not a teller or manager in sight, just a very nice woman who keeps saying, I think, "May I help?" She even knows where the "lavatory" is—for all the good it does me. In the seventies and eighties I drove a diesel car and when you drive a diesel car you better either be aware of where you can get fuel, or keep a very sharp eye out for a diesel pump and fill up whenever you see one. Now, with my tummy trouble, it is a matter of keeping a very sharp lookout for handy "lavatories" and not letting "the call" become too urgent. In this case, if it hadn't been for the "handicapped" booth, I have no idea what I would have done. The "sit down" stalls (women's, too, I learned later from Marion) have this rather bizarre tiled appliance in the floor. It's only a few inches high. What on earth . . . ? Is it to squat? And just how do you manage that? (Marion said it was ok going down; it was the getting up that gave her pause.) A moment of panic until I spy the sign for handicapped. I certainly am, and make myself at home.

Then I break down—who can blame me?—and grab a bite at McDonalds. In this part of the world, us foreigners order by pointing at pictures on a card. As usual, the fries had to be made up specially, but then were delivered to me in the downstairs dining room.

Finally find an Internet facility and try to call up Dan's website. Instead, get a full menu of porn flicks and other junk and can't get rid of it. Turn the rotten machine right off and re-boot. Unusual Yahoo screen, unusual blanks for ID and password, and ultimately, no go. Do it again and again. Still no go. Everything in Japanese of course. Given the size and nature of this automatic city, I suspect some new-fangled bells and whistles have been added making the whole affair impenetrable to me. Head back to the *Sonnamiya* LRT station, which is part of the central rail complex, having only the vaguest memory of which way to turn, where to cross the street, what door and what escalator, etc., but vagueness is often the best way: I just let my sort of under-conscious compass guide my steps, and voila! finally arrive at the automatic ticket machine. I do stop on the way and try the automatic phone for Ellen. Bad idea! She'd just gotten the latest automatic telephone bill and could not be placated (it's her Scottish ancestry, I think). "$3.15 a minute from China, and $5 to set up the call!". She now loves the e-mail with unbridled parsimony. Well, I'll do my best but I'm not sure she quite understands the concept of wandering through Oriental streets—streets bedecked with a million pictograms in Thai, Arabic, Viet Namese, Chinese, Korean, or Japanese—looking desperately for something resembling "PC" or "Internet". I don't mind a friendly ramble when I have plenty of time, but today we sail at 1600;

185

deadline for return is 1500 and I ain't at my best doing the e-mail trudge. Actually, this will make the big surprise easier. Let's see: e-mail from Yokohama, maybe from Hitachi saying we're off trans-Pac-ing, then maybe something from Long Beach, being really vague about length of stay, possible other ports, time through the Canal, etc. etc. then nothing until a phone call from Long Harbour on Salt Spring, with apologies for using the phone, but . . .

Well, ship is all loaded and buttoned up. Other three not back yet: still looking for postcards and stamps I'll bet.

Funny sensation yesterday. Up on the bridge deck I glance upward and from the mast is flying that erstwhile "dreaded symbol of all that is sneaky and evil"—the red sun on the white ground—the Nippon flag. The big red zero. How things do change. But I doubt that we will ever be able to take the awful swastika with the same equanimity.

Actually, the Kobe LRT is not. It may be "light" and it is "transit" but it is not particularly rapid, except that it's above the traffic. That's because it doesn't run on rails, but on rubber tires rolling on elevated wooden roadbeds just wide enough for the wheels. Switching requires side guide rails to move the train from one "track" to another. There are guide rails all the way along, of course. Wonder why they opted for this. Let's see: two "tracks", two guide rails and a "third" rail for the power, plus the cumbersome switching. All instead of two steel rails plus the "third". Cheaper? In Japan with its massive steel industry? Hmmm. Plus, I would think there'd be the risk of the occasional flat tire. Of course the cars themselves might be cheaper, not requiring the heavy steel "trucks" and wheels needed for rail travel. Still, very nice trains.

We're off and running—literally! Running before a sizeable ty-phoon, with winds rumoured to be around 260 k., that is predicted to overtake us about 2100 tonight. Nobody is announcing it formally. (They never tell us nothin'!) but everybody's talking about it and scuttlebutt is sometimes, once in a while, occasionally, right. Just in case, will double batten all my hatches and put the valuables on the floor. Yokohama is less than 24 hours away by my reckoning.

I am never quite sure whether to credit the latest news or instructions. Our last—Korean—shore pass stated "Next Port: Osaka". In fact, the next port was Kobe. It is true that Osaka is but a stone's throw from Kobe, but we won't be stopping there. So I just watch and wait. Matter of fact this lovely bay is home to the following cities—and they're all ports with no space between them at all: Akashi, Kobe, Nishinomiya, Amagasaki, Osaka, Sakai, and Kishiwada. So, once again, a bit of misinformation is gobbled up by this passenger who is thirsting for the hard stuff. Humbug!

47.

Well, we're in it now! Rain, wind and rolling to beat the band. My leaky front window is running a small stream. Everything secured—I hope. Klaus wanted a typhoon; he's got one! Hope the Captain won't regret not staying in the bay until this was past. A day more would have done it. Well, we have no deck cargo, so nothing to lose overboard this time. But the CD player goes merrily on—a little Mahler, a little Brahms. What would I do without it?

Just before midnight: ALARM BELLS SOUNDING! One - two - three - four - five - six - seven - - - - - - - nothing! Not the emergency signal that would have us all on the poop deck—in this case, the "weather" deck! There should have been a long one after the seven shorts. I dress anyway. Nothing happens. Five minutes go by. Then 12 rings in a row—doesn't mean anything. The ship still gambols along, rocking and rolling like there's no tomorrow. Nobody's been asleep. Are you kidding? Still nothing happens. A door slams someplace. Five more minutes. Now nine rings in a row—means nothing (I keep telling myself). The guy in the next cabin, the 3rd engineer, is on watch, and his closet door is banging in rhythm with the ship's motion. Nothing else is happening. I peek out into the corridor. Nothing. There is no danger to the ship; she has been through much worse, I'm sure. Just damned uncomfortable and inconvenient for sleeping—or anything! Does seem like a funny—or *not* so funny—time to test the damn bells! Now I'm up and dressed and no place to go—thank goodness! Lights were turned on in the lounge below me, illuminating the river-running deck and frothing bow wave. Now they've gone off. I'm going back to bed, "perchance to . . ."

7/10 Violent rolling stopped during the night, probably with a course change. Still stormy out there with heavy sometime rain and a wonderfully flowing leak in the window! Wind and mist over the gray sea. But we charge along, heaving spray right and left and giving no quarter. Dropped off to sleep sometime and actually did quite well. Hope Marion, two decks up, is faring well, too. 3rd engineer, off watch at midnight, quickly secured his errant door and then I could hear only my own creaks and groans—and those of the ship as well. Will try for some more sack time.

Still rain, but we are ahead of the lagging typhoon and should be safely in Yokohama in three hours or so when it passes by. Weather is at our back as we head up into Tokyo *Wan*, and we are making 20 knots! Slept most of the night; leaky window has left

187

huge patch of soaking carpet, but—hey—this is a ship and it's only water. Will dry off in a week or so (actually it was gone in a couple of days) but must contrive to get the thing fixed.

The city of Hitachi—36°30' x 140°37'—appears to be north of Tokyo near Mito and a good way inland. This—or a port nearby—will be our final stop before the Pacific.

They say—pulling teeth again —two days in Yoko . Will head immediately for Internet café.

And I did discover two things: (1) because of the downpour last night, the big hatch between the house and the funnel housing, usually open to help ventilate the engine spaces, was closed to keep out the rain. This caused a buildup of hot air which set off the automatic fire alarm. I needn't have worried, but it was exciting all the same. And (2) that wasn't the real typhoon, only a preview; the real thing is still lurking off to the south, but heading our way.

Entering Yokohama roads where we will anchor overnight to ride out the typhoon. All large ships in this harbour will either put to sea or anchor out, even those now berthed. Typhoon due at about midnight. We should be able to enter the port tomorrow afternoon. Then two days here put us into Hitachi not before Saturday the 13th. Don't know how long we'll bc there. It's a relief to be in a safe anchorage for the bad weather.

So the Captain was quite correct in getting us out of Kobe and into Yokohama before the real typhoon hit. Good for him! (I do believe he knows a bit more than he lets on.)

The rolling ship causes stories to be told. Almost all of us have chased oranges around the floor as the capricious ship continues to roll them off in new directions, but Klaus had a tale he called "Chain Reaction". At the height of the tumult last night, he went into his fridge for a can of beer, set it on top, as he needed both hands to close and lock the fridge. When he looked up, the beer was gone—rolling across the floor. He chased it, grabbed it, and opened it with a flourish: a geyser of foam erupted, covering him nicely. He adjourned to the bathroom for a rinse, but not before pouring the rest of the beer into a glass. When he returned, there was the glass: gone! Nothing for it but to start again—this time successfully.

In the anchorage now; I count at least 26 ships on the hook.

At anchor. Another sleek pilot boat with, I'm sure, a female deck hand. The pilot, who clambers over the rail in any weather, and up or down a rope ladder, must have been in his 50s. The Captain says we could now go in tomorrow morning or noon time.

Yes! The window is fixed No leaky! You see, there are four clamps that hold the window shut, one at the top, two at the side and one at the bottom. The top three can be loosened easily as they have large turnable steel rings, but the bottom one, for some reason, requires a special "key" or wrench—just like the one that was missing from the cabin. I managed by sheer ingenuity to loosen the lower clamp, but could not tighten it firmly again. Thus, perhaps, the leak. Borrowed Klaus's wrench. Voila! But I must get one of my own. The sign above the window says ESCAPE WINDOW, but without the wrench . . .

Rain has begun and we, and the now 40 or 50 ships at anchor, await the big blow.

Lamb for supper. Not bad.

Well, this trip seems to consist of "almosts", and that idiot leak is *almost* fixed. Can't screw the clamp any tighter, but still there is a steady slow drip. (Maybe it's me!) But it is really bucketing down now—a genuine typhoon rain storm, and the leak is not nearly so bad as last night. Wind has also picked up, can feel this great hull being buffeted.

Real rivers of rainwater run down the deck at either side of the holds. No place for it to run off except aft and the river is as wide as the walkway. I can see all this because every floodlight on the ship is lighting up decks and hatches and cranes and the slashing currents of rain. To sleep.

7/11   Moving! Tug! Brilliant sun—blue sky. Typhoon? What typhoon? All gone.

35°06'N x 139°45'E (Yokohama)

Tied up—Japanese puttered out in a small boat again and fetched our first line. A mounted black and white checkered flag signals: "This is your berth". Generally we just look for men waiting, cargo laid out, trucks lined up, etc. We are almost underneath one of the two beautiful suspension bridges spanning the harbour area.

To tugs KATORI and MYOKO MARU, Yokohama:

THE TUG: She appears from nowhere, is suddenly there, impatient and muscular, shouldering aside the sea in order to get closer; keeps pace, lifting, falling away, nosing in; then, nearly at quayside, takes a line and waits 'til you are at just the right place: a nudge, a push, a pull, then puts her nose to the hull and with great thrashing and roiling simply pushes the 584 feet of this ship sideways into its waiting berth. Oh so

189

gentle, ready to pull back if needed, then when you touch the quay, she leans against you, going no place, just pushing,, holding you against the pier until she gets some invisible sign that all lines are made fast. Then she relaxes, drops her line, backs away, lifts her skirts and shows you her sleek, low rump as she skates off to make the next ship snug and welcome.

Stevies here all wearing white puttees! Very chic! Later in town: school girls wearing thickly-bunched white socks around their ankles—looking like the stevedores—except for the legs.

Trip into town, but back aboard to sail at 1900. Same day! Yokohama is far and away the most explosive retail city I've ever seen! Enormous department stores—three in a matter of blocks—we're talking multi-story emporia here—all thronged with people. Never saw such a selection of stuff: thousands of pairs of women's shoes, four and a half floors of "Ladies fashion" in one store alone. In the *Sogo* Store I come upon a delightful Tea Lounge and, sitting in the middle of it is a sleek Yamaha grand piano playing all by itself! Electronic, of course, and I am tempted to sit at it, make my fingers move, and impress the gentle guests.

Absolutely acres and acres of shopping, plus underground "BAZAR" and then there are all the streets and avenues with more. Nothing poor about this city—this country! Pay $18.32 (2,100 yen) for Internet time—the most expensive yet anyplace, and have some trouble at first getting an English Yahoo screen. When I do, I e-mail everybody I can think of only to discover later that all the messages came through in total gobbledegook. Rats!

Spend all the money I have with me ($20.00) at this place and no bank in sight will honor any of my three Mastercards (one Platinum, another Platinum Plus) for a cash advance. Have just enough cash for a small packet of not very good Oreos. But as usual, wonderful people-watching and an adventure with a violin:

She is carrying a violin case.
Obviously heading someplace
A rehearsal? A concert?
If I follow her, maybe she could lead me to
A rehearsal? A concert?
Always looking for music—
Live music, real music,
Maybe some sort of
Rehearsal or Concert.
Loose cover, that's my game.
Too loose: she ducks into a dress shop,

190

And is gone!

Not put off by the disappearing violinist, I follow the signs to what just might be a concert hall on the top floor of this store. I ride up about nine stories by escalator, and here is the large, multipurpose hall! People are milling about; smiling young ladies sit at tables outside the main doors. I approach one of them; she smiles, says in English, "May I help you?" I say, "What is going on here?" I am ready for a recital— koto? shakuhachi?. "This is a job fair," she replies. We laugh. "May I go in?", I ask. "Certainly." I do. Yes, it is a job fair. I come back out, turn again to her wonderful smile, "Nothing for me," I say, and, both of us chuckling, take my leave,

I wander around, watching, listening; sit under a tree and read a bit, then amble back to our meeting spot, sit down in a busy plaza at the edge of a garden.
Write:

> *My feet hurt.*
> *I am sitting on the*
> *Stone rail around*
> *Some outdoor sculpture.*
> *I look down at my feet.*
> *I think I'll take my shoes off.*
> *My shoes are resting on the ground;*
> *The ground is paved with bricks laid*
> > *out in pleasant patterns.*
> *I look at the bushes.*
> *People walk by.*
> *I hear a voice speaking a language*
> > *I don't understand.*
> *Children play a little distance away.*
> *I understand their cries and laughter.*
> *I raise my eyes.*
> *More people go by.*
> *Old people, young people, students,*
> > *businessmen.*
> *One large lady,*
> *Many small ladies.*
> *An airplane flies overhead.*
> *A car horn toots.*
> *The subway disgorges more people.*
> *Music! I hear music!*
> *It's gone.*
> *More people go by.*
> *I am in front of a large department*
> > *store*
> *With an interesting name: TAKASHIMAYA.*

I look closely at these ordinary, everyday
special people.
They are all Japanese!
Every one of them!
No wonder:
Here I am in Yokohama!
I take my shoes off.

Here comes the group and we move to the cab stand. Japanese taxicabs; WOW! All black, all of them. All Toyotas—large ones like the Cressida but not called that. One called a "Comfort". All very shiny, immaculate inside and out, white lace covers on all seats. Driver with white shirt, coat and tie, he can open the back doors from his seat. *Very* impressive cars. Hate to get out when we reach the ship.

We all rush to the bridge after supper to catch a glimpse of Mount Fuji. And there she is! Not snow-capped at this time of year, just standing magnificently with a layer of clouds wreathing her, but not obscuring that famous peak. I glimpsed her when we came in this morning, but, without the snow, I thought it was "just a mountain".

48.

Twelve hours to Hitachi—which I still have not seen on a chart or map, only in a directory a few days ago. Apparently this is a very small port, but with quite a lot of cargo for us, all going to Newport News, Virginia. (I'll just have to trust them to get it off by themselves; I'll be gone by then. *sigh*)

Well, damn! Our favorite officer, Chief Engineer Andrezej Solohub (he of the gallstones) left the ship today and we—at least I—never bade him farewell. We were so eager to flee the ship this morning that we never gave it a thought. Of course, he was supposed to leave in Singapore, I think, but kept hanging in 'til they found a replacement, so after asking him at every port, we began neglecting to do that). I feel badly. He was such a sterling fellow.

Just up on the bridge. *Still* haven't located this Hitachi place! Next chart will probably show it. It is still a strange feeling: this great 17,000 ton ship hurtling through the night without being able to *see* anything! Pitch black out there, not a light to be seen. Of course the reliable radars are hard at work seeing 10 or 12 miles in every direction. Still, "looking" out those windows, feeling the ship plunging through the seas, and seeing nothing at all can be a bit unnerving. In the darkness of the bridge itself, with its eerily glowing consoles, even the talk is quiet and low, and quite cozy-sounding.

We are gradually leaving Tokyo *Wan* or Bay and turning north again into the broad Pacific. My guess is that the leftover typhoon swells will give us some unpleasant movement tonight. Will batten down again.

For some reason one of the deck lights just went on and I could see the terrific smashing these waves are taking off our bows. There is a stiff breeze blowing out there and occasionally a bow wave smasheroony comes right on board. It could be an interesting 12 hours to this mysterious port of Hitachi.

7/12 The mystery is solved. Hitachi is, indeed, a city inland from here. The actual point of land to which we are now headed is Kobachi Hana, but our berth will be in the "Port of Hitachi" and is, as noted, north of Mito. This is our final "foreign" port (for me anyway); from here we head straight across the vast Pacific. Let's hope it lives up to its pacific name! We'll remain at virtually the same latitude—36° to 37°—all the way across to Long Beach, our 20th port, including Houston.

Another lovely day—the night was indeed pacific, except in my gut, but it settled down after while. Bad day for eating and drinking yesterday. Must do better. Nothing to drink from 0800 to 1800 and really felt the loss. And nothing to eat either except those unfortunate Oreos. Stupid me—took only $20 with me; usually—*always* take $50. Dumb!

The flying fish are out in welcoming fleets.

36°30'N x 141°30'E (Port of Hitachi)

And here we are! This may be a small port, but it has the biggest derrick I've ever seen—an enormous orange boom with HITACHI printed on its flank. And the Japanese stevedores, so fond of working together in groups, are a study in teamwork as they hoist and attach the huge slings and shackles to lift a gigantic box into our hold.

There is a small, charming, delightful, inspiring, cozy Japanese village called Kujihama just a stone's throw from the ship. The Kments ride their bikes (for the first time) into the village; Klaus and I will go in by cab this p.m. Looks like we sail tomorrow evening.

My dream has come true! This place is the real thing: gardens, topiary, "proper" roofs, Finches in a cage by the front door, shoji screens inside. And the quiet! Just an ordinary country village, but after more than three months of almost ceaseless noise and tumult, it is a dream!

Klaus and I taxi in in the usual spiffy black, shiny cab and when we get out of the car, I just stand there, basking in the quiet. Quite an experience. We part as usual and I meander. A huge crow, just naturally mouthing off, but in Japanese, with a voice so like a woman's I think somebody is in trouble! Tiny railway station with regular one-car electric "trains" gliding silently in and out (the really fast trains can be seen whizzing along in the distance on the side of a hill).

I purchase two lovely rice bowls in a little shop with the sweetest proprietor imaginable. She watches me, smiling and curious, as I tour her shop, looking over all the bowls and finally choosing two. She wraps them carefully and, eschewing the usual plastic bag, smiles with delight and gives me a special paper "shopping" bag. She is most interested that the bowls are going back to Canada, and even gives me a discount.

I find myself back at the little railway station. Trains and ships run neck and neck in my affections and after, shilly-shallying for a while and unable to read a word of the schedules or prices (ticket office open 0645 to 0940 and 1551 to 1956), can no longer resist, so muster up my courage and just get on the next "train" that comes in. The conductor seems to understand my ticketlessness and allows me to pay him. After 4 stops or so (about a twenty minute ride) I jump off to wait for a returning train. Just a wee crossroads, almost no activity about, and when exactly will that "returning" train arrive? No idea. Klaus and I are to meet at 1700 for the taxi ride back and I look nervously at my watch. I pace and peer up the single track that curves away into the woods. Suddenly, there it is—silently moving into view. I get on—back on, really: it is the same train, but now a second car has been added and is full of school girls. We roll through the countryside and when we reach Kujihama, I pay again and depart.

Oops! My financial resources are running a bit low. I didn't count on the silly train ride.

I meet Klaus who beckons to me from across the street. He has discovered a *Kendo* class for very young children. All dressed in black bottoms and white tops, cloth bands around their heads, these meter high warriors take turns beating on their master—invisible behind all his padding—with bamboo sticks, and shouting something "frightening". What a delightful racket. Cutest thing yet!

This afternoon is the perfect way to end my stay in Japan—and my trip through foreign parts: the quiet, the birds singing, children laughing, people chatting. Perfect!

I do not have quite enough yen to cover the cab fare back (Klaus paid when we came in), so I ask Klaus to cover for me. I pay him right back when we return to the ship—an accustomed occurrence among us four.

Never mind . We are back, and something very technical is going on on the pier next to the ship. We all had to be back by 1800, though we probably won't sail until tomorrow evening.

Well, here's a new one. Both the Captain and the Chief Officer advise us—at separate times—that we are confined to the ship for the night while two giant boilers (or something) on the quay are X-rayed. We thought they wanted to detect any flaws before they put them aboard tomorrow, but in the end, they don't put them anyplace! They just stay there, covered with tarps and a rough housing.

7/13 Nobody got caught in the X-Rays last night.

I just now took a stroll around this big quay, watched the folks fishing, checked out a tug that came foaming in to empty its trash, and came across a sign on a gate in English: DO NOT KEEP OPENING.

The last box is about to go into #3—probably the last piece of cargo to be loaded until the ship gets to Europe. ('Til then it's all discharging—Long Beach, Houston, New Orleans, Newport News.) It's a big moment—and just a bit scary. It means we're ready to tackle the world's largest ocean—11 days without a stop or a sight of land. But after those 11 days I'll be home, really. Speaking fluently, instead of sort of grade schoolese (I'm sure the Germans aboard will feel the same way, after I've gone; they can get back to the real thing) and spending money without having to convert it, and best of all I will, soon thereafter, be on my island, in my little house, with my lady. It will have been four months. Who would have believed it?

"Beginning of sea passage"—official entry in ship's log. All of us stand now on the bridge wings to say farewell to Japan, Asia, lovely Kujihama—and land! Tugs pull us out backwards, swing us about and head us on our way, then with a burst of foam under their tails the EITAI and the KAMAKURA scurry back into the harbour to await their next guest.

Every time we leave a port, I have the feeling I've forgotten something.

Course now 90°—due east, but we'll do a little northing, I think, after a bit—the circle route, as they say. Very romantic when a ship sails—even a beat up old tramp like our BIBI. People watch from shore—just wondering, I suppose: where she's going, where she's been, who are those two old geezers with the gray beards? I'll put on John Arpin's *Muss i' denn* when I go down. The Kments sang it on the bridge as we pulled away: "I must go . . ." I hummed along.

49.

7/14   "Bastille Day" finds us under brilliant sun and hazy cloud cover plunging into the Pacific, 12 hours on our way with a following sea and a gentle roll. The weather looks good for the crossing; we will head slightly north to skirt a building low—as Ocean Routes suggests. No special prep last night for the long voyage—we just sailed away as we have sailed away 20 times before.

We have two new officers on board now, both the Chief and 2nd engineers, both Polish, the 2nd with courtly manners (he kissed Marion's hand when he met her) and nice strong face, and the new Chief who arrived in Kobe, and is still a bit shy. Found out why: he had only been home a month from a previous one-year contract, when they grabbed him again. Mind you, we are never introduced to these new people, and know who they are only from where they sit at mealtimes. I have not yet met the new Chief, but at least so far he seems a far cry from his rollicking predecessor with the gallstones. So far on this trip, these two, plus the fitter, the electrician, the Chief and 3rd officers, and 2 or 3 seamen have come aboard as replacements.

Sunday on the ship: a day off when possible and "*eis*" (ice cream) for lunch.

We recalled yesterday that the ship was built in Japan—don't know just where—and its original Hitachi engine still powers us. Speaks well for Hitachi if its engine can run virtually non-stop for 23 years!

Good sleep last night. Up and down a couple of times, but no real reason to get up, so . . . much reflection on the trip and more.

38°N x 146°30'E (at sea)

I am sleeping the whole day!   (Seems always to happen after we leave a port.) All morning, then lunch, then all afternoon! A real sleep deficit, I guess—plus that old cradle-rocking motion of this fine ship. Outside, pea soup fog! Can't even see the bow, yet it is a shallow sea fog and the sun does penetrate now and then.

Despite the fog, the barbecue tradition goes on. No idea what it will be like on the poop deck.

196

BBQ was all right—stacks of pork chops. The others still down there, but I "have a meeting" (Marion—ultra-perceptive Marion—says, "Yes, I know—you always have a meeting at this time.") Still heavy fog. Tomorrow may be our "repeat" day—the International Date Line approaches.

7/15 Still fog! Reminded the Captain that we, the passengers, were unable to *see anything* in this fog. He apologized, but said it wasn't very interesting to see anyway. Still the sea remains calm, little motion to the ship, just enough so you are aware that you are moving and being gently rocked. It may be hard to get used to sleeping in a stationary bed after 100 plus days at sea.

40°07'N x 154°51'E (at sea)

At lunch, conversation about Han's Czech (*Sudetenland*) roots, the Kments' friends escaping to the West from Leipzig (Marion still won't say how they did it!). Fascinating.

Also news (rumour!) that today will not be repeated; next Sunday will, so we shall have two July 21sts.

Tonight I feel very lonely and depressed—I am (again!) weary of this routine, I desperately want some pancakes with maple syrup instead of the everlasting beef and sauces and stuff. I don't want to eat, but must, and I don't think we'll ever get across this ruddy ocean, plus we have to add a day, and I get afraid that my "inner" resources are drying up. For the first time, I didn't have music in the afternoon—maybe that's it! There are now certain CDs that I don't want to hear any more. No sun all day, just fog and mist and gray, gray seas and sky. And this gut thing just keeps on. Am taking double calcium at Ellen's suggestion, but no change yet.

7/16 Ah, the invisible Pacific! More fog and occasional rain. but we plow ever onward, taking a northern circle route. Mood improved. Finding that I rather dread going down for meals—the necessary camaraderie gets on my wick after a while. But my music, even if it's all pretty familiar, helps. Sometimes it carries over, even to meal times when I will enter humming, or unconsciously hum a bar to break my slight prandial tension.

Sometimes I wonder if it might not have been better to have fellow passengers who were more or less tyros like me, rather than vastly experienced adventurers who've seen and done it all. Sort of like, "We've seen the world; now we'll go around it. " And in Klaus's case—again!

Well, the big news today—out here in this mind-bogglingly enormous expanse of water—will be (a) whether the Kments get their

197

toilet fixed, and (b) whether Klaus got through to his son, Uwe, last night. (Yes and yes.)

Fog has lifted for the moment, and the Captain was right again: it's not very interesting out there—all water and sky!

Omigod! The scrapers are at it again! Just what we need to make this scintillating ocean crossing more enjoyable.
Sun!
A ship!
(small pleasures)

40°51'N x 163°38'E" (At sea)

We chat some more about "money-making ideas: McRice for McDonalds. and the "Orange-opening School" on Salt Spring. These two ideas should, Marion feels, make us "very rich".
We are nearing our closest point to Hawaii—and are not letting the hapless Captain forget it!

7/17 Arose for brekkies—a little bit of fluid for the pills and, to start the day, some (splendidly rediscovered) scrambled eggs! Klaus told us of his sighting of a school of dolphins this morning. Must keep an eye out.

41°34'N x 172°216'E (At sea)

Hey! *Fog!* What d'ya know? What a drab day!

7/18 We are about to cross the International Date Line (IDL). Our position now is 179°43'E which means another 17 minutes of longi-ltude—i.e., 17 miles—to go, about an hour. So, at about 0900, it will suddenly be yesterday again. Don't know how the Captain will arrange it. Obviously, we won't have two Sundays, as one rumour had it. I prefer just to say, "set your calendar back a day."
Still overcast and smooth. What a crossing! Perfect—ok, perfect for sleeping!—just a lulling rock in the great cradle of the sea. Gut still weird, but can't seem to do anything about it, so . . .
No brekkies today—no real appetite—even our OJ doesn't appeal—water will do.

7/17 Bingo! It is now yesterday! Instead of my being 19 hours ahead of Ellen, I am now 5 hours behind her and will gradually catch up until we reach Long Beach when we will be, again, on the same time. I will have reset my watch at least 24 times, losing an hour each time—except for that reversal after Singapore.

Fascinating! Imagine somebody "inventing" this whole system. Note that the IDL—the line itself—never passes over land, never crosses populated areas, always over uninhabited water so it can never affect daily activities or business. So now it is Wednesday the 17th all over again. The GPS on the radar moved from 179°59'59"E almost immediately to 179°59'59"W and is now moving "backward". The Captain has ordained that Thursday, the 18th will be the day repeated. It really doesn't matter a hoot out here. I prefer to think of it officially, but Klaus! Klaus wants to think of it—and virtually insisted that I think of it—as the *Kapitan* wishes. "You can't set your watch back without the permission of the captain! You just go out of your way to be different!" says he. I don't think so, really; I just don't go out of my way to be the same.

50.

39°52'N x 178°46'W

No sooner had we crossed the line than the weather began to clear. Now bright sun, blue skies and a lovely aquamarine sea. Walked the deck for 45 minutes, then sat on the bow enjoying the wonderful breeze, the sea and the birds. (No dolphins.) *Must* escape the party tonight—the "IDL Party"(?). Any excuse will do. Have told Marion that I feel *"ein bischen krank"* so she'll be ready for me to make my excuses.

7/18 Nice sleep. Nice gut (not perfect, but better), nice haircut, shower—but now we have stopped! In the middle of the Pacific Ocean, we are adrift! *Warum?* (Why?) Surely it is too early to be early at Long Beach. Problems? Will make a trip to the bridge.

Well, we've stopped to change an injector in one of the cylinders of the main engine. Should be finished about now. Must say, I prefer almost any motion of the ship over this idle drifting. Another overcast day with, however, very smooth sailing—when we're moving.

Pleading slight, incipient, possible minor illness, I kept away from the party last evening. Today, for the ship, it's the 2nd July 18th—Thursday. I had two Wednesdays (which, as I say, drove Klaus bananas), but at midnight last night it became Thursday for everybody so we are all in sync once again.

Klaus is becoming more convinced (and more irritated) that I am an "intentional revolutionary" and, after the Kujihama taxi business, an "opportunist". He obviously has not had a lot of experience with "difference", nor has he a great deal of tolerance for it.

199

(Reading John Sandford's SUDDEN PREY; a splendid writer, and I noted a line, which may or may not fit our own experiences here. "The dawn came—cold, sullen and stupid!")

We move! Laundry in. All's well.

No, we stop! Turns out it wasn't the injector, it was the exhaust valve, which they are now fixing. Captain said we could have continued to California at reduced speed, but he opted to stop and fix it instead. I backed him up on that.

38°13'N x 171°05'W

Still stopped, valve being fitted. We go in one hour. Laundry in dryer. Bad lunch: rice and beef!

Laundry out and drying on the Siegfried line, but the ship is still in the same place—a-rockin' and a-rollin'. Last laundry and last haircut for the trip—5th laundry and 4th haircut. Marion, at lunch, said, "Richard, you don't look happy . . . I think you are homesick." She's right, of course. I'm not only homesick (something I've never experienced)—I'm *here*sick! The damn tummy tumult, a combination of this long haul, the seemingly increasingly inedible food (for me), the somewhat wearing nature of this camaraderie, the damn scrapers, and my longing to talk to somebody in normal English. Plus, I *miss* it all—Ellen and Dan and Jen, the cozy house, friends, the French horn, the computer, and—once in awhile—the TV, but certainly the radio and the CBC. At least the sun has reappeared. For a moment.

Still immobile! Obviously the problem was not so easily remedied. We have already lost nearly 7 hours. By the way, the party last night went on until 0200 (0300 when the clocks were advanced). The Kments just chuckled when I asked if they had been down for breakfast, but Uncle Klaus, with some asperity, replied: "Of course!"

Still sitting quietly in mid-ocean. The popcorn popper is becoming a real lifesaver. Meats at meals are getting a mite strange. We've had duck twice now (Yech!), fish of various sorts (whole fish, eyes and all) a number of times, and tonight pork knuckles for the second time. The meat on them is quite good, but the spectacle of that huge knuckle on the plate doesn't leave quite enough to the imagination. Too much for Marion; she returns it with thanks. Calamari, too—not bad.

Also, the kitchen crew apparently feels that LARGE helpings are a rule—and indeed they may be for the working crew. I hate to waste food, but even when I ask for a small portion, I get a walloping wad. Erlito, the cook, makes the best chicken I've tasted since Swiss Chalet, but at the moment the hens seem to have flown the coop. We think—hope?—that the "two tons" of watermelon are finally gone, and instead of the fresh fruit—apples, pears, oranges, bananas at nearly every meal, the fruit is now canned—peaches, apricots, pears—which is ok. So the popcorn, almost daily now, is turning out to be a real boon. And I think I have enough corn and butter to last.

I waited at supper to see if anyone—the Captain, the Chief, etc.—would voluntarily tell us what the hell is going on. Nope. Finally asked the Electrician. Guess it wasn't the valve after all, but they are fixing whatever it is. The fact that these clever fellows are actually able to repair that monstrous engine, that they know what to do and can do it, is next to miraculous to me.

We move! Wonder what this does to our "schedule" re: Long Beach's already short stay.

7/19 Still moving, still overcast, still a smooth ride. Speed increased a bit to try to make up some time. Captain says we'll be "on time". My gut seems to be settling down a bit, but scrapers and grinders still at it—though getting further away.

38°N x 164°W (at sea).

Did not go down for lunch. Napped until after noon, and had no appetite, plus mealtime is sometimes getting to be a bit of a drag. I promise never again to take mealtimes for granted. Wonder what would happen if I sat someplace else once—maybe in one of "their" chairs. (Maybe Klaus is right: maybe I am a revolutionary!) (Maybe?) Am reading yet another book—the third this trip—about Germany (two of them were in the ship's library), and, of course, about the war, the Wall, the trials, the attrocities, etc. etc., and I simply cannot help thinking about the unbelievably monstrous things that were perpetrated by Hitler and his henchmen—and countrymen. While we have talked about the war and its privations and hardships, no one has (dared?) mentioned the camps and the ovens—almost as if they didn't really happen, or they happened somewhere else. The old story told after the war: if you listen closely, as Germans—officers, soldiers, industrialists, even the man on the street—are interrogated, it becomes "apparent" that "there were really only three Nazis in Germany—and nobody seems to know who they were". And of course the presence of those smoking, sprawling camps and the incessant

201

lines of boxcars that fed them seemed to be a complete surprise to everybody.

Am also struck by the haunting similarity between the apparent desire to be told what to do—and the willingness to do it, and the similar Canadian penchant for strong government and paternal overseeing—and also being told what to do. The idea, too, of thinking for yourself seems to be, particularly with Klaus, a very suspicious activity. He can be downright insulting, in his rather blunt English, at the idea of my doing things my way. I take the "guff" for obvious reasons, but if we were just neighbours in the conventional way, I would long ago have given him a blast.

Yes, I am homesick, perhaps for the first time in my life, though still so glad I am taking this trip.

(Most beautiful music on now: Schubert Mass #3 in Bb. Exquisite soprano—not an everyday find.)

Glorious afternoon! Popcorn, a little solitaire, a great new book, and music—now the Shostakovich 5. More and more I realize how much I need time to be by myself. I wonder if more people really feel this way, but hesitate for some reason. Call it whatever you want, but I guess one of the reasons for this trip was just that—time by myself. Yet I keep falling into my own trap—my feeling that I must participate, co-mingle, engage, etc. etc., and it always gets me into trouble—a brown funk of discouragement and depression. Yet, I have only to put my mental foot down to chuck it all—as I used to at Ohio Wesleyan, and just for a while do exactly what I want to do.

Ah, more glorious music—what would I have done without it? (Rimsky-Korsakov, Symphony 3.)

There! I put one of the calling cards that Dan made for me in each of the paperbacks I'm leaving in the ship's library. Hey, why not? Somebody might find one and decide to write. I'm keeping two of the books I brought along, and "borrowing" two or three from the ship.

Popping thoughts:
I must be especially careful. There is this lurking suspicion—based partly on past experience—that looking too much forward to something—in this case arriving home—will lead to disaster of some sort. My continuing internal problem might, I suspect, develop into some major thing that would either do me in, or necessitate an emergency flight home and consequent failure to complete my vaunted circumnavigation. So I try to take it one day at a time and try not to think about the home fires with too much longing or excitement. Sometimes my expectations are so elevated

that I become convinced that it will never really happen. I'll be careful.

7/20   *Der Zwanzigsten Juli*—the 20th of July, the 58th anniversary of the almost successful attempt on Hitler's life. Count von Stauffenburg placed his briefcase under the conference table at *Wolfschanze* where Hitler and his cronies were meeting. The bomb was provided by the Allies, according to my friends here. It went off, but Hitler was only slightly injured. In the wake of the event, 5,000 people were executed, including many high-ranking officers who were in on the conspiracy. In 1966 I saw the building in Berlin where the mightiest of them were strung up with piano wire and hung from meat hooks to die slow and exquisitely painful deaths. In 1955 while stationed in Germany with the U.S. Army, I saw, at the village "*Kino*", a film depicting the whole thing. (And bought some of the best chocolate I've ever eaten!)

Bit harder going this morning under gray skies, and over—and through!—those rough and tumble seas which, every once in a while, jump straight up in the air and come aboard over the bow. Obviously pushing our timetable to get to Long Beach by around noon on the 24th for that ten hour stay—just long enough, we figure, for a run to the Queen Mary for a quick looksee. Our berth is apparently close to the middle of town which will be nice indeed.

Enough rock and roll in the ship so I secured the popper and any other loose items last night. It will be nice to get to the point where you have identified and squelched every squeak and rattle in the room, and, by golly, I think I'm almost there!

Well, by my usually expert calculations, I say we're in Long Beach at 1400 on the 24th if we keep our present speed of 18 knots.

Might fast today! Tired of this business. It may be too   much meat in my diet. Some meals, like the BBQ, that's all I eat. Other meals, the fruit, potatoes, and the occasional veg that I like. Try to balance it with corn, but that may not be so good either. Just a constant ache in midsection (mine) and Old Faithful down below.

38°N x 155°58'W (at sea)

Whooee! The heaviest weather yet! Regular bashes on the snout (the ship's), rivers of spray running down the walkways, and crashing waves—white horses everywhere—absolutely mesmerizing to watch. What a magnificent tumult as we blast our way through. And yet, a remarkably smooth ride—nowhere near the rolling we've undergone in the past. Waves, wind, and seas from the SW buffeting

203

our starboard quarter—a nice kick in the rump, actually, helping us along. For this ship, this is nothing—a playful jaunt.

But my window is leaking again—or still; I've got to find a wrench to tighten that lower clamp.

Wind down, rain lets up a bit, ship settles down. I nap.

At supper I ingest: 2 plus glasses of water
2 pieces of beef
1 small helping of rice with butter
19 peas
2 slices of bread and catsup
1 cal./mag. tablet
7 apricot halves

Ship's horn sounding. Why? To the bridge. Man missing—well they can't find him—Romeo Melo. Horn sounds, again—Captain, Chief Engineer, Klaus, and I on the bridge wing looking. More horn. Where is Romeo? The ship is scoured and finally, here he comes—looking a bit sheepish. He was in the engine room—odd for him, a deck crew A/B—and couldn't hear the alarm horn. Romeo, one of my favorites, and a real craftsman around the bridge—repairing, painting, inventing gadgets. Great fellow. Glad we didn't lose him—but serious concern until he showed up with his shy smile. The Captain, scowling and smiling, said simply: "Romeo!" It was Renand who told him he was "missing".

51.

7/21 Up at usual time. Bright sunny Sunday—even on the ship it feels like a special holiday kind of day. We know there will be no scraping or grinding today, and no one gladder about that than the guys who have to do it. The sea, a mill pond for the ship, though small swell and small waves tickle her bottom from the SE.

37°57'N x 147°23'W (at sea)

Lovely lunch—quarter chicken, canned peaches, ice cream.
Klaus to me: "You missed the morning preach—Cookie made the morning preach, and Renand washed his hands in unguiltiness."

Lovely day, too. Should make "*ein spaziergang*" around the deck.

BBQ tonight. Don't really want to go; I always eat lots of meat (chicken, steak, pork chops) and drink lots of Coke. Not good. We'll see.

Clocks ahead again tonight—am only, now, one hour away from "home time."

BBQ finished. Gorgeous evening. Had one small piece of beef, 2 hot dogs, 1 7UP (Blecch!—no Coke left). Maybe now some popcorn left over from this morning. I asked Marion if it was possible to eat too much meat. Answer: yes. I think maybe that's what the problem is—about three times as much meat as I'm used to: 2 helpings a day, instead of 2 or 3 a week. So am cutting way back. Basically, one meal a day—chicken if possible. Still would give a lot for a plate of pancakes or a big bunch of Kraft Dinner. (Don't start!)

7/22   Brilliant sun and, exactly as predicted by Ocean Routes, the wind has gone around to the NE and picked up. So now we take the sizeable seas on our port bow. No big deal, just the familiar rocking motion that tends to put one to sleep. Was wondering how much I had spent in seasickness remedies, let alone how much time was spent talking about them. Here it is day 105 and not one pill has been touched, let alone the bracelets, the suppositories, and all the other rigmarole I didn't really dare leave without. Maybe I'll put an ad in the Gulf Islands Driftwood: "Free preventive pills for people preparing to put to sea in a pea green boat."

Found a whole clutch of books in the library that either are new or that I just hadn't seen before. They should carry me through. I have a genuine fear of running out of reading material. These items were donated by Freighter World Cruises—my very own freighter travel service.

The grinders are at it again. It's still like being inside that 50 gallon drum with the busy dental crew trying to get in.

Feeling more normal. Klaus missed breakfast! A first!, and arrived sleep-drenched and half an hour late for lunch. Heavy drinking at the party (BBQ) last evening. "Not used to hard liquor, but beer was gone, so I had to drink it!" says he. Marion missed her breakfast and is off her feed for lunch. Party! (Worth it?)

Reg'lar Nor'easter blowin' up out thar'. Ol' BIBI pitching very nicely. Will batten everything down before supper. Our course is 99° now, but we must come down to 104° tomorrow. That'll be interesting with the seas more broadside.

New sked: into Long Beach at night—the 24th, pilot at 0400 on the 25th, discharge starting about 0800, sailing @ 1800. We've been unable to make up enough time after our 10 hour repair job. But this is better: we get a whole day ashore.

Clocks ahead tonight, the last time for me—the 24th. That's one way of going around the world, I guess—by the hours as well as by degrees.

205

Marion still not eating. I think the motion of ship bothers her, too, though pitching is far better than rolling. So, two more full days at sea—that'll make 12 in all since we left Japan.

This ship is fair leaping across the Pacific! The bow rises 20 or 30 feet, then drops into the next wave trough with almighty torrents of water catapulted out from the bows. Mountains of spray whipped by the wind into a frenzy of foam and flying sheets of white water. It's one way to get the mud off the anchors! (Though each of the hawse holes is fitted with a nozzle that sprays chain and anchor as they are raised.)

7/23 Misty morn; wind and seas down considerably, sun and blue sky breaking through. Rain squalls lurking in the distance—good! They may clean my windows of salt spray. Think I'll go down for breakfast: eggs, peanut butter toast, juice.   Marion still off her feed.

Still life—wan Marion, friend, bucket, new pilot ladder

206

Poor Renand. Spent all day yesterday moving furniture and cleaning the carpet in the officer's lounge and last night some idiot tramped in with his oily, greasy, dirty, sooty, rusty work boots on and klutzed the whole thing up again. There are signs all over the ship commanding people NOT to wear work shoes and boots into living areas.

But there's always somebody.

We've had to turn a little south to 104° or so, so we are crossing the NE seas and rolling a bit more. Wind has also picked up some; nothing to worry about except my drapes are sliding again.

36°33'N x 131°19'W (at sea)

Well, the comfortable pitch has become a pesky roll and this Nor'easter is slowing us to around 16 knots. No wonder Cappy changed the sked. I keep thinking we are "close" to L.B. (we *must* be!) but still have 600 miles to go, so we're still 'way out to sea.

Doesn't seem possible. Marion still off her feed.

Wind down, sea down, weather fair, so—A DRILL! Lifeboat this time. Everybody down to the MUSTER STATION (all painted afresh after the other one was "disappeared" by the grinders-chippers-painters) on the poop deck. Poor Marion, roused from her semi-sickbed, clad in huge orange lifejacket, looking a bit wan and forlorn. Boats lowered, but not into the water, just over the side. Chief Officer must again "make photo" of all drills and all maintenance—like greasing the davit cables. This will probably be my last drill.

A ship! Tanker or bulker off to port, fairly close in. First sign of life in 10 days!

7/24 Amazing. Just woke up. Sun shining and the sea looks like the lake back home. Very slight swell which can be felt rather than seen, with blue sky overhead, a few clouds. Today is, by gum, the 24th—Long Beach Day!

The gut slowly returning to normal, I think. Calcium? Less meat? Less food? More popcorn? Who knows?

Holy doodle! We've stopped. Now what? Killing time, or breaking down?

Ah. Only routine engine and steering tests required by the U.S. Coast Guard before we enter the port. Takes about 15 or 20 minutes to get up to full speed again, but we're soon on the way.

The constant creak of cargo lashings, an echoing metallic sound, or maybe it is the ship herself, her covers and doors, all tight and secure, still working just enough to make this unique sound. The constant vibration of engines and motors and generators and pumps, the rumble and pulse of the big diesel that drives us, the revolutions of the shaft that spins the huge propeller: there is no mistaking this ship's heartbeat. The tiniest hinge, hook and hasp will come alive and buzz, tinkle, rattle and bang if given half a chance. Everything on a ship from dishes to doors to railings and radars loves to give voice—challenges you to damp it, to find and stop its sound. A ceiling light fixture that never rattled in its life will, at 0347, begin to buzz and sing; the door to the loo has defeated me. Stuffing tissues, draping towels—all to no avail; the ticking in the "holdback" latch never stops. Listen! You can hear it now. A healthy clout on the TV/VCR every once in a while silences that unit's buzzing. A hat brim stuffed in the jamb of the main cabin door does the trick there—when you remember to do it—but after while, all these little preventions become simply routine. These are the sounds of life on the ship. We wait for them, miss them when we stop, breathe easier when the ship again begins to move and the rattles and squeaks take up their chorus. Nothing could be more depressing than a ship, dead in the water, all power off, all machines stopped. Like that great liner under tow, simply waiting for rigor mortis to set in.

For supper T-bone steak, assorted other goodies and, for me, something the Kments had heard about but never actually seen: a peanut butter and jam sandwich!

In an hour or so I'm going to start looking for Point Conception, our first landfall. Then another 5 or 6 hours to go along the coast. . .

LAND HO! The California coast in plain sight across the port bow: mountains, buildings: Point Conception. Only 120 miles to go now, past Santa Barbara and L.A. and into L.B. Pilot at 0400.

Down in the lounge: three Polish crew members are watching an American movie, dubbed into German, with Chinese subtitles.

For the first time in weeks, the moon is seen. And it's full. Shining a path across the sea as we head for L.B. Quite stunning. And I know Ellen, a convinced "lunatic" is seeing it, too.

7/25 Up at 0330 to have a look. The guys are putting the pilot ladder in place, so I stay to watch. Long Beach gleaming off to port.

Pilot is aboard.

33°45'N x 118°20'W (Long Beach)

We are tied up in a very narrow slip having been unceremoniously flipped around and towed in backwards. I watch for a while, then go back to bed, fall asleep.

Big knock on the door! It is 0630! It is Renand. (At first it occurs to me that he is inviting me down for ice cream! No.) The Customs people are waiting in the Captain's cabin. I am fast asleep, but get dressed, climb up to E deck, to find two obnoxiously cheery agents smiling broadly and trying to make banal conversation as we blearily fill out customs declarations. I am slowly beginning to steam! No explanation, let alone apology for dragging us out at dawn. The woman is the cheeriest, the man just plain nosy. "Ah," says he, "I see you were born in the U.S., but left for Canada. Why?" I snarl: "How much time you got?" and go back to bed.

Fifteen minutes later, the Chief Officer knocks, wants passport to copy. What?

Hey, there are at least ten oil wells right on this huge concrete pier—pumping oil!

We set off at an early hour to find a cab—the customary procedures in force: try to make the gate man and/or the cabbie understand where we want to go in a foreign city. The way this is done is by TALKING LOUDLY, or drawing pictures. It does not occur to the other three that we are now in the United States, an English-speaking nation (more or less) and that I can make a fairly valid claim to actually *speaking English!* I let them fumble and mumble, realizing with a chuckle that the Mexican cabbie doesn't speak much English either—his is as broken as theirs.

But, such a day we have. Fine chat with Ell and set her up "real good" for the big surprise. Promise to call her again from Panama.

Also spend 3 1/2 hours on the venerable and quite unimaginable QUEEN MARY, which as we all know, sailed into Long Beach in 1967 to a permanent birth and retirement, and has since been lovingly cherished and protected, and established as a first class hotel and absolutely glorious attraction. I have been super impressed by our 584 foot ship with her 15,000 hp engine. Imagine

209

my dropping jaw at the sight of this 1019 foot behemoth with her *four* 40,000 hp engines! I have been quite proud of our 18 knot speed; this Queen at times made 44 knots—nearly 50 mph (almost 80 kph). For a reasonable package deal rate, I am allowed simply to wander this great ship at leisure, almost stem to stern, bridge to morgue, plus a tour of my choosing. I select the "Grey Ghost" jaunt—the ship during wartime when she was converted to troop carriage—at one point ferrying some 16,000 men! Our guide is also quite unimaginable and should immediately be charged with a "412". "A FOUR-TWELVE—WHAT'S A FOUR-TWELVE?" "Overacting; let's go!" (What? You don't know Stan Freberg's DRAGONET?)

In the engine spaces of the Queen is stationed a gentleman engineer who had actually served there when she was in service. Among other things he informs us that the QUEEN MARY II is even now under construction in Scotland and will be in service by 2004.

But what a scene! What a ship! And how superbly this city has worked to preserve not only this magnificent ship but her spirit and ambiance! To get there, a free shuttle bus from downtown Long Beach.

My package also includes a tour of the Russian sub tied up under the bow of the Queen; I pass—have already been through one in Victoria, and, I mean, you see one Russian submarine, you've seen 'em all. Right?

Then we bust a gut (so to speak) getting back to the ship to make a 1500 curfew in order to sail at 1600—that's what the man said. We are full of the day's events, but the first thing we hear on coming aboard is that we sail not today, but *tomorrow!* At supper I say to the Captain, with a wry smile, "OK—so what happened?" And he replies: "That's California! Now you know why I was not pleased to come to California." It seems the stevedore's union took a look at our cranes and derrick—the same ones we have been using to load and unload at the previous 19 ports—and "disallowed" their use. Even the big jumbo. Nobody seems to know quite why. There are no shore cranes here, so: gridlock! Marine surveyors and the Coast Guard were called in and it was finally decided that the big Stuelcken derrick could be used. So while our five cranes lie idle, the 250 ton derrick S - L - O - W - L - Y (in its lowest gear it seems hardly to be moving at all) lifts 8 ton crates out of tween decks #4, and the unloading moves at a pace the local snails would find enviable. It is said that the happy stevedores will finish at noon tomorrow. So we will sit idle for 13 hours tonight, and pay a heap more dough to stay in the port another day—or portion thereof. As Epaminandas's Mammy might say, "Dey ain't got de sense dey was bo'n wit'."

I may go back downtown tomorrow if there's time—only a $5 cab ride. I need chocolate, butter and a crossword puzzle book. Maybe Internet, too.

52.

Hey, from my cabin window I can just see the top of one of the QM's funnels!

Just watching the unloading of the huge crate we brought from China. One man operates the big derrick (V - E - R - Y   S - L - O - W - L - Y, of course), probably two men in the hold, 2 on shore to loose the slings and a man on shore to direct. In Asia there would be one man on the crane, one man beating a stick on the hatch coaming to direct the operator, 4 or more men in the hold, *35 guys on shore—and nobody to direct!* Well, maybe a few to direct. Instead of the motorized California broom that quickly dampened and swept the quay this morning, there would be 15 guys with reed brooms moving the dust around. Well, it all makes work for the working man to do. And why not?

A flight of pelicans swooping over in tight formation—maybe a "plunge" of pelicans—or a "bill" of lading. I have also noticed these flights zooming along in the middle of the night. Heading for a Pelican party? Wonder if they ever get stopped for FUI—Flying Under the Influence.

Aha! A forklift dropped a box! First "accident" I've seen on the trip. Small box just tumbled off the load to the ground. So here comes a second, smaller forklift, picks up the small box, puts it down again in a different place. Now a man comes along, sees the small box, bends over, picks it up, and puts it back on top of the pile.

A little walk up Pier D, Berth 30 as the sun sets in the west. Which is surprising since this is California where they could easily have disallowed it for some idiot reason. After the supper explanation of our plight, the Captain allowed as how in California, "It's always something!" Last time he was here, the pilot came aboard, took one look forward from the bridge and refused to take the ship in: too many cranes! They waited another 24 hours for another pilot.

Speaking of which, I have discovered a splendid 24 hour National Public Radio classical station from U. of Southern California. Great! We can stay here as long as need be.

Hot damn! The Mahler first symphony!

Being an inveterate closet conductor, do I "conduct" the opus? Hey—is the sea salty? The orchestra sometimes has trouble following me, as the performance is nominally led by Lenny, whose interpretation can only be termed bizarre from time to time. I know the Kments love Mahler so I call them the moment it is announced. "Ahh", says Marion, "we are just listening to Mahler's *Lied von der Erde!*" Next morning I ask what they thought of the symphony. "Oh, we heard only the last few minutes—after the *Lied* was over." I said, "But . . . the *Lied* was on disc, right?" "Yes," said Marion, "but we couldn't interrupt it in the middle!" Ah, me! Once again, good old *Deutsche Ordnung* rears its head.

I've heard that symphony a couple of dozen times, and played in it thrice, but now realize that practically the entire thing is based on the interval of the 4th. No wonder Mahler's cuckoos sing in 4ths—as opposed to Beethoven's 3rd!

7/26 Well! We got some company overnight! An E N O R M O U S Hyundai container ship—probably Panamax (the largest ship that can transit the canal) or larger—was snuggled up next door in this narrow gap between piers. Then, later, as I watched, another huge HANJIN container ship came gracefully into the harbour—it turned out to be the very first ship Klaus had sailed with—the one with the funny (ha ha) captain. He will go over later (at vast taxi expense) where he will find not a single familiar face aboard, but is welcomed nonetheless.

Hooray! My tummy's back to normal.

They have finished loading the 10 ton crates with the 250 ton derrick; now our guys have to flip the derrick, change slings, etc., so it can work out of #3 hold, all the time those five cranes are sitting idle.

We are now 24 hours late leaving. These idiot clowns, now lifting little boxes with the jumbo! Unbelievable. Talk about stupid! (Except for their pay cheques, of course.) ETD now 1800, but at this rate—aargh! I can't bear to watch them.

1745 and not finished yet. One more big generator (at least). Will they do it tonight? Will they try? This sort of stupidity writ large is just what drove me out of this country. We have been around the world—20 ports—some of the most "developing" countries on earth—with not a single loading mishap, and I've never seen anything like this! This country is, pardon my native candor, stupid (i.e.: willfully ignorant) from the top down and from the bottom up, and all night, too. I have not felt this deeply outraged and insulted since I left this bloody place 30 years ago. And the U.S. just can't seem to figure out—or doesn't give a tinker's dam—why it suffers its contcmporary reputation.

Ready for this? We sail *tomorrow! Afternoon!* Hearing this news, Klaus immediately took off for Hollywood. Not having heard the news, the Kments, who had walked over to the Queen Mary, had to beetle back to the ship to "sail at 1800" tonight.

Talked to the bosun: tomorrow, one more generator (goes on a railroad flatcar), several other crates, and they have to flip the derrick again! We could be 45 hours late. Kments have already made arrangements to meet friends in Houston, and now we learn that two locks in the Panama are under repair, so who knows? Who cares, really? As Super cargo Dirk said earlier about the passengers waiting in Hamburg, "When you stop earning money, what's another few days?"

ODE TO POPCORN

What a miracle is the corn that pops,
The kernel that explodes!
Take along a bag of these wee seeds:
Heat them up and up—
They POP!
Become ten times bigger, and fluffy, and,
Like the less edible snowflake, no two are
Ever the same. Never.
The aroma of popping corn can fill a ship,
      tantalize dozens of taste buds.
Take the exploded inside outside, drizzle on
      some butter, add a dash of salt
      and, one small morsel at a time, pop
      the corn—again!—into the mouth!
Ah, the taste, the texture, the crunch, the crush,
      the tingle of tasted seasoning!
Lo! You are chewing and gnashing the fluffed up stuff
      right back to its original size!
A handful of seeds—a mountain of puff—a handful of
      crunch!
Popcorn: doesn't fill you up, doesn't fill you out!
All that scrumptious flavour, then
Almost nothing in the tum tum.
Popcorn: real cereal, real bulk, real taste, real good.
Popcorn has it all!
(And it's fun to watch!)

213

7/27   An overcast morning—the giant contship still here—unusual. Will find out about our sailing time—would like to visit Wal-Mart for some basic supplies. . .

Looks like we go at 1500 today, so I'm off. We are forbidden in this port to walk; must call for a shuttle bus to take us to the gate—safety measure, not a bad idea, but of course we four have been walking ports all around the world and are fairly knowledgeable about avoiding moving vehicles, etc. But I sneak around the end of the quay—walking boldly to demonstrate that I know where I'm going and what I'm doing. Too bad I don't have a clipboard.

The California Clowns are at it again: a short aluminum ladder—one a kid could probably lift easily—is lashed carefully (the Chinese dudes could learn something here) to the giant hook of the 250 ton derrick and lifted S - L - O - W - L - Y aboard and down into the hold. The foreman of this bunch is, to me, particularly annoying: arrogant, officious, inflated—the American eagle in person.

Back from town, and a lovely ride on the zippy LRT train all the way into Los Angeles and return—2 hours, 90¢. Didn't get off; just wanted a train ride. Saw again the "Watts Towers"—visible from the train! These are a couple of 80 foot spires made by a fellow in his back yard from bottles and other found objects. Took him years, and they are still standing.

Not enough time to catch a bus to Wal-Mart, so settled for Top Value where I invested in: 1 12 1/2 oz. bag Ruffles Ripple Chips
1 lb. butter
1 13 oz. bag Hershey Kisses
1 32 oz. bag Jolly Time White corn

All the necessities of life! And back home in time for lunch— quarter chicken.

And now the Brahms 1 on the radio!

Now we are 48 hours late! Will we depart in 20 minutes as hoped? Feel like flipping the bird to these clowns. Somebody ought to do something!

Tugs are here, cranes put to bed, derrick moving S - L - O - you know the drill, into place. We may make it!

We pull away from the United States..

Last view of the majestic Queen. Our ship now carrying 6556 tons of cargo, having left probably 1500 tons to the Yanks. We were never more than about 80% full. More stuff went to L.B. than I imagined.

Word is that tonight "we make barbecue"—with, they say, *roast suckling pig!* I don't doubt it for a moment!

53.

Is this Catalina Island I see approaching through the haze? Could be.

Radio: Hindemith, S.M.T.C.M.v.W. No, I 'm not going to write it all out. Oh, all right: the Symphonic Metamorphosis on Themes of Carl Maria von Weber. One of my favorites. Ahhh. Don't fade out on me . . .

Piggy

And I tell you; roast suckling pig is exactly what they say it is. Wow! Succulent, tender, juicy—oooh—and unbelievably tasty. Renand—the "special events" cook—BBQs and such—got the fire started and the spit rigged around 1600 and the boys took turns rotating the pink piglet until it was brown and bursting. Apparently they routinely pick up a frozen piggy in Singapore and save it for the Pacific finish line.

Just passing San Diego off to port—a band of light on the distant horizon.

Here's the poop (from the poop, as it were). We'll be in Panama one week from tonight—August 3rd. Inspection, etc. will take most of the evening and on Sunday, the 4th—with good fortune—we will pass through the famous waterway. Should finish in the early evening, then it is 3 days and 6 hours (!) to Houston—the 6 hours are for the Houston Ship Canal, I think, or maybe it's 6 hours plus the canal. Which makes Houston arrive on the morning of August 8th. Could be back on my island that very evening! Will be able to make final plans after Panama.

7/28   Rather dull day—overcast with a slight swell coming from—can't really tell, except it's fore or aft so we sort of delicately gallop in "slo-mo"—not at all unpleasant.

28°13'N x 116°24'W (at sea)

Well, I'm afraid this leg of the trip may prove the most difficult. Beautiful day after all as we galumph across the sea heading SSE for the Canal, but though it is near perfect sailing, my impatience will rear its head. Six days left to Panama, then a day in the Canal and three plus days to big H.

More popcorn (the new stuff!):
The reader may become suspicious that the ship, the sea, the trip itself are becoming decidedly onerous to me. Not in the least! My brother, Dave, has six children; they have children; the visits to the homestead by this assembled tribe are wondrous to behold—I speak from personal experience. Dave and his incomparable wife, Carol, love to see them arrive, eat, engage in the usual Moses banter and hilarity, but when the last car pulls out of the driveway, the visit is over, and calm descends, Dave, with a contented sigh, reflects: "The kids are great, but I sure love those tail lights!"   Well, me too, on this trip, only writ large. Four months away, a head full of hundreds of adventures to share, dozens of people to greet, activities missed and ready to recommence. I don't want this trip to end—ever—and I will yearn for the rest of my days for the feel and the sounds of this ship, for the first glimpse of land and then the view once again of open ocean, but right now the Port of Houston, Turning Basin Terminal, Pier 16 beckons with a Siren song that is irresistible. So, bear with me in my lonely and longing meandering as we approach—unbelievably—the end of this dream.

216

7/29 Bright, sunny morning with, for us, a calm sea running right in our direction. Almost like a raft trip in the rapids—waves and swell carrying us along. I figure it adds at least a knot to our speed. Otherwise, water, water, everywhere.

22°41'N x 119°19'W (at sea)

Flying fish are back! Getting tropical here. Of course: just crossed the Tropic of Cancer—again.

My hand-written journal says for this day and time: "Insulted at supper by Klaus. Took a walk on deck—a pair of dolphins said hello." What happened at supper: shortly after the start of the meal, he turned to me, and with some ire in his voice asked: "Do you know what consideration is?" I said, yes, of course. He replied, "I have asked you not to hum and whistle at the table and you continue to do it!" We were quite shocked at this outburst. Humming? Whistling? I had no idea I was committing these offences. The Kments and I all love music and occasionally in fun break out in some old tune, but only rarely and then only briefly. Sometimes I do come into a meal humming something I've just heard on a CD, or perhaps, even during the meal, I will "mutter a small hum" of some theme, but again only very briefly and certainly *sotto voce*. I doubt the Kments across the table even hear it. But he obviously does. And he doesn't like it. I put his comments behind me and strive over the next few days to regain his good will. And by the end of the week, it is all forgotten.

7/30 Bright and blue this a.m. with the wind and sea having gone around to S-SW. Time is moving as slowly as the jumbo derrick. Was sure this was Wednesday. Nope—it's Tuesday—all day. Don't know whether to hurry it along or let it lag. Am on my 27th book, but am afraid I'll run out. Have combed the small library pretty thoroughly, and saved a Dean Koontz paperback for the trip home—"borrowed" from the ship.

Grinding so unbearable ("3 or 4 hours"!), I retire to the conference room on E deck. When I return "home"—*a ship*! We are overtaking another general cargo ship off to starboard. No, she's going to cross our bow. She's the GREENWIND "out of" Limassol, Cyprus; same hailport as the BIBI, but she's probably never been there either.

18°33'N x 104°55'W (at sea)

217

The popcorn I bought in Long Beach is the really tiny kernel white stuff that comes only rarely to B.C. It is *so* delicious, I cannot forbear and polish the whole 2 pounds off in a week or so.

A little post-prandial deck trek—no sign of the dolphins, but another magnificent sunset. Weather warming up after rather chilly(!) California.

7/31 Well, another fantastic dawn coming "up like thunder". Sky begins to lighten, then turns dark. Then great bolts of lightening and heavy black clouds lie ahead. We plow right on into it all, and meet another ship coming out. Now the rain begins and thunder rolls even through my heavy windows. Lets see if my new wrench *(yes!)* will keep out the drips. Ah, a real drencher, and so far no seepage.

This is great—washes all the salt off the deck, cleans the windows.

Off to port the sun is driving right on through the squall, just lighting up the clouds. Come on, sun!

But it never made it! Just couldn't get all the way through the cloud cover. Now a brisk breeze has sprung up from the SSE though the rain has gone.

15°14'N x 98°17'W (at sea)

At lunch, the latest sked:

8/3	1600	arr. @ Canal
8/4	0200	get in line
8/4	0600	start through Canal
8/4	2000(?)	leave Canal
8/8	0400	Houston pilot
8/8	1200	Arr. Pier 16

A hundred birds and dozens of dolphins cavorting off the starboard bow. Oop! Gone. Only the wandering birds.

I'm hangin' on to this trip by the skin of my teeth. Ain't *nobody* or nothing going to spoil it for me—including *me* and my pestiferous, petty fussbudgetiness! And guess what (things get even better!): Friday is a *party*! "I couldn't live without parties", says Klaus.

Hang on and hang in there, Moses, only seven days to go! You can make it. I love the sea and the ship and my new popcorn and the music and the books and even the Coke (though I am really a Pepsi man). I am so excited about arriving home, yet I don't want to rush this fantastic voyage. Talk about conflicting emotions!

218

8/1   Bright sun, calm sea and a book by John Mortimer—so pithy and gorgeously written, that I must either read it aloud (to myself) or pause every few lines just to celebrate his prose and laugh aloud. Mortimer created the "Rumpole of the Bailey" books and TV series.

The first of August—here at last and in a week I might be home. Think of that!

Blue fish jumping. Early lunch. (No, not the fish.)

Will wait 'til we clear the Canal to make plane reservations. Several options, but want to get away as soon as possible.

8/2   Another morning!   Will take some ginger, along with the breakfast popcorn. (I know, I know!) Tomorrow the "channel", as the Kments persist in calling it. (I finally did suggest—making something of a joke of it—that everybody—including the Captain—might consider that the pointy end of the ship is called the "bow" as in bow wow, rather than "bow" as in "bow tie"—the only time I have "corrected" anyone on the ship—unless asked. Now all we have to do is tell the Captain.)

Great news!   Have found a whole new clutch of readable books in the stash downstairs. I think I'll make it!

Phrases from my current tome, a novel that attacks the Internet-ization of the world, etc. "Information is not knowledge—there is so much unregulated, unreliable information that there is no longer any knowledge!" "American moral exceptionalism." "Mundus vult decipi"—the world wants to be deceived, the "threshold moment"—that moment when new technology begins actually to alter the way life is lived.

9°05'N x 85°32'W (at sea)

Big brown birds—white bellies, white beaks, bigger than gulls. More Boobies or Gannets.

These birds, seemingly accompanying the ship, wait for the hundreds of small fish frightened by our headlong rush, into dashing—almost flying—away from our smashing bow wave, then they swoop down, either grab one, or dive after it—going quite deep—several feet down.

A ship! A roll-on freighter heading the other way.

Costa Rica! Plain as day off to port.

For supper I had "lunch": peanut butter and jam sandwiches. Too much fancy cooking. Tummy has turned on me again. Also took

219

a couple of ginger pills. Am going to Klaus's party tonight. I suggested that maybe I could actually bring the corn popper to the party. Not only will we have fresh popcorn, but everybody can see how it's done. Will not stay long, however.

Party's over—for me. Popcorn went over great—four loads and everybody gathered round to see it pop—then two loads more (and a big bowlful up to Renand in his cabin).

Funniest moment: Marion and Hans told the true story of a woman who came in and wanted glasses to read with. Hans fitted her, tested her on a number chart. Fine. Week later, woman comes back, very angry. Can't read with these glasses. Tried the number chart again. Fine. Checked the lenses. OK. Woman's son was along and finally admitted that the woman was in fact illiterate, had heard about "reading glasses" and was sure that with a pair on, she would be able to read. I said, "That's a true story, but there is an old joke: man breaks his arm, asks doctor 'will I be able to play the piano when it's healed?' Doctor says, 'Yes, indeed!' 'Good', says man, 'I never could before'" When the laughter died down, the Chief Engineer, who has, since his arrival, turned into a real party animal, is fond of fetching a drum from the crew's lounge and beating the tar out of it in "rhythm" with the Captain's singing, and who has also "had a few" tonight, says *he* has a joke, and in his wonderful broken English, says: " Man breaks finger, asks doctor 'Will I be able to play piano?' 'Yes,' says doctor' 'Good,' says man, 'I could not before!'" We all sort of look at each other and then crack up! The pitfalls of a multilingual gathering.

Most of them are still down there, the Captain singing lustily and raking his guitar—quite well, as a matter of fact, and the Chief Engineer "playing" his drum. He so wants to join the music!

54.

8/3   Panama off to port now. The Captain saw a large whale yesterday, quite close to the ship. We should have had ice cream! Water temperature now 33°C.

Headed almost due north now (16°) across the Golfo de Panama, and should reach the area of the Canal by about 1300, I think (but I'm always wrong!). Bit of rain in the air; several ships here and there.

Will call home from the ship at about noon, keep my promise to Ellen, try to catch her daughter, son-in-law and the new granddaughter now visiting from St. Albert, lay more groundwork for the big surprise, etc.

8°43'N x 79°78'W (at sea)

Well, dammit all to hell and back! The g.d. ship's phone is busted again! Can't call Ell, can't call the airline. Somebody shut its damn power off which means the PIN must be inserted again and a number of people tried to use the thing, and in dialing phone numbers inadvertently inserted what the idiot phone thought was the wrong PIN and after three "wrong" tries, the whole thing constipates and that's the end of it until—something. Nobody told the Captain until I did after trying to use the bloody thing at noon. Why don't they tell him? He could've put the PIN back and we'd be off to the races. No chance of fixing it now until Houston. It really screws him up, too; he has to send and receive faxes galore, and he won't be able to confirm our ETA without the phone/fax.

Well, anyway, we are here—at the Canal anchorage. Lot's of ships around.

9°30'N x 79°30'W (Panama Canal)

At anchor, watching the guys put little awnings on the bridge wings for the Canal pilot—one of the requirements here, as are the lights for Suez. Protection from sun and rain, I suppose.

Suddenly, right over head, six great pelicans, very low, giving us the once over. Several passes in and out of formation, then off they go: four here, two there, then one comes back so Klaus can sketch him. Panama City—tall buildings—through the mist and rain squalls; Balboa next door to it—the real entrance to the Canal. A couple of dozen ships anchored here now.

Still feel rotten about the damn phone. None of the cell phones—all European—work here either. Well, as the man said, Gotta be able to flex!

For supper tonight fresh fish. And I mean *fresh!* Caught only minutes before off our very own stern. They "bara-bara" or "jig" for them using a long line with several hooks, some of which carry something shiny or light coloured. Just drop the rig over the side and pull rapidly up, over and over. Renand said sometimes there were five or six fish on his line at once. Only small fish, mind you, six or eight inches, but fried in butter—yum! Of course, they gut the poor thing, but otherwise it's the whole magillah right there on your plate. I had four—could have had more. Delicious flavour. Several kinds were caught and these guys know exactly what to do with them. A good time was had by all, except for the fish, and the Captain, who—a man who spends his life on the ocean—does not like fish. Better this than the Master on one of Klaus's earlier ship who really loved red cabbage, so red cabbage was served at least three times a week.

Pilot arrives at 0600 tomorrow and we exit the Canal at "1910", said the official. It will cost the ship somewhere around $1.50 per gross ton, or about $30,000 to go through.

Just went down on deck for a photo of our fisherfolk crew. They are pulling in some big ones—12" or so, but while I was there a real whopper—5 lbs. or more—with catfish-like "whiskers" came over the side. Still bothers me to see things killed. These guys sure do love to have their picture's taken and when I appeared each grabbed a fish from the bucket and lined up with big smiles. A grand troupe! Just looked out the window to see them toss the big fellow back; don't know if he'll make it, though—too long out.

Filipino fisherfolk

8/4   Sky turning from black to blue; 3rd officer and Romeo waiting for pilot boat to come alongside. Then we're off. Lone butterfly, lone pelican swooping in—even in the dark! Romeo, as usual, seems to be where the action is. Coincidence? Assignment? Or just alert?

Thought it would be clear this morning—seemed to be at night—but now it's hazy and misty. Sun may burn it off.

Ah—here's the pilot boat. Beautiful as always. A line over to bring up the pilot's duffles (one a big orange case), and here he is.

Miraflores: the first flight of (2) locks, each 1,000 ft. long, now behind us, another flight right in front of us. Nifty little electric engines—3 per side, 2 lines each—move along tracks, guiding us into the lock and keeping us centred as we move into and out under our own power, shepherded by tugs. After this first set, we have been lifted about 50 ft. And as we move from the Pacific into the Atlantic, we are of course going from east to west in this unique Panamanian geography. Yes, strange as it seems, the isthmus of Panama turns around on itself in a big "S", forcing you to move from the Pacific Ocean, now on the East and birthing the rising sun, westerly to the Atlantic, which will anon receive its setting.

A visitors' centre on the bank has a large balcony filled with people watching us, and the two ships with us, go through. One, a MAERSK container ship is probably a "Panamax". Many newer ships will not fit through this canal and are doomed to remain in one ocean or the other, or make a trip around the Horn or the Cape.

Here we are at the approach to the 2nd flight—called Pedro Miguel. About 12 guys have come aboard to tend the lines. Lots of sailboats moored and berthed in marinas, usually near locks. Very hot up on "G" deck right in the sun; came down to cool off. These cute little engines have bells just like the old trolley cars. We are also watching the immense Frigate birds soaring high overhead, riding the air currents and seeming never to flap a wing.

Another 25 to 30 feet higher now and we are in "Cucaracha Reach". As far as I know, that means "cockroach". The linesmen depart and we head for the Gatun locks at the other end of the Canal, which will drop us back to Atlantic Ocean level—about three inches above the average, but tidally variable, Pacific level.

Here is the enormous Culebra cut in the Continental Divide making way for the Canal. High hills on either side needed to be blasted away and dug out; I am told that technology had to be invented and developed over a span of some 40 years to get the job done. The shore on either side is "terraced" back in huge steps, and right along the water's edge, wires are strung as landslide warnings. A dramatic place this Canal—the largest construction project in history by 1914. The 44 year effort to build it—a failed French project followed by the American success, makes, to my mind, one of the most fascinating stories in the history of human endeavor. (See Note 3.)

Just spent an hour-long lunch talking with one of the pilots. Great guy! Excellent English, former tug boat driver (eat your heart out, Moses!). Now he is one of about 300 Canal pilots. Turns out the tolls have gone up some and we will be paying not $30,000 but more like $38,000!

Was telling him about the Suez baksheesh, which made him shake his head, but recall a story he'd heard: a Suez pilot asked the captain for Marlboros, found out that the ship was clean out of cigs, so said, "Well, all right, just give me $10!" More head-shaking. Also about the California nutbars including the pilot who wouldn't take the ship in because he couldn't see around the cranes and derricks—and this fellow said,"Well, as a matter of fact, because you have all that paraphernalia on deck, you must go through the Canal in the daytime—you and the big, big ships. All the regular traffic goes through at night." Night navigation here requires that the pilot be able to see the lights and buoys along the route; with all the cranes, he can easily lose track. No good. So—aha!—good for BIBI! I mean, who wants to go through the Panama Canal at night?

We are now anchored and waiting in Gatun Lake—a backup at the last locks, I guess. This is the huge body of water that floods nearly 200 square miles of the Isthmus. It was created by damming the ferocious Chagres River, and it now makes up of most of the Canal, carrying ships across the Panamanian midriff.

For lunch: a giant turkey leg. That's all, except for the chocolate ice cream for dessert. Rain, as we moved across the lake. Klaus made sure to explain to the Captain yesterday that if he mentioned to the pilot—beforehand—that there were passengers aboard, the pilot would bring along maps and brochures of the Canal. But in the press of activity, the message didn't get through. The pilot was sorry, too.

Asked the pilot if he had a cell phone. Yes, but only for local calls. Rats! Well, I trust that Ellen will remember the key word in all of this: "FL - - - ", you know.

We should be moving soon.

Real thunder and lightning and a downpour blotting out all sight and sound, but for the flicker and boom of the squall. Here come the linesmen for the locks. The mist clearing now. They bring their lines—heaving lines, actually—right along with them.

Ah—we move. Yikes—I count 18 guys coming aboard. More "Jobs for Everyone". Yet more: as we approach the first lock in this flight of three, two men *row* out in a little boat to get the first line and carry it ashore. We all think, Gee, for $38,000 maybe they could afford a little motor for these guys. Then: on each of the nifty electric engines that help the ship through, there is a little "front porch", and on this "front porch" just enough room for a plastic lawn chair. A man sits in the chair and rides back and forth. At the end of each run, he gets down, takes the two steel cables with their bights, and when the lines to the ship are loosed, loops each of the bights over hooks on the front and back of the "little engine that could"—or just did. Then he gets back up on the porch and sits down in his chair for the ride back. I'm sure he has a title—maybe Looper, 1st Class—and a fair salary.

Just about to leave the last of the three Gatun locks. We are running quite early. Another hour, I think, and we'll be at sea again. Sked called for 1910; we'll be out by 1745—my guess. (But then, I'm . . .)

Just occurred to me. These two German fellows seem rather reticent about conversing. Klaus is hopeless: every response is a terrible pun or some other attempt at humour. It is most difficult to talk with him. Hans seems ill at ease and is also given to sort of short-circuiting a conversation with odd *"bon mots"*. Maybe it's this old man-to-man thing: "men don't talk". Would love to have a real chat with Marion, but she's almost never without Hans. I really miss good conversation—the chat at lunch with the pilot was a fine thing.

Here we are at the end of the Canal—Cristobal and Colon and Manzanillo off to starboard, harbour cranes, and so forth, but we head straight out through the breakwater into the ocean and make for Houston. Three days, 6 hours to the pilot station, 6 hours more for the ship canal. That's 84 hours by my reckoning. That makes it Wednesday, August 7, about 2300, plus the six hour Ship Canal ride: 0500. The Captain mentioned noon on the 8th. We'll see.
Looks like the pilot boat approaching. (Terrific lightning!)

Wow! This is the Atlantic all right! No! It's not the Atlantic all right; it's the Caribbean Sea! Never mind. There's a big swell coming in from NNE. We won't be westering any more so this minor pitching should not turn into rolling.

Klaus did it again at supper! That's twice. I'm trying to maintain a modicum of *gemütlichkeit* here—for just a few more days, but he is apparently unwilling to meet the situation halfway. This time it was: "Can't you just eat? I've told you, I don't like humming and whistling at the table!"—in a very aggressive tone. Was not even conscious I was doing it—if I was—and in any case, he must have been listening very closely.
This time it was more difficult to swallow his insulting manner, but once again, I determined that this oddball was *not* going to rain on my parade. I took a long walk around the deck, talking myself down and blistering the paint off stanchions and hatch covers. This seems particularly strange behaviour for such an experienced traveler. All of us are conscious of the occasional strain of close quarters and crossed paths, but it seems to get to him much more.

225

55

8/5   Bladder call in the wee hours (no pun intended); upset by the Klaus Case, and obsessed with packing plans, so—the hell with it!—I get up and start packing! Can't do a whole lot—I *use* almost everything I have, but I get the bags out of the drawer under the bed and start sorting and planning. Can't do a damn thing about anything of course until I can actually get to a phone on land in Houston. Then it will be airline first: get me on my way, 1st class if necessary, then a taxi. It's not that I am dying to leave the ship; it's just that I hate saying goodbye. Am hoping the other guys will, as usual, take off immediately for the sights and their friends so I can drift away unobtrusively.

Quite rough outside, but getting better, must get latest ETA from skipper in the morning.

Have put aside $120 for Renand as an (inadequate) tip; $30 for Erlito, the cook, as per TravLtips suggestion. I tried to keep Renand's "service" to me to a minimum; he cleaned the cabin not every week, but twice during the voyage, etc. Still I feel badly; wish I could afford more. Discovered early on that while the ship had a mechanical dishwasher; it was busted, so Renand did all the dishes by hand!

Well, it's after four a.m.; the watch has changed upstairs; I'll try to get some sleep. Still concerned about Ellen not hearing from me. Maybe she will call FWC and find out where the ship is. (In fact she did just that!) I won't call her from Houston, unless I'm stuck there for some time—still want to surprise her with a call from Long Harbour on Salt Spring.

Very windy day, big waves from NNE, choppy sea, rough and tumble, but no big deal. We take the seas on the starboard bow and just plow through, though the ship does have a sort of random motion—at least no rolling to speak of.

Hmmm. Much smoother ride, though wind still seems to be pretty stiff. Sunshine, blue skies, puffy clouds as we bash north toward the Gulf of Mexico.

14°42'N x 80°34'W (at sea)

Straight from the Captain's noon report: "PAX Moses, Richard will complete his voyage and disembark in Houston." Well, that's it. Also: "Houston PLT 0600 8/8/02" which means berthing about noon or 1300. Then my fun begins!

Wind down to almost nothing. Sea flattens out, ride becomes steady and smooth (boring!).

The Captain offered to ask the agent in Houston to book my airline flight, so I took him up on it. Very nice offer indeed! After careful thought about the trip home—particularly the other end, I have suggested an early flight for Friday morning, the 9th. Could possibly get out of Houston late on the 8th, but then I'd be stuck in Vancouver with no ferry to the Island until the 9th. So, I'll hang around the ship until Friday morning. I really want to arrive on Salt Spring (by Harbour Air seaplane if necessary) before Ellen visits her client at 1600. Plus, this would allow for any arrival delays. But, then, why would I think there might be delays?

Also, the Captain said the telephone will be working soon but at 3 times the previous rate per minute. Still, will call Ellen ASAP; just a very short message to reassure her of my welfare.

Wow! More big lightning! Another storm brewing? Hope so—get the salt off the windows.

2200 Fairly severe pain starts in lower left quadrant. Consider taking some Tylenol 3, but hold off. Go through day's intake of victuals, opine a few self-diagnoses. Nothing definitive.

2230 Two Tylenol 3.

8/6 0100 Pain eases after T3s, but has now spread to general lower abdomen. Nothing seems to help. Am having flushes (of all kinds!). Must have slept for short while. No specific spot or area sensitive to pressure.

0105 Pain now definitely easing. Food poisoning?

0303 No pain, but now it begins sneaking back, L.L.Q again, but not as much, not enough to prevent sleep.

0459 Fair pain still, in L.L.Q, but starts to fade until by 0530 things are back to "normal". Yowser! What a scare! Was sure this was it! Would be on painkillers to Houston, then rushed to hospital, etc. As with the beginning of the trip, I won't believe I'm home until I step in the door of #30. Still think it might have been something in the food. Januscz, the electrician, next door, has been up and down, too.

Just coming light outside, smooth sea. 2000 tonight should see us pass into the Gulf of Mexico

Pain gone—what a night! But beautiful morning, flat sea (for us), bright sun, blue sky.

Packing virtually finished.

20°46'N x 85°04'W (at sea)

Hot dog! Called Ellen. Decided, with the triple rate satellite phone and its "one way at a time" speaking, to go with the "Over" protocol. That is, she speaks, I make not a sound, she says "Over", then I speak, etc. Worked just fine! Everything is OK. Told her "Next time I call, the ship will be in Houston"—true enough, but of course *I* won't be; I'll be in Long Harbour, about 3 miles from her! As Dan would say, "Hee hee!"

Apple pie for supper—first time—not like Mom's, but bless our Cookie all the same!

8/7 Bright, sunny, but sprinkly morning—rained a bit a while ago. Great piles and stacks of clouds, and of course, not a ship in sight. Calm seas; my last day at sea! This time tomorrow we'll be well into the Houston Ship Canal. No word from the agent on plane res. Could actually be home tomorrow. *Tomorrow?!?*

From my expert calculation (I keep doing this) we should arrive off Galveston at about 0300 tomorrow morning to await the pilot at 0600. Quite exciting to see that we are back on the same chart we used four months ago when we left this place. Eight new crew members since then. At least one debarked to be missed by me only a week or so later: Albert, one of my favorites, got off in Singapore. Albert and Romeo seemed always to be the ones "on hand" when something extra was needed. I often think about Waldek, too, and wonder how he is doing. Back at sea, I hope.

Am all packed, as much as I can, and have had to unpack a couple of things.

26°02'N x 90°36'W (at sea)

Well, the agent did it! My plane reservations are made. Leaving Houston at 0800 CDT tomorrow, arriving in Vancouver at 1315 PDT giving me plenty of time and options for getting to Salt Spring Island. Perhaps I can catch the non-stop Bowen Queen ferry to Long Harbour and get that free hot dog! (The charming snack bar lady noticed me taking this summer round trip several times in previous years, and one day when I ordered my usual second hot dog she said, "This one's on the house!" I always offer to pay; she always smiles and won't have it.) Many thanks to Matthew Richards,

228

the Rickmers Agent. I had put on my "order" paper "Taxi to get to airport for flight", but have heard nothing of that. Bit much to ask him anyway, I thought.

We are surrounded now by the lights of hundreds of oil rig platforms! Had no idea there were so many. Each one appears as a black square on the chart and as we approach Galveston, they get thicker and thicker, glowing and glittering in the night. The Captain is on the bridge; we are steering manually (can't see who the helmsman is—too dark); it will take some cautious maneuvering to get through this forest. The oil field stretches all the way along the Gulf coast from Mexico to Florida. Unbelievable! Billions and billions of dollars must have been spent to put them all up. And each one is mammoth. Yikes!

8/8   Well, my calculations were not far off; we have just taken on the pilot, the Galveston shore is now our horizon, and the guys are lifting the cranes and lowering the derrick in prep for the journey up the Canal. This means we will probably arrive at Pier 16 before 1100.

Ahead: a roadway of bell and light buoys: "red right returning"—the sailor's mnemonic—and green to port, leads across Galveston Bay. The melancholy clang of the bells as we rush by is signaling the sad end of this journey—this unbelievable, unimaginable journey to the ends of the earth and back—at least 25,000 miles.

29°30'N x 95°W (Houston)

At 1045, we are tied up at Pier 16 in Houston—in the precise spot where I first found this great, lovable hulk. The Captain and I were on the port bridge wing as the final lines were made fast. I said to him "Well, you picked me up; you took me around the world, and you brought me back!" And I shook his hand.

I did it! No, *we* did it! I took the trip, but Ellen and Jennifer and Dan and many others let me do it and encouraged me, and waited for me and will welcome me home.

Our tug's name is FRANCES E. HADEN; it's the FRANCES E. that caught my eye: Ellen's mother's name and initial.

After some bother—both taxi numbers given me by telephone information last week in L.B. were bad, I've lined up a cab for tomorrow at 0600. Renand insists on being there then to help with the bags—he won't take no for an answer. I wish I had $1,000 to give him.

229

The Captain says the ship will be leaving tomorrow evening. Somehow I doubt it. Didn't realize the #5 tweendecks had to be emptied, too. 8 pipes at a time and there are hundreds and hundreds of them. Plus, two other holds are working. And now it rains and everybody quits! Listen to me: still doing it! Still calculating and "worrying" this ship. I won't even be here!

Rain stopped, back to work. Most of these Texas stevedores appear to be about 20 lbs. overweight and decidedly middle-aged. They sort of scramble and stumble around over this great load of pipes—as I would! (I mentioned this fact to Dirk once—it also applies in England; he said the young dudes just won't take the jobs anymore.)

I dunno—all 5 of our cranes are working, plus a big shore crane, and the jumbo derrick when needed. They may do it. Will they work at night? (STOP IT!) Lots of cargo on shore to go, including some for Algeria! Nice stop for next trip. (I CAN'T STOP! Will I ever stop sizing up ships and cargo and wondering ?)

Before supper, I deliver to Renand and Erlito my humble thank-you gifts, and return the glass, the knife, the salt shaker, some leftover butter, and the rest of the unpopped corn. They are a rare pair.

Afterwards, a long walk—I find the Seaman's Centre—really nifty! Buy a Pepsi, or two, and two Almond Joys. Come back, pay my phone bill ($7.62 for that brief call to Ellen), say goodbye to the Captain, tour the ship to say other good-byes, but hardly nobody is "to home". Ship probably won't sail 'til Saturday now. Much to do, and unloading is going much too slowly.

By golly, the pipe crew *is* working tonight! Unloading 8 at a time—after experimenting with a number of different rigs. I'm still watching cargo, reading labels, checking ships—but it's all over!

Penultimate goodbyes—to the Kments—up to their suite for a last glass of wine. Klaus at the Seaman's Centre. Fond farewell tomorrow to Renand.

8/9 0155 Can't sleep. This never happens. Maybe it's the two candy bars, the Hershey Kiss (1), the Coke and the two Pepsis, but stuff like that has never bothered me before. It is also just maybe that I am a bit keyed up about actually having to leave my ship, getting home, surprising Ell, etc.—and meeting the *two* taxis in the morning (the Agent lined one up after all, but, hey nobody tells me nothin'!) and having to send one away and apologize.

But, I also may read the letter from Klaus he gave me when he came down "to say goodbye" a couple of hours ago.

He actually handed me a small wrapped package; we had a few nice words at the door; I bade him farewell, and decided to put the package away for perusal on the plane. But here I am wide awake. So, why not? I open the packet and there is the Texas roadmap—returned to sender! And here is a rather strange letter that solves all the mysteries of his change in mood and my (correct) feeling that I had somehow offended—several times, as it turns out—not only with the "worthless" map, which he did not consider a proper gift, but the Japanese taxi "fuss" when I couldn't pay the fare—plus, of course, the "music" at meals. In my hyper-excited state, I am stunned, and some distraught, not only at my own apparent lack of sensitivity and consideration, but at the fact that this man had harboured his resentment for weeks, unable to get beyond it, unable to make his peace. Well, despite being born on the same day, we are obviously not peas in a pod. He was a fun guy and a bold adventurer and maybe meeting me was a new adventure with which he can regale his pub friends. I hope so.

I *hate* waiting! Three and a half hours to go.

Maybe I should have taken off yesterday, but then I would have knocked around one Vancouver terminal or another all night, or spent a bundle on a room, so I was "intelligent" and now I get to be sleepless in Houston!

I sleep for a couple of hours, off and on, keep waking up, and finally it is time. I do about three final checks of the cabin, then schlep the bags to the elevator and out onto the main deck, where four months ago—to the day!—in the dark, I arrived breathless, finally to stand on this deck. The Bosun and the 2nd officer are there now—standing their watch, and getting ready to start the cranes. The Bosun is a capital fellow, a bit older than the rest, and one of the smallest crew members. But he can do anything, and now he hefts the biggest bag to his shoulder and strides off down the teetering gangway like it was solid concrete. (I remember the day I finally learned to tread this gangway "no hands"!) Then the next bag goes. It is still only 0540. I take a walk across the flat quay to look at BIBI as I first saw her lit up like a Christmas tree.

When I get back, Renand has appeared. I give him the keys to my kingdom; we shake hands, pledge eternal missing—and suddenly both taxis (in fact double cab pickup trucks!) are here. We straighten out who called who and the Agent's cab gracefully gives way—he gets all the calls for Rickmers ships anyway. He leaves me in the hands of surely the talkiest Texan in tarnation! What a dude! A grandfather

231

with a bunch of kids and grandkids and two dogs and he "jes kep
up a stiddy straim o' Texas blather" all the way.

And here I am at the George Bush Airport.

We arrived at 0640 or so, I was moved smartly to an empty
America West counter and in a jiffy I was in. Then—guess what!—a
Big Breakfast at McDonald's, and here I sit, with 50 minutes to go
before boarding.

And I still don't really believe *any* of this!

CODA

8/9   2100 I am standing now outside the small ferry terminal
building at Long Harbour, Salt Spring Island. I just placed a phone
call to Ellen. My usual whimsical greeting—which had come to her
from all parts of the world—her relief and pleasure at hearing it,
then my commentary for this day: "Well, the ship is in Houston! In
exactly the same place as when I got on. Fascinating coming up the
Canal, seeing things I distantly remembered." Etc., etc. "Now," says
I, "we'd better make some plans for your meeting me. Got a pencil
and paper?" "Yes," she says. "All right," says I, "first thing is go out
the front door and get in the car; then drive to Long Harbour where
you will find this ancient mariner waiting for you!"   (Long silence.)
Then: "I *knew* you were going to do something like this!"   And then a
lot of laughter and a tear or two, and—oh, my, here she is! And
home we go.

The trip from Houston was absolutely unmemorable.
Everything right on time: the planes, the bus to Tsawwassen, the
Bowen Queen to Salt Spring—with the usual periods of waiting in
between of course. But the weather was perfect, my fellow
passengers all congenial(!) and even Christine, the snack bar lady on
the ferry was bowled over to see me. Alas, she was very busy so no
free hot dog.

At home and still agog at this small house we live in. I realize
that during the past four months I (or perhaps some other person)
have lived an entirely different life in an entirely different
"house"—almost everything about it, let alone the fact that it never
stopped moving (in one direction or another) was—well—not this, at
all!   I am gently stunned to find everything I know and love, yet
everything totally "different", too. It is very exciting. Babbling my
head off—*in full-blown English*—I   mention my regret at not making
Dan's concert on the 5th. Ellen says, well, he is playing another one

232

tomorrow in Nanaimo. So, of course plans are made to head up island. Then a call to Jennifer with my big surprise to discover that she will be driving down from Comox for the concert. A reunion!

Next day, we arrive in the park, find a blanket spot and spy Dan, in white tie and tails, sitting on the outdoor stage, warming up. I head his way, stand beside the platform and give my little whistle. He looks up—beautifully startled ("What? That sounded like Dad's whistle—but it can't be—he's somewhere in the Gulf of Mexico!") But he looks up, sees me, and catapults himself in my direction for a big hug. Jennifer's had come a bit earlier, and, my final zinger accomplished, I join her and Ellen for the big show.

I am well and truly home now! In some ways it seems I have never left, but there is this big "thing" in the middle of me now—this great package of feelings and joys and experiences and people and places that is just there—and there to stay. If at times I seem to drift off, if my eyes glaze over, it's probably because I have—just for a moment—found myself back on board that other life, standing on BIBI's bow or her stern or just gazing out my salty window at the endless, timeless, ever-varying sea.

I'll be back.

BIBI on August 9th as I left her

233

POSTLUDE

10/10/02   After two months of getting back into "civilian" life, a time during part of which the ship trip seemed gradually to fade into the background: "did I really do that?", with the ship sort of sailing away into the mist, things now seem to be changing. I remember before the trip, trying to imagine myself on the ship, moving across the sea, touching ports, even weathering storms. It put me to sleep at night pretending I could feel the roll of the ship, the throb of the engines. I was, in short, romanticizing this voyage. And for the most part my imagination proved accurate. I felt that "the other passengers" might prove "interesting", the food might be "an adventure", and it all proved out. True, I was always a bit ill at ease during meals—my essential shyness coming to the fore; true, travels ashore were sometimes more than I really wanted to handle, etc., etc. and true, upon my return, I was glad to be back in the land of convenience, easy living and easy popcorn. Great relief to be shut of all the "problems" of travel. Now, however, I find myself re-romanticizing the whole thing. I look back with nostalgia at the huge ship as it plows across oceans. I can feel its motion again. Most of all, perhaps, I yearn again for the detachment and non-involvement the trip made possible. I feel again that "there is too much on my mind". I am getting too involved in "things". Even my pleasure at playing the horn is waning. I can see why seamen begin to become anxious to get back to the sea. I find myself, suddenly going quiet, gazing off and recalling some moment on shipboard, or just sensing the size and motion of the ship. And even now before I sleep, I once again, pretend to feel the ship's motion, the pulse of her engine, and the amazing idea of being part of her, but this time remembering instead of imagining. However, alas, it took me no time at all to get used to a stable bed, and floors that didn't tilt, and doorways I didn't have to step up to get through! I tried to inveigle Ellen into donning a white jacket to serve my plate at regular times on a linen tablecloth, but it was no go.

However, the idea of doing it all again—a la Klaus—does not (yet?) appeal, but I am a lot closer to understanding what motivates him than I was before. And my fears about the trip putting me off ships and sea? Groundless. Ferry rides are still exciting; the sighting of a freighter grabs me and won't let go, and I know now I will never be able to live very far from the sea that carried me into that other life.

Interestingly, and very pleasantly, while there were moments during the voyage which may not have been perfect, it is now only the marvelous moments I remember. All else has just faded away and the voyage in my head is just as I imagined it during the planning stages.

10/26/02. Just found out what was going on in my tummy all that while. It was—still is, until I finish all these pills—a parasite called *Blastocystic Hominis*, and it did not come from China or Thailand or any of those exotic places; it apparently came from right here on this "exotic" island, and may be in the drinking water the town gets from a local lake. Imagine that! Another "almost"!

Incidentally, when I got home and stepped on the scale, I discovered I'd *lost* about 15 lbs. No wonder I had to keep tightening my belt!

5/1/03 More than a year now since I left for the big trip, and I remember it with increasing fondness. The Kments and I have communicated several times—Marion actually calling once. In fact, they sent along a video tape of DINNER FOR ONE, the 20 minute play they raved about on the ship, which neither I nor, it turns out, a single Brit around here had ever heard of, which was actually recorded in Germany, and the showing of which has become an absolute German New Year's Eve tradition! I have made several copies for friends here.

No one seems to have heard a word from Klaus. I still find myself smarting slightly over his attitudes, though Marian suggests that since he is, or was, a teacher, he "knows" only one way to do things.

I sent a FAX to Steward Renand in the Fall, never knowing whether it actually arrived or not, but shortly before Christmas, with the BIBI once again in Houston, I think, he called. There, on the message machine was his winsome voice and delightful accent (no one was home at the time, alas) wishing me a Merry Christmas, and ending with a plaintive "I miss you!"

The parasite is long gone, but it has perhaps left me with a nifty case of IBS (Irritable Bowel Syndrome). Ah, well, another rather unusual way of reminding me of those halcyon days aboard ship.

9/10/03 In an effort to locate Steward Renand in order to send him a copy of this book, I learned that the MV BIBI, her two sister ships plus the other two Rickmers ships making "my" circumnavigation have all been replaced by six of the new Rickmers "super" freighters, BIBI finishing her final trip on March 20, 2003—less than a year from the time I left her. The last three "supers" will come on line in September and October, 2003. More details on the Internet along with pictures of the new ships.

NOTES AND OTHER ODDS AND ENDS

Note 1: The "hat" joke. A doctor was asked to give a lecture to a women's club on the subject of sex. He agreed, but, concerned lest she try to give him pointers and cautions on the subject, told his wife he was talking to the group about sailing. She was not able to attend the talk, but a day or so later ran into a member of the club who said to her, "You're husband's talk was wonderful! We all learned a great deal from it." "You know," said the wife, "I'm a little surprised; he really doesn't know that much about it; he's only done it twice—and the first time his hat blew off!"

Note 2: Flipping the Stuelcken derrick. The derrick is of course a 100 foot boom mounted on a pivoting base and supported by cables and blocks running from the top of the boom to the tops of towers on either side of the ship. From the upper end of the boom hangs a hook supported by two arrangements of blocks and cables attached to a sort of bridle or yoke to which is attached the actual hook. One set of supporting cables hangs down the port side of the boom, the other on the starboard side. Now the hook itself is either on the forward side of the boom—thus ready to serve hatch #3, or on the aft side, to servc #4. But how to "flip" this enormous hook from forward to aft sides? It turns out that, in addition to the two great shackling pin holes on either side of the "yoke", there is also central hole. To flip the derrick, both port and starboard blocks are detached from the yoke as it rests in its cradle. One of the blocks is attached to the central hole, the other can now be swung around the base of the derrick. Now the derrick is operated to lift the hook, using, of course, the block and cables attached to the centre hole. When it is out of its cradle, it, too, can be swung around the other side of the derrick, placed in the new cradle, and the blocks reattached to their proper holes in the yoke. Voila! The derrick is now ready to serve the other hatch. It requires several men to effect the flip and may take half an hour or so.

Note 3: The Panama Canal. I put very little in the actual journal about the Canal because I didn't know much. Now I know much more, but this opus is not the place to expound on one of the most fascinating stories in history. Instead, let me recommend a book called THE PATH BETWEEN THE SEAS: THE CREATION OF THE PANAMA CANAL, 1870-1914, by David McCullough, published in 1977 by Simon and Schuster. Its more than 600 pages, its notes, extensive bibliography, photos, and index, present this almost unbelievable story of vision, courage, scandal, death and triumph in exemplary fashion.

(MY) ITINERARY

(4/9/02	0630	Dep.	Salt Spring Island, B.C.)
(4/9	2310	Arr.	Houston)
4/10	0001	Arr.	MV BIBI
4/11	0045	Dep.	Houston
4/11	2200	Arr.	Beaumont, Texas
4/13	0300	Dep.	Beaumont
4/15	0330	Arr,	Tampa, Florida
4/16	2030	Dep.	Tampa
4/26	2045	Arr.	Newport, Wales
5/3	2250	Dep.	Newport
5/5	2145	Arr.	Immingham, England
5/7	2205	Dep.	Immingham
5/9	0015	Arr.	Hamburg, Germany
5/11	0200	Dep.	Hamburg
5/12	0630	Arr.	Antwerp, Belgium
5/14	2330	Dep.	Antwerp
5/20	2030	Arr.	Livorno, Italy
5/21	0800	Dep.	Livorno
5/24	1700	Arr.	Port Said, Egypt (Suez Canal)
5/25	1530	Dep.	Suez Canal
5/30	0800	Arr.	Salalah, Oman
5/31	0920	Dep.	Salalah
6/8	0430	Arr.	Singapore
6/9	0930	Dep.	Singapore
6/11	0700	Arr.	Ko Sichang, Thailand
6/13	1300	Dep	Ko Sichang
6/13	1430	Arr.	Laem Chabang, Thailand
6/14	0400	Dep	Laem Chabang
6/16	1200	Arr.	Ho Chi Minh City, Viet Nam
6/17	0920	Dep.	Ho Chi Minh City
6/19	0200	Arr.	Hong Kong, China
6/21	1600	Dep.	Hong Kong
6/24	1430	Arr.	Shanghai, China
6/25	0900	Dep.	Shanghai
6/27	0600	Arr.	Xingang, China
6/28	1930	Dep.	Xingang
7/1	0600	Arr.	Shanghai
7/3	0200	Dep.	Shanghai
7/4	1345	Arr.	Masan, Korea
7/7	1400	Dep.	Masan
7/8	0745	Arr.	Kobe, Japan
7/9	1600	Dep.	Kobe
7/11	0715	Arr.	Yokohama, Japan
7/11	1850	Dep.	Yokohama

7/12	0730	Arr.	Port of Hitachi, (Kujihama)
7/13	1900	Dep.	Port of Hitachi
7/25	0515	Arr.	Long Beach, California
7/27	1615	Dep.	Long Beach
8/3	1430	Arr.	Panama Canal
8/4	1730	Dep.	Panama Canal
8/8	1030	Arr.	Houston, Texas
(8/9	0600	Dep.	Houston)
(8/9	2100	Arr.	Salt Spring Island)

DAYS AT SEA   79
DAYS IN PORT   43

DAN'S WEB SITE: While I have included a few excerpts from Dan's incomparable web site covering the trip, I have tried not to duplicate it unnecessarily. You may still access it at:

<http://www.chalumeaudio.com/richard/freighter.html>

REASONS MINE WAS THE BEST CABIN ON THE SHIP.
1. double room (suite); space for map, popcorn makings, storage
2. 2 windows facing forward, one to starboard
3. 2 incandescent light fixtures (not all fluorescent as in smaller cabins)
4. desk chair with four legs (not wheels) to put on coffee table for "throne"
5. new, or nice, curtains
6. great movable arm chair
7. great movable sofa
8. located on C deck—doesn't roll as much as E deck owner's suite, and is closer to dining room
9. larger fridge than owner's suite
10. cut rate price due to change of ships
11. able to shut off incoming chilled air when necessary (other cabins' fixtures old, worn, unshuttable)
12. fine bed

S H I P ' S   P A R T I C U L A R S

Name	**B I B I**
Nationality	CYPRUS
Port of Registry	LIMASSOL

Official nbr.	710647	IMO NBR.:	7722126
Call sign:	*P 3 S X 6*	SatC ID: 420900991	Sellcall: 210985000
		SatM ID: 763,033,425 763033428	763033426 FAX

Owners: DOUBLE C SHIPPING CO - LIMASSOL CYPRUS

Operators:	TECHNOMAR SHIPPING INC	Phone:	301-6233670
	MENANDROU STR 3-5	Fax:	301-8084224
	145 61 KIFISSIA, ATHENS, GREECE	Tlx.:	216964 DGRA GR

GRT	17128	PANAMA	18228	SUEZ	17965.71
NRT	9448		14562		14108.07
L.O.A.	178.27 m *555*	L.b.p.	168 m		
Breadth	26.5 m				
Depth	14.20 m				

Built:	HIROSHIMA WORKS INNOSHIMA	Yard nbr.:	4613
Keel layed:	24.07.1978	Launching date:	02.11.1978

Class:	100 A 1 + LMC/UMS	LLOYD REGISTER
L.V.	9559	

Propeller draft:	6.40 m / 21'	Propeller dia	5800 mm
Anchor weight:	6900 kgs *7<2m*	Chain	605 m /64 mm

Dist.Bridge to Stem:	139.8 m	Bridge to Stern:	38.5 m
Air Draft :	53.50 m /Jumbo *175.5'*	Under 45 deg./	44.80 m
Bridge Mast	46.90 m	Fwd antenna	45.60 m

CAPACITY:

17703 M3 GRAIN	in	Holds		
13891 M3 GRAIN	in	TD'S		
816 TEUS			CONTAINERS	
4913 M3	WATER BALLAST		330 MT	FRESH WATER
1760 MT	IFO	345	MDO	80 MT L.OIL

	Freeboard	Draft	DWT
Tropical Fresh	3,419 m/11,22'	10.834/35' 06.5"	23148 mt/22782 lt
Fresh	3,635 m/11,92'	10.618/34'10"	22339 mt/21986 lt
Tropical	3,629 m/11,91'	10.624/34'10.2"	23159 mt/ 22793 lt
SUMMER	3,845 m/12,61'	10.408/34'01.7"	22337 mt/ 21984 lt
Winter	4,061 m/13,32'	10.192/33'05.2"	21521 mt/ 21181 lt

ENGINE:	HITACHI B&W 8L67GFC	Output 15000 HP/119 Rpm
		Service 13600 HP/115 Rpm
SPEED:	18.5 KN / Ballast	17.5 kn cargo
CONSUMPTION	IFO/41 MT - 110 Rpm	MDO : Sea/3.7-Port/3.8 mt
BOW THRUSTER:	KaMeWa: 800 HP	

Master m/v Bibi

MV BIBI

Flag: **Cyprus**
Port of Registry: Limassol
Call Sign: P3SX6
Fax: 763033426
      Phone: 763033425

HOUSTON 11.04.2002

Dear Mr.Richard Bradley Moses

Welcome aboard MV BIBI
We hope you have an enjoyable voyage and a pleasant stay with us.

To begin with we like to give you a brief introduction and some
information about the ship, ourselves and normal procedures aboard.
Please take the few minutes required to read this introduction, it will
help you to familiarize yourself with the vessel, will probably answer
many of your first questions and introduce you to important safety
regulations.

MV BIBI is a cargo vessel, a „working ship" and not a cruise ship.
This is probably the main reason you are travelling with us. Please
keep in mind that, while we do what we can for you, our main
objective is the transportation of cargo and the work connected with
this.

First we should like to introduce ourselves and the other passengers
on board for this voyage, if any, as we all will be ship mates for the
months to come:

Master	Grzegorz	Wasielewski
Chief Engineer	Andrzej	Solohub
Chief Officer	Waldemar	Watracz
Second Officer	Eric	Velarde
Third Officer	Dominador	Unida
Second Engineer	Tadeusz	Ziolkowski
Third Engineer	Ernesto	Arellano
Steward	Renand	Mercado

         No doubt you will get to know the other
crewmembers in due time yourself.
The common language for everyone on board is English.

Passports / Travel Documents

Please hand your passports and vaccination documents to the Master after embarkation and show him your passage contract. The passport will be returned to you for shore excursions after immigrations clearance in each port of call.

Communication

The vessel is equipped with satellite communication (phone and fax), which you may in urgent cases, at your own expense, use to send or have messages sent to you. Depending on the geographical location different satellite codes have to be used to reach the vessel. Inquire on the bridge for the currently applicable code.

Safety

Please familiarize yourself with the safety regulations, the emergency signals and assembly points, locate your life jacket, the emergency exits etc. Detailed emergency procedures are on display at bridge as well as Safety Manual at off'srec.room
If you have questions please ask Domonador Unida = Safety Officer, who will go through the emergency procedures in detail with you in due time after joining.

If ever you hear the general alarm (seven short and one long blast), take your life jacket(s) and proceed to the nearest assembly point!

You will find a detailed ships plan on display at the ships corridors. You are required to attend emergency drills which take place on a regular basis. You will be informed accordingly by the Safety Officer.

Please keep in mind that this vessel, like any other cargo ship, is liable to roll and pitch heavily, not only during bad weather but also in certain sea areas with heavy swell. Therefore please secure all your belongings prior to departure. This includes all cabin furniture which may shift otherwise. If you need assistance: the Steward will help you.

Also remember, that you yourself need time to adjust to the ship's movements, and be aware of the fact that unpredictable and erratic movements can occur at any time. So be careful when walking through heavy doors, on the stairs, on deck etc.

Do not walk on the cargo deck after dusk or during the night: the Duty Officer cannot see you on a dark deck and could not help you in case you slip or fall.

In general, please adhere to all instructions from Master and Officers as well as all signs posted!

Pollution Prevention

Merchant ships are subject to strict rules and regulations with regard to the protection of the marine environment. In compliance with these regulations you will receive a brief instruction from the Safety Officer. Please follow those instructions as heavy fines can be imposed against the vessel and individuals in case of violations.

<u>Please do not throw anything overboard!</u>

Your Cabin

We hope you feel at home and comfortable in your cabin.
It will be cleaned once a week by the Steward, who at this time will also change linens and towels. If this is not sufficient and you require additional cleaning, towels or linen change, please ask the Steward.

Valuables

You may deposit your valuables in the ship's safe. Just ask the Master.

Meals

Meals are taken in the Officers' Messroom on A-Deck. Dress is informal. Meal times are

Breakfast	0730-0830
Lunch	1130-1230
Dinner	1800-1830

You can make yourself coffee or tea at any time in the Officer's Pantry.

Bonded Stores

In our „Slop Chest" we carry a small selection of wine, spirits, beer, soft drinks, cigarettes, toothpaste etc. If you wish to purchase anything, please ask the steward who is in charge. Opening times are posted in the mess room, please note that you cannot buy anything while the vessel is in port.

Settlement of Accounts

The accounting currency on board is US Dollar, all charges are to be paid in this currency. Please settle your account at the end of each month and on dis-embarkation.

Medical Care

At the time of booking this voyage you will have been informed that there is no medical staff on this vessel. The Master, as well as some of the other Officers, have completed a first aid training, and the vessel is equipped with a first aid room/hospital, and carries basic medicines for emergency use.

In case you require medication regularly, be sure you have a sufficient supply to last you during this voyage. Advise us immediately if a medication emergency should arise.

Officers' Lounge/Facilities
Since this vessel does not have separate facilities for passengers, you are invited to use the Officers' Lounge and all other recreational facilities. So we all share the public rooms and we thank you for observing normal social rules.

Video/Library
In the officers lounge there is a selection of video films as well as a small library which you may use. Please return videos and books afterwards.
You are welcome to add any of your own which you can spare.

Ships time
We will be travelling through different time zones and will correspondingly adjust our time on board. You will be informed of such time changes by second officer. The electric ship's clocks are adjusted from the bridge and always show the current ship's time.

Electric Supply
The ship's voltage is 110 Volt at 60 Hz. And plugs and sockets are American type. You will find an adapter in your cabin to connect your own appliances.
If you are not certain or encounter problems, ask the Electrician for advice.

Fresh Water
Fresh water is of vital importance. Please do not waste it and use not more than you require. Avoid leaving taps running unnecessarily and report leaking faucets to the Steward.

Washing Machine/Clothes Dryer
The Steward will show you the washing facilities you may use and explain the handling of the utilities, if necessary. He will also supply you with detergents. Please save water and energy and use washing machines to the maximum effect – full loads if possible.

Luggage
The Steward will show you where you may store your suitcases and other luggage during the voyage.

Deck Chairs
Deck chairs with cushions are available for your convenience. Please make sure chairs and cushions are returned to their storage space and secured after use.

Moving about
Please take great care when walking on all external decks. Be sure to wear adequate footwear!
This is a working ship and can be dangerous for the unfamiliar. For your own safety, the Main Deck is strictly off-limits for passengers while the vessel is in port, even when no loading or discharging operations are in progress.

At sea, you are requested to inform the Duty Officer before going onto the Main Deck. Even during moderate weather conditions, this deck is liable to be wet with spray and can be very slippery and therefore dangerous. Also, the deck is being used for carrying containers and general cargo, and while the various lashings secure the deck cargo, persons moving about can easily trip and fall.

<u>Never move on the Main Deck during dusk or darkness!</u>

Be aware of the fact that decks of cargo vessels tend to be dirty, rusty, oily, greasy and sooty. Choose your footwear and clothing accordingly.
Please remember also that grease and dirt will stick to your shoes and is likely to be carried into the ship and into your cabin, where it is almost inpossible to be removed from the carpet.
Since your cabin will be your home for weeks or months to come,

<u>please leave your dirty shoes on the door mat!</u>

Navigation Bridge
You are welcome to the Bridge resp. the Wheelhouse at any time unless a special manoeuver is in progress. This might be the case when entering or leaving port or during a difficult passage.
Try to be aware of situations when your presence at the bridge may be distracting or disturbing to the Duty Officer. He is responsible for the safety of the entire vessel and you must follow his requests or instructions without delay or hesitation.

<u>Please do not touch any navigational instruments!</u>

Engine Room & Machinery Spaces
Passengers are not allowed to enter the engine room and machinery spaces on their own. You may ask the Chief Engineer for a guided tour of the engine room, he will be glad to show you around.

Schedule/Itinerary
You will be kept informed of our itinerary by the Master. Part of the special charm of a voyage on a cargo vessel are frequent changes of schedule and ports of call, which you should be prepared for in our special cargo liner service.

Port Areas/Shore Excursions

Please be very careful when proceeding from the ship on to the dock. These are dangerous areas due to cargo handling by forklifts, trucks, cranes and other vehicles. At some docks it may therefore be required to use a shuttle bus.

Be sure you know the exact name of the terminal/dock, port area, berth, where our ship is located, to enable you (or your taxi driver) to find your way back. It is also useful to have the name, address and telephone number of the port agent with you.

Always inform the Duty Officer before going ashore and make sure you know when you must be back in order not to miss the departure of the vessel. Make sure you return in ample time since the vessel will definitely not be able to wait for you, and report back to the Duty Officer.

While ashore do not flaunt your valuable belongings and adhere to the common sense rules of prudent travelling.

Security

In port it is necessary that you keep your cabin door locked at all times. While the ship's crew makes every effort to keep unauthorised persons out of the accommodations, thieves may get in after all. You should also lock your cabin at night in port when you are sleeping.

Finally

Again, welcome aboard, we trust you will have a pleasant and enjoyable voyage.

If you have a question or do encounter any problem, inform the Duty Officer or the person most likely to be able to assist you like the Steward, the Electrician or others. This way you meet different people and get to know the crew. If none of them can help you, you can always ask the Master.

Bon Voyage!

RICKMERS - LINIE

DOUBLE C SHIPPING COMPANY LTD., Owners

TECHNOMAR SHIPPING INC., Managers

THE MASTER

....
(Ship's stamp + signature)

245

"FINISHED WITH ENGINES"

ISBN 141200507-8

28903137R00137

Made in the USA
Lexington, KY
06 January 2014